W9-AJM-344

AMERICAN
JESUS

VOLUME THREE:
REVELATION

MARK MILLAR
STORY

PETER GROSS
with TOMM COKER
ART

JEANNE MCGEE
with DANIEL FREEDMAN
COLOR

CORY PETIT
LETTERING

MELINA MIKULIC
DESIGN AND PRODUCTION

JODIE MUIR
COVER ARTIST

SARAH UNWIN
EDITORIAL PRODUCTION MANAGER

LUCY MILLAR
CEO

Created by Mark Millar and Peter Gross

IMAGE COMICS, INC. • Robert Kirkman: Chief Operating Officer • Erik Larsen: Chief Financial Officer • Todd McFarlane: President • Marc Silvestri: Chief Executive Officer • Jim Valentino: Vice President • Eric Stephenson: Publisher / Chief Creative Officer • Nicole Lapalme: Vice President of Finance • Leanna Caunter: Accounting Analyst • Sue Korpela: Accounting & HR Manager • Matt Parkinson: Vice President of Sales & Publishing Planning • Lorelei Bunjes: Vice President of Digital Strategy • Dirk Wood: Vice President of International Sales & Licensing • Ryan Brewer: International Sales & Licensing Manager • Alex Cox: Director of Direct Market Sales • Chloe Ramos: Book Market & Library Sales Manager • Emilio Bautista: Digital Sales Coordinator • Jon Schlaffman: Specialty Sales Coordinator • Kat Salazar: Vice President of PR & Marketing • Deanna Phelps: Marketing Design Manager • Drew Fitzgerald: Marketing Content Associate • Heather Doornink: Vice President of Production • Drew Gill: Art Director • Hilary DiLoreto: Print Manager • Tricia Ramos: Traffic Manager • Melissa Gifford: Content Manager • Erika Schnatz: Senior Production Artist • Wesley Griffith: Production Artist • Rich Fowlks: Production Artist • IMAGECOMICS.COM

AMERICAN JESUS, VOL. 3. First printing. March 2023. Published by Image Comics, Inc. Office of publication: PO BOX 14457, Portland, OR 97293. Copyright © 2023 Netflix Entertainment, LLC. All rights reserved. Contains material originally published in single magazine form as AMERICAN JESUS: REVELATION #1-3, "American Jesus," its logos, and the likenesses of all characters herein are trademarks of Netflix Entertainment, LLC, unless otherwise noted. "Image" and the Image Comics logos are registered trademarks of Image Comics, Inc. No part of this publication may be reproduced or transmitted, in any form or by any means (except for short excerpts for journalistic or review purposes), without the express written permission of Netflix Entertainment, LLC, or Image Comics, Inc. All names, characters, events, and locales in this publication are entirely fictional. Any resemblance to actual persons (living or dead), events, or places, without satirical intent, is coincidental. Printed in Canada. For international rights, contact: contact: lucy@ netflixmw.com. ISBN: 978-1-5343-2499-2.

®
image

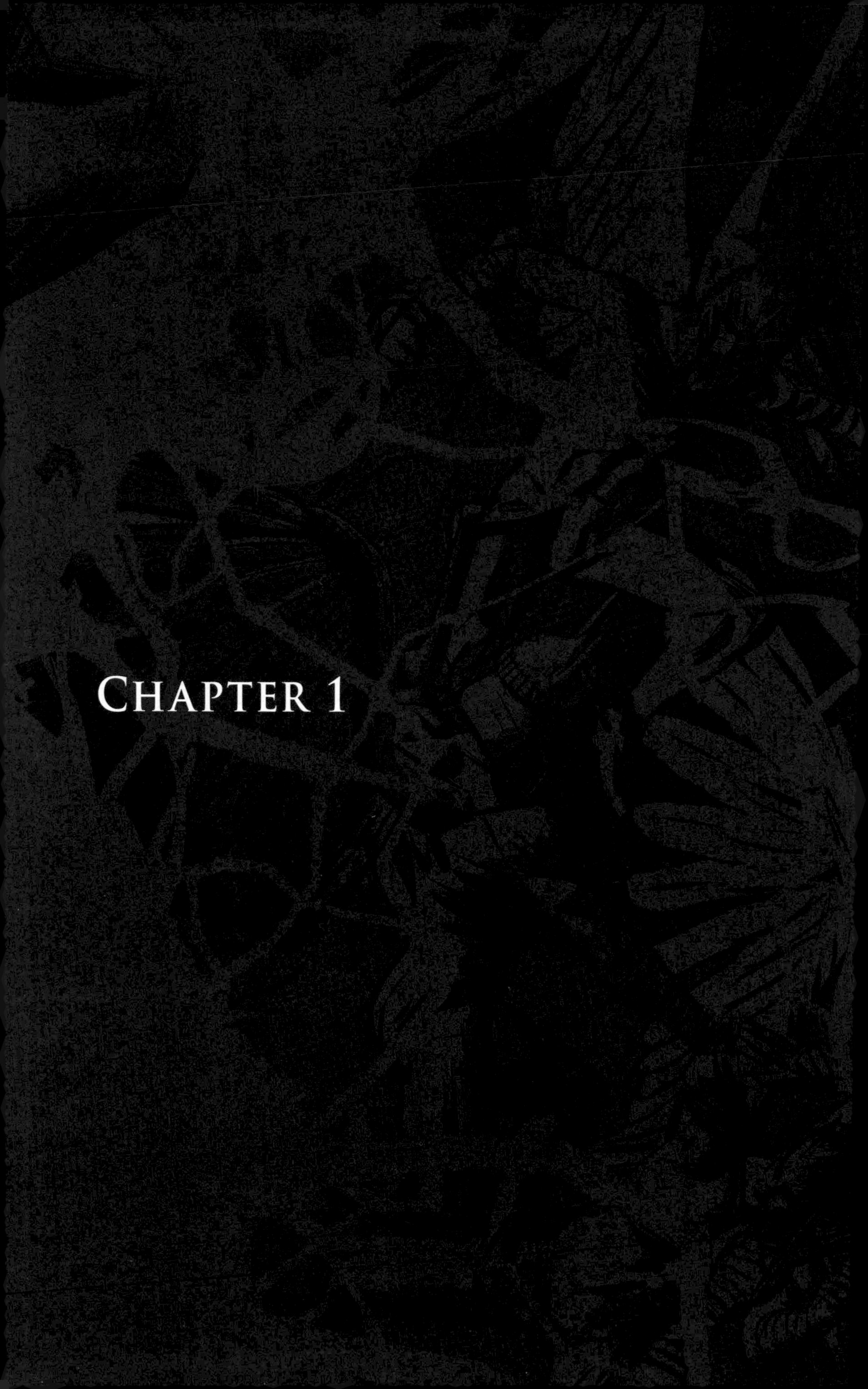

CHAPTER 1

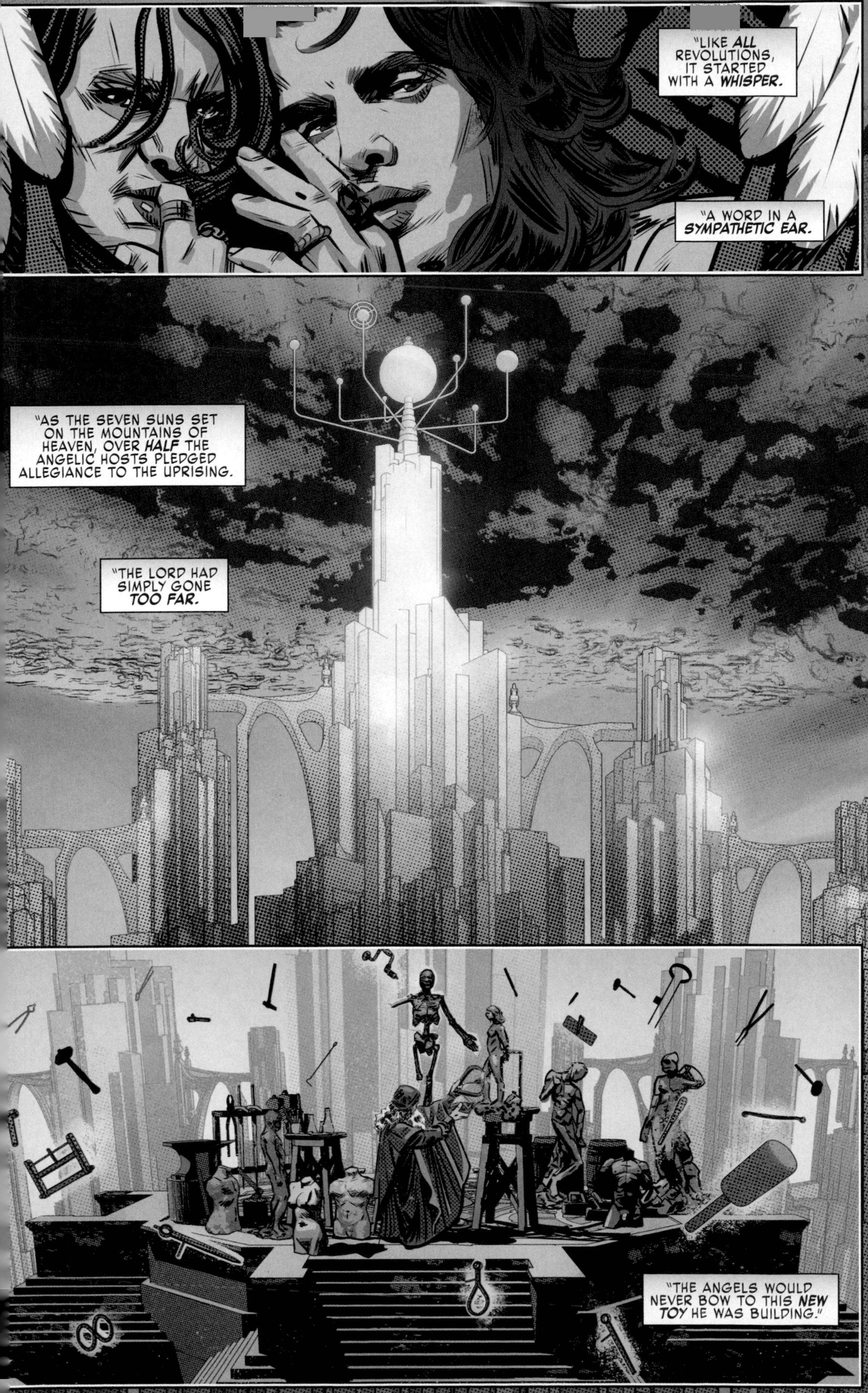
"LIKE ALL REVOLUTIONS, IT STARTED WITH A WHISPER.
"A WORD IN A SYMPATHETIC EAR.
"AS THE SEVEN SUNS SET ON THE MOUNTAINS OF HEAVEN, OVER HALF THE ANGELIC HOSTS PLEDGED ALLEGIANCE TO THE UPRISING.
"THE LORD HAD SIMPLY GONE TOO FAR.
"THE ANGELS WOULD NEVER BOW TO THIS NEW TOY HE WAS BUILDING."

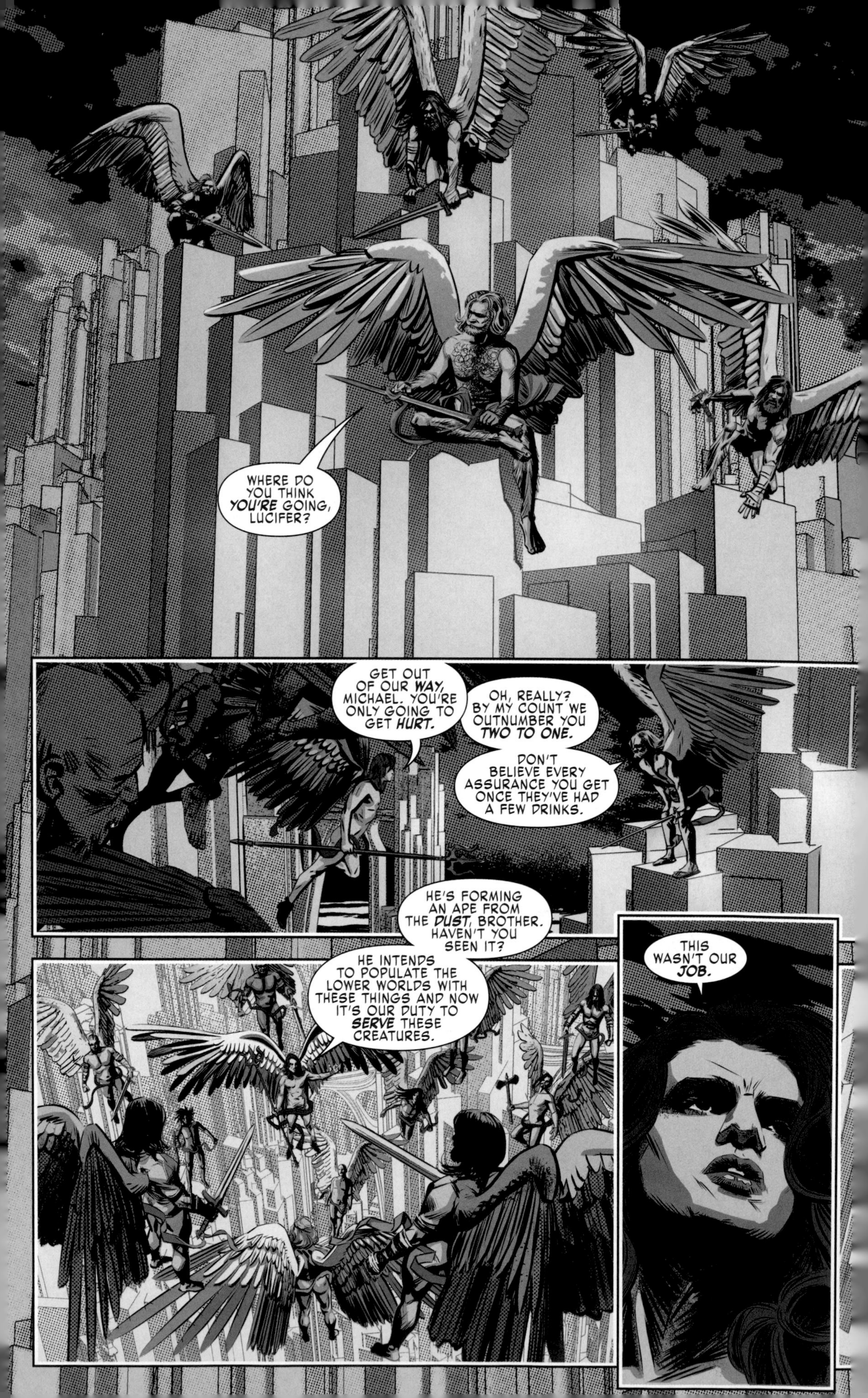
WHERE DO YOU THINK YOU'RE GOING, LUCIFER?
GET OUT OF OUR WAY, MICHAEL. YOU'RE ONLY GOING TO GET HURT.
OH, REALLY? BY MY COUNT WE OUTNUMBER YOU TWO TO ONE.
DON'T BELIEVE EVERY ASSURANCE YOU GET ONCE THEY'VE HAD A FEW DRINKS.
HE'S FORMING AN APE FROM THE DUST, BROTHER. HAVEN'T YOU SEEN IT?
HE INTENDS TO POPULATE THE LOWER WORLDS WITH THESE THINGS AND NOW IT'S OUR DUTY TO SERVE THESE CREATURES.
THIS WASN'T OUR JOB.

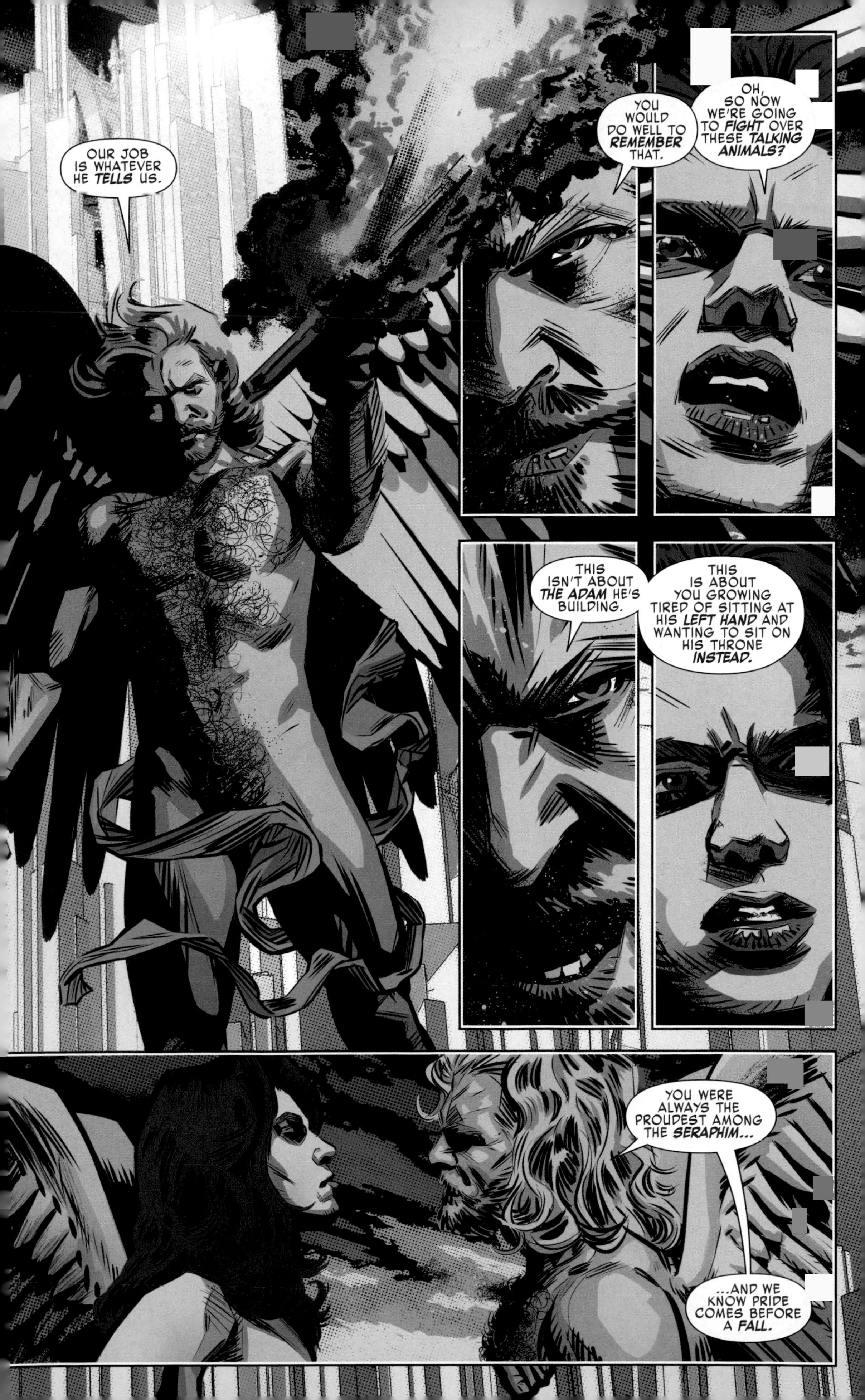

OUR JOB IS WHATEVER HE TELLS US.
YOU WOULD DO WELL TO REMEMBER THAT.
OH, SO NOW WE'RE GOING TO FIGHT OVER THESE TALKING ANIMALS?
THIS ISN'T ABOUT THE ADAM HE'S BUILDING.
THIS IS ABOUT YOU GROWING TIRED OF SITTING AT HIS LEFT HAND AND WANTING TO SIT ON HIS THRONE INSTEAD.
YOU WERE ALWAYS THE PROUDEST AMONG THE SERAPHIM...
...AND WE KNOW PRIDE COMES BEFORE A FALL.

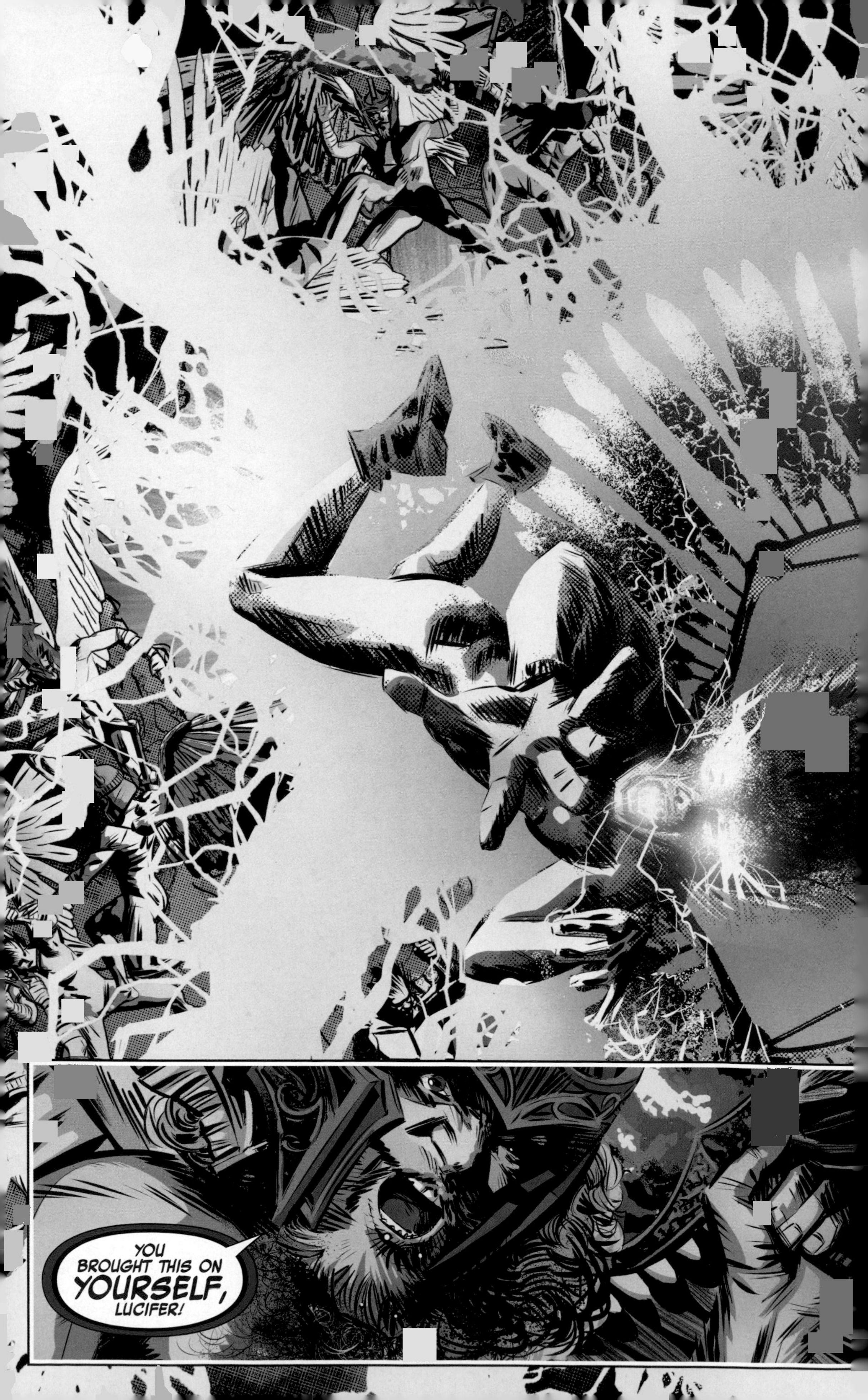
YOU BROUGHT THIS ON YOURSELF, LUCIFER!

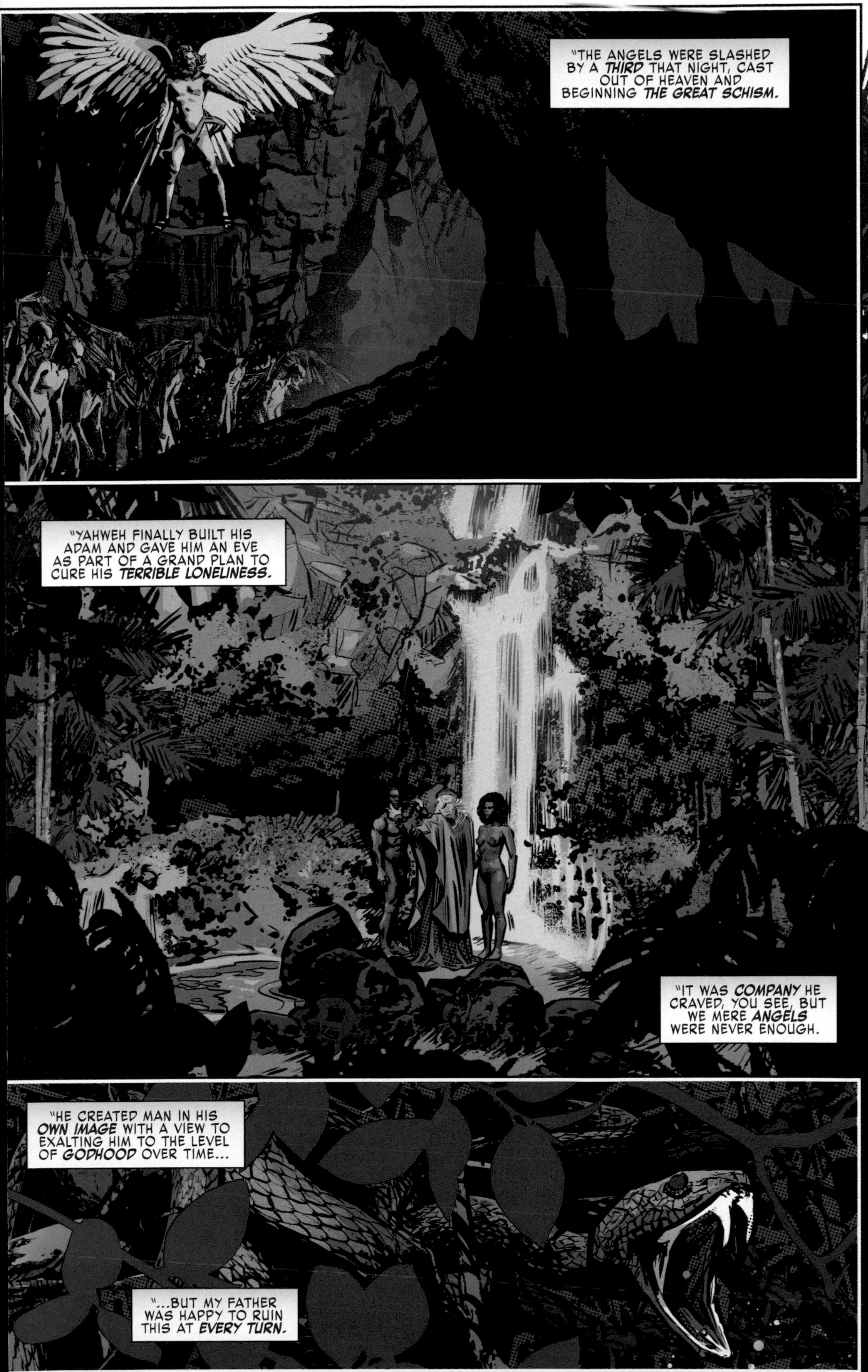
"THE ANGELS WERE SLASHED BY A THIRD THAT NIGHT, CAST OUT OF HEAVEN AND BEGINNING THE GREAT SCHISM.
"YAHWEH FINALLY BUILT HIS ADAM AND GAVE HIM AN EVE AS PART OF A GRAND PLAN TO CURE HIS TERRIBLE LONELINESS.
"IT WAS COMPANY HE CRAVED, YOU SEE, BUT WE MERE ANGELS WERE NEVER ENOUGH.
"HE CREATED MAN IN HIS OWN IMAGE WITH A VIEW TO EXALTING HIM TO THE LEVEL OF GODHOOD OVER TIME...
"...BUT MY FATHER WAS HAPPY TO RUIN THIS AT EVERY TURN.

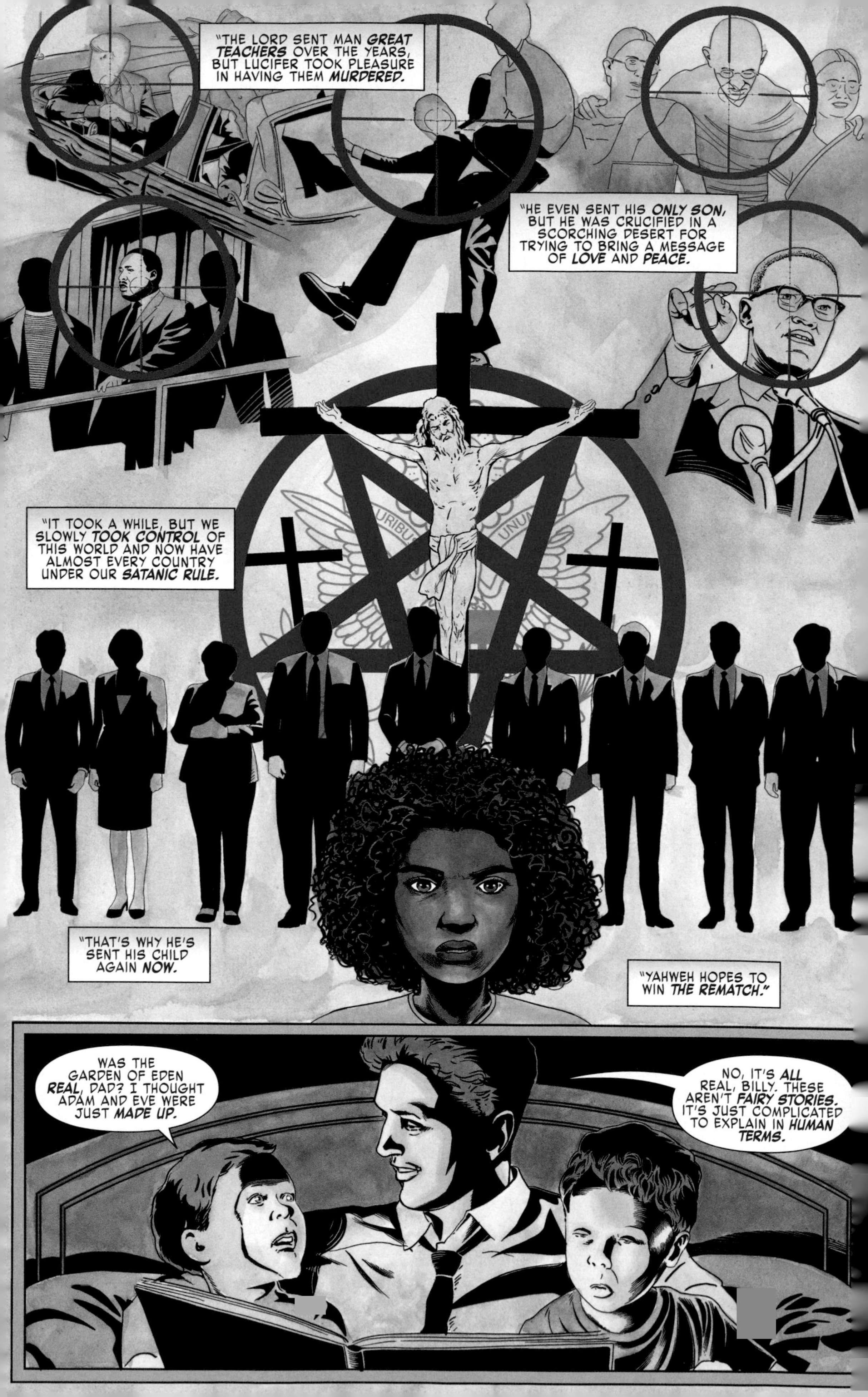
"THE LORD SENT MAN GREAT TEACHERS OVER THE YEARS, BUT LUCIFER TOOK PLEASURE IN HAVING THEM MURDERED.
"HE EVEN SENT HIS ONLY SON, BUT HE WAS CRUCIFIED IN A SCORCHING DESERT FOR TRYING TO BRING A MESSAGE OF LOVE AND PEACE.
"IT TOOK A WHILE, BUT WE SLOWLY TOOK CONTROL OF THIS WORLD AND NOW HAVE ALMOST EVERY COUNTRY UNDER OUR SATANIC RULE.
"THAT'S WHY HE'S SENT HIS CHILD AGAIN NOW.
"YAHWEH HOPES TO WIN THE REMATCH."
WAS THE GARDEN OF EDEN REAL, DAD? I THOUGHT ADAM AND EVE WERE JUST MADE UP.
NO, IT'S ALL REAL, BILLY. THESE AREN'T FAIRY STORIES. IT'S JUST COMPLICATED TO EXPLAIN IN HUMAN TERMS.

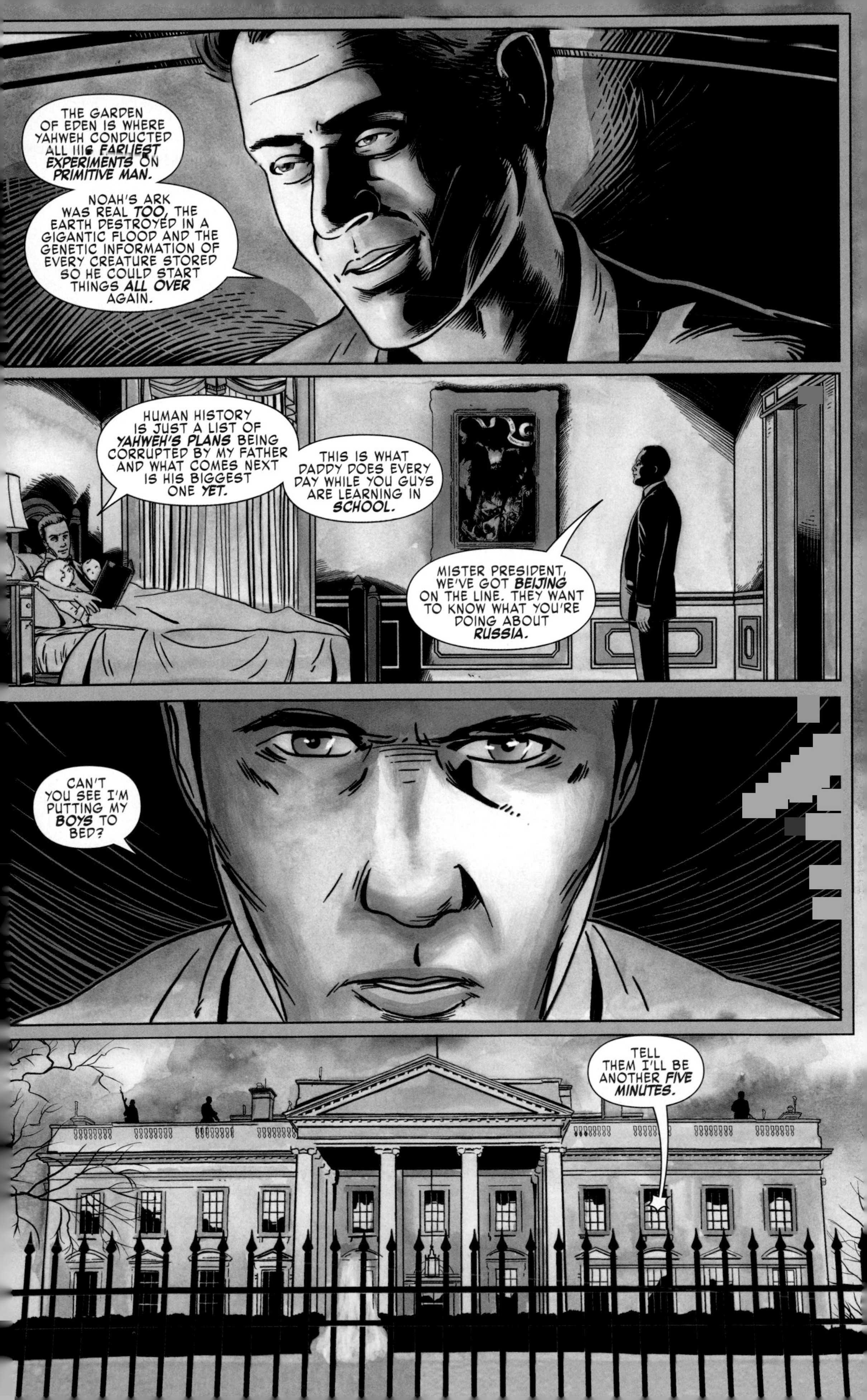
THE GARDEN OF EDEN IS WHERE YAHWEH CONDUCTED ALL HIS EARLIEST EXPERIMENTS ON PRIMITIVE MAN.
NOAH'S ARK WAS REAL TOO, THE EARTH DESTROYED IN A GIGANTIC FLOOD AND THE GENETIC INFORMATION OF EVERY CREATURE STORED SO HE COULD START THINGS ALL OVER AGAIN.
HUMAN HISTORY IS JUST A LIST OF YAHWEH'S PLANS BEING CORRUPTED BY MY FATHER AND WHAT COMES NEXT IS HIS BIGGEST ONE YET.
THIS IS WHAT DADDY DOES EVERY DAY WHILE YOU GUYS ARE LEARNING IN SCHOOL.
MISTER PRESIDENT, WE'VE GOT BEIJING ON THE LINE. THEY WANT TO KNOW WHAT YOU'RE DOING ABOUT RUSSIA.
CAN'T YOU SEE I'M PUTTING MY BOYS TO BED?
TELL THEM I'LL BE ANOTHER FIVE MINUTES.

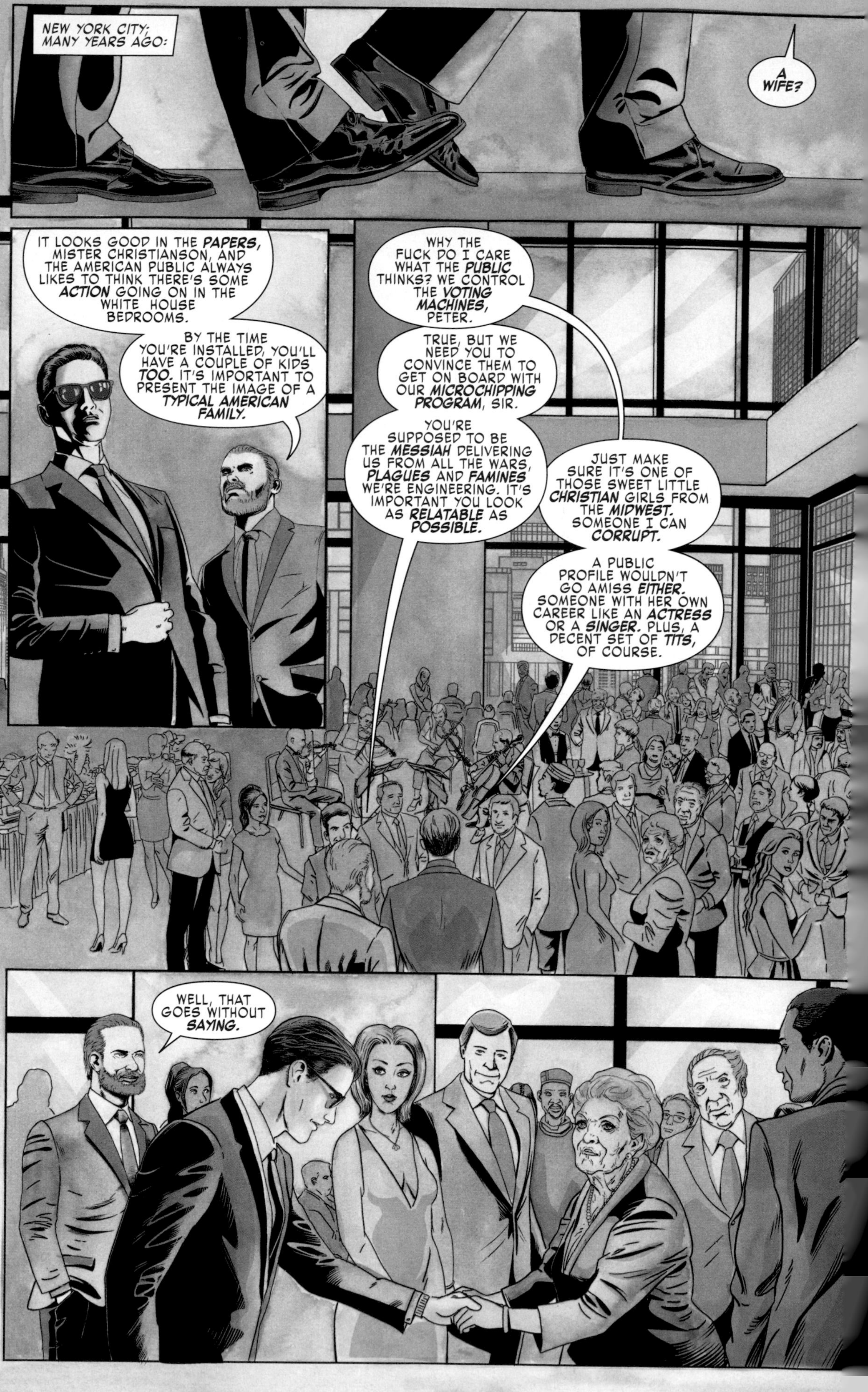
NEW YORK CITY; MANY YEARS AGO:
A WIFE?
IT LOOKS GOOD IN THE PAPERS, MISTER CHRISTIANSON, AND THE AMERICAN PUBLIC ALWAYS LIKES TO THINK THERE'S SOME ACTION GOING ON IN THE WHITE HOUSE BEDROOMS.
BY THE TIME YOU'RE INSTALLED, YOU'LL HAVE A COUPLE OF KIDS TOO. IT'S IMPORTANT TO PRESENT THE IMAGE OF A TYPICAL AMERICAN FAMILY.
WHY THE FUCK DO I CARE WHAT THE PUBLIC THINKS? WE CONTROL THE VOTING MACHINES, PETER.
TRUE, BUT WE NEED YOU TO CONVINCE THEM TO GET ON BOARD WITH OUR MICROCHIPPING PROGRAM, SIR.
YOU'RE SUPPOSED TO BE THE MESSIAH DELIVERING US FROM ALL THE WARS, PLAGUES AND FAMINES WE'RE ENGINEERING. IT'S IMPORTANT YOU LOOK AS RELATABLE AS POSSIBLE.
JUST MAKE SURE IT'S ONE OF THOSE SWEET LITTLE CHRISTIAN GIRLS FROM THE MIDWEST. SOMEONE I CAN CORRUPT.
A PUBLIC PROFILE WOULDN'T GO AMISS EITHER. SOMEONE WITH HER OWN CAREER LIKE AN ACTRESS OR A SINGER. PLUS, A DECENT SET OF TITS, OF COURSE.
WELL, THAT GOES WITHOUT SAYING.

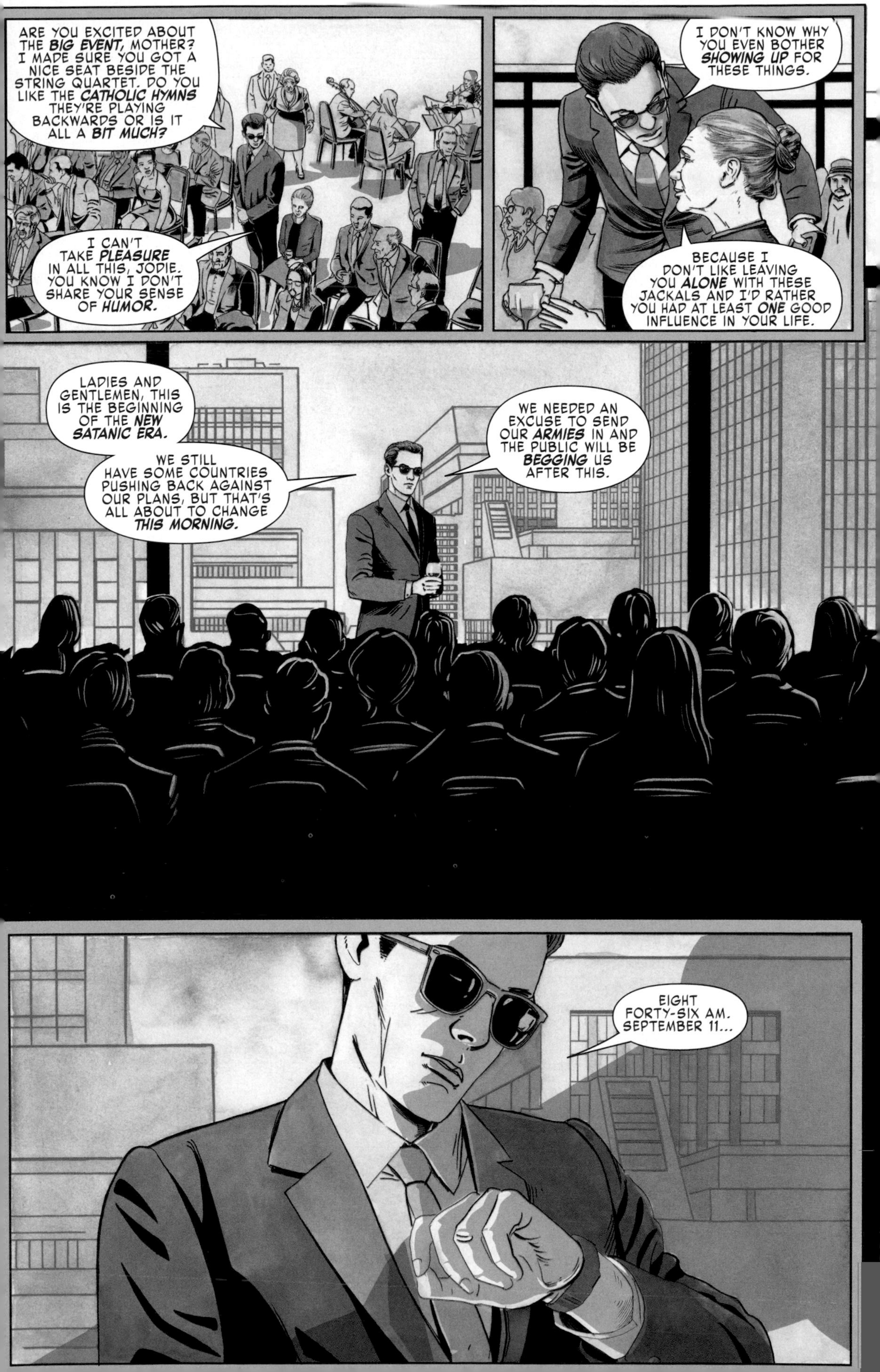
ARE YOU EXCITED ABOUT THE BIG EVENT, MOTHER? I MADE SURE YOU GOT A NICE SEAT BESIDE THE STRING QUARTET. DO YOU LIKE THE CATHOLIC HYMNS THEY'RE PLAYING BACKWARDS OR IS IT ALL A BIT MUCH?
I CAN'T TAKE PLEASURE IN ALL THIS, JODIE. YOU KNOW I DON'T SHARE YOUR SENSE OF HUMOR.
I DON'T KNOW WHY YOU EVEN BOTHER SHOWING UP FOR THESE THINGS.
BECAUSE I DON'T LIKE LEAVING YOU ALONE WITH THESE JACKALS AND I'D RATHER YOU HAD AT LEAST ONE GOOD INFLUENCE IN YOUR LIFE.
LADIES AND GENTLEMEN, THIS IS THE BEGINNING OF THE NEW SATANIC ERA.
WE STILL HAVE SOME COUNTRIES PUSHING BACK AGAINST OUR PLANS, BUT THAT'S ALL ABOUT TO CHANGE THIS MORNING.
WE NEEDED AN EXCUSE TO SEND OUR ARMIES IN AND THE PUBLIC WILL BE BEGGING US AFTER THIS.
EIGHT FORTY-SIX AM. SEPTEMBER 11...

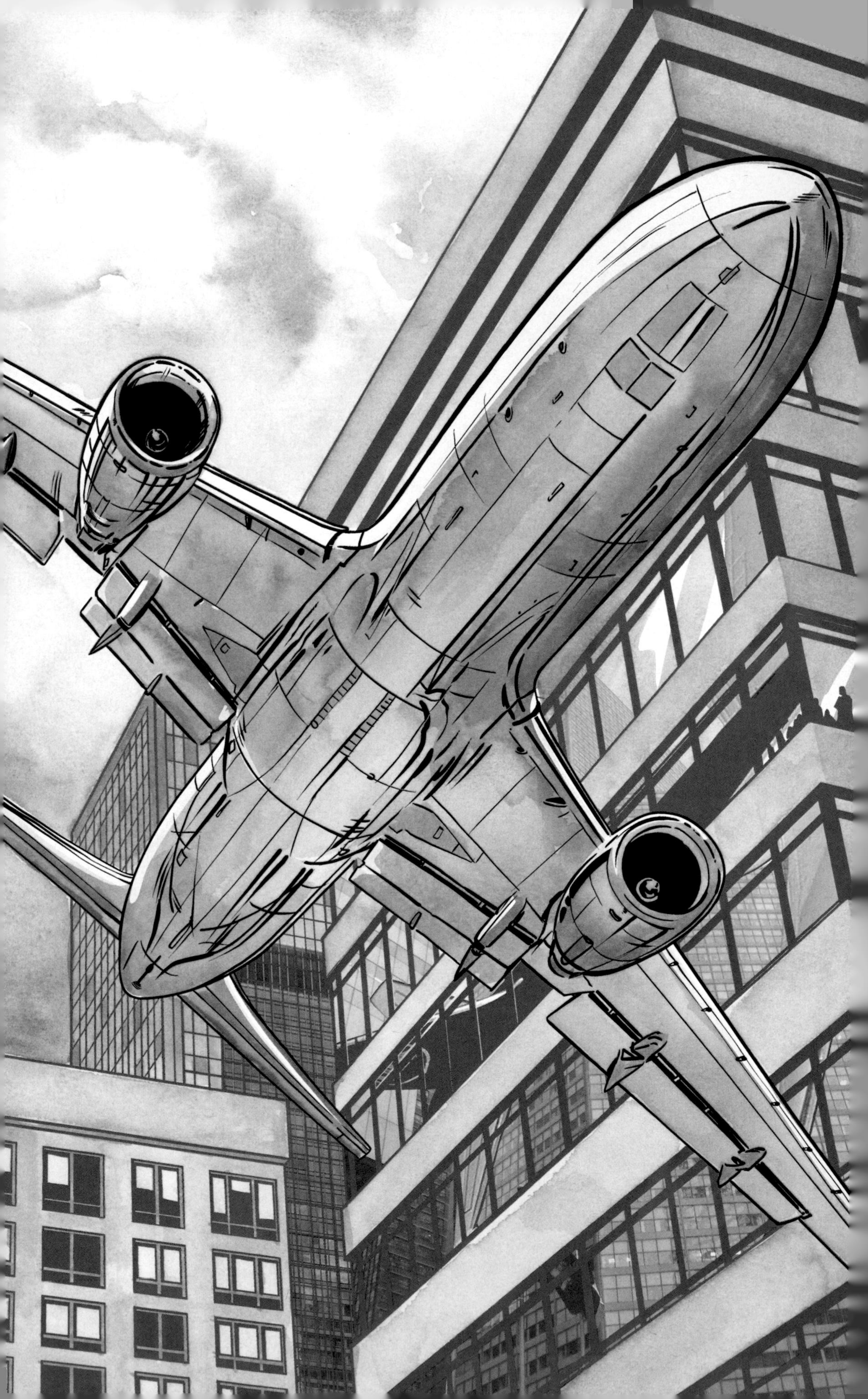

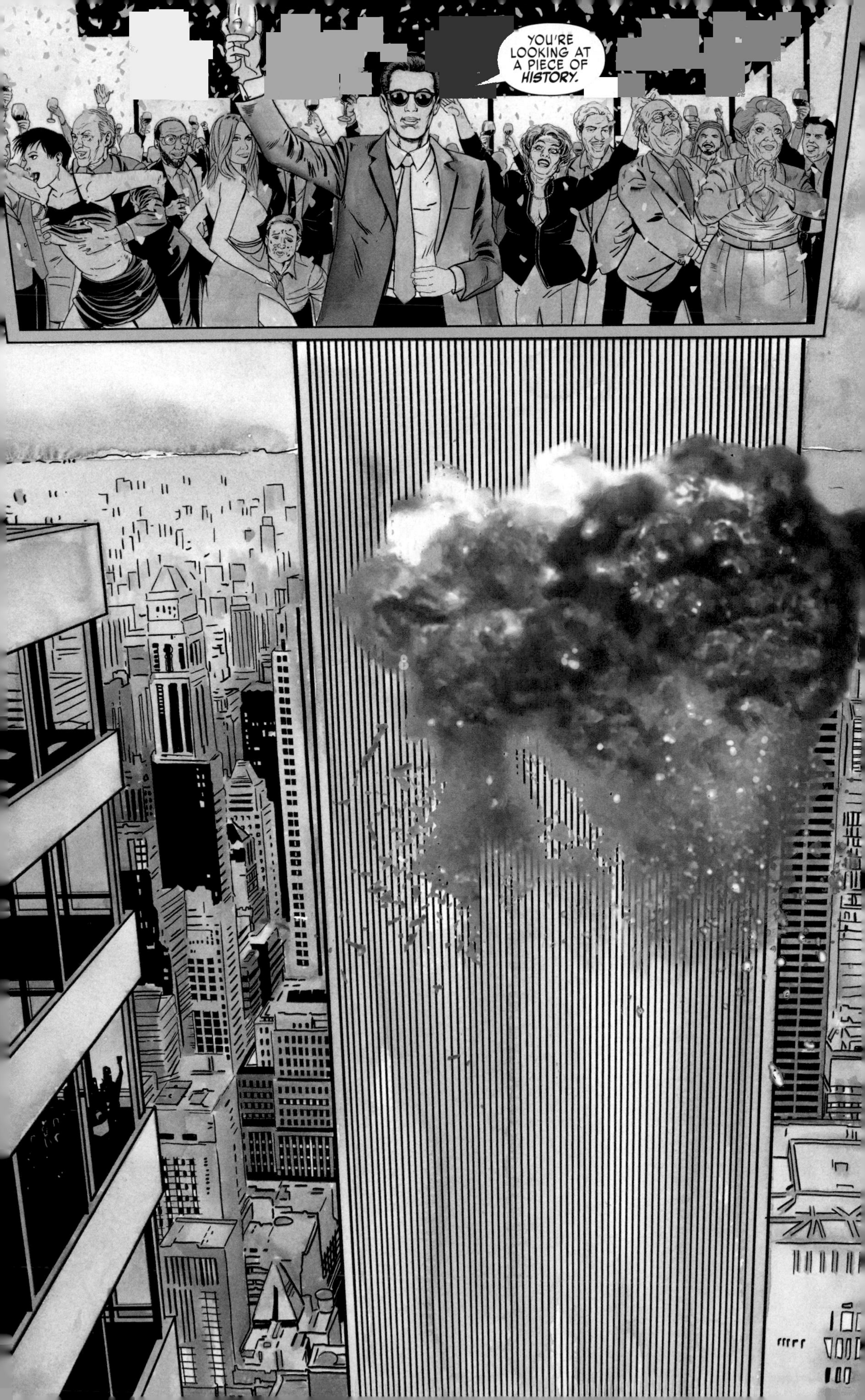
YOU'RE LOOKING AT A PIECE OF HISTORY.

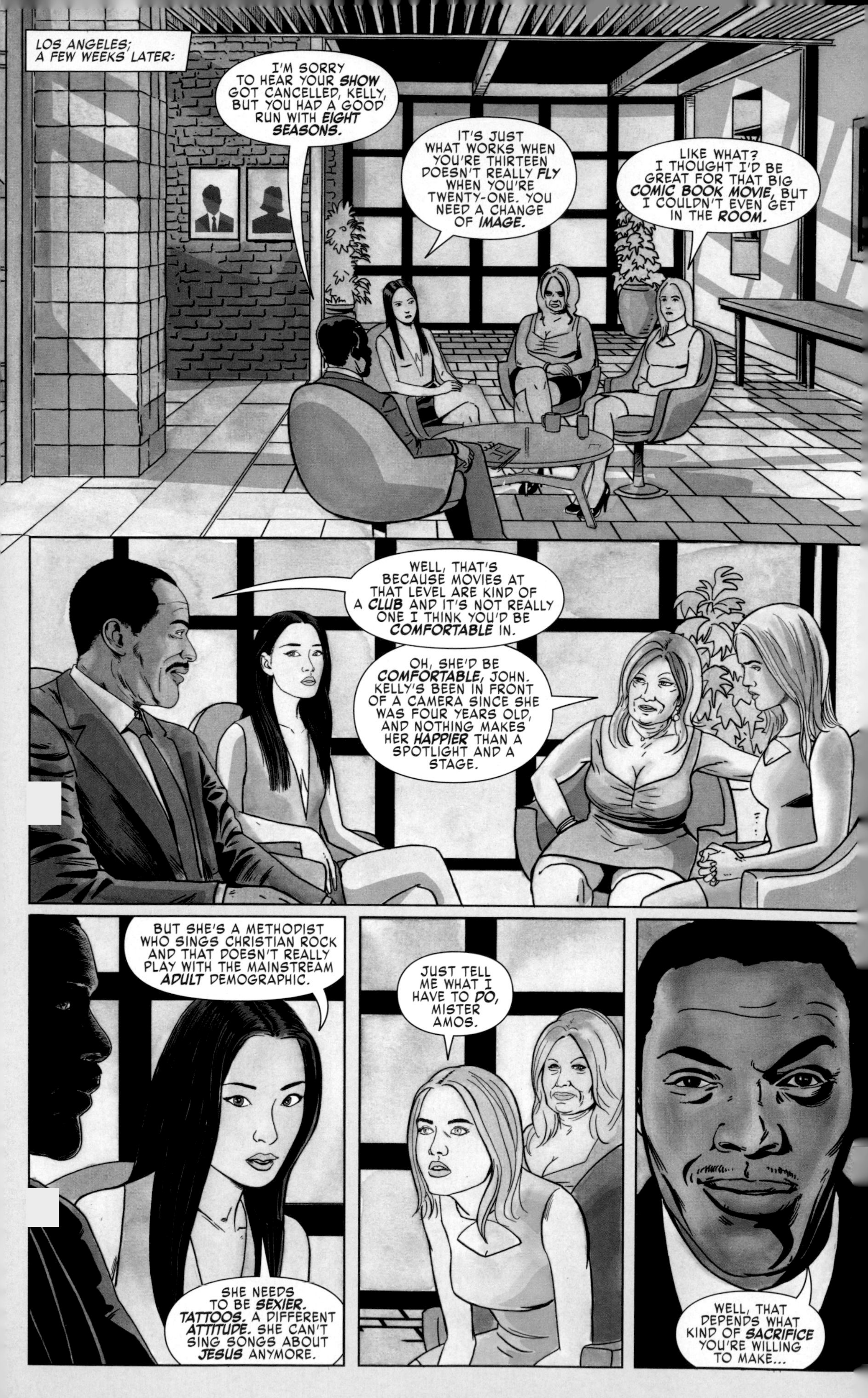
LOS ANGELES; A FEW WEEKS LATER:
I'M SORRY TO HEAR YOUR SHOW GOT CANCELLED, KELLY, BUT YOU HAD A GOOD RUN WITH EIGHT SEASONS.
IT'S JUST WHAT WORKS WHEN YOU'RE THIRTEEN DOESN'T REALLY FLY WHEN YOU'RE TWENTY-ONE. YOU NEED A CHANGE OF IMAGE.
LIKE WHAT? I THOUGHT I'D BE GREAT FOR THAT BIG COMIC BOOK MOVIE, BUT I COULDN'T EVEN GET IN THE ROOM.
WELL, THAT'S BECAUSE MOVIES AT THAT LEVEL ARE KIND OF A CLUB AND IT'S NOT REALLY ONE I THINK YOU'D BE COMFORTABLE IN.
OH, SHE'D BE COMFORTABLE, JOHN. KELLY'S BEEN IN FRONT OF A CAMERA SINCE SHE WAS FOUR YEARS OLD, AND NOTHING MAKES HER HAPPIER THAN A SPOTLIGHT AND A STAGE.
BUT SHE'S A METHODIST WHO SINGS CHRISTIAN ROCK AND THAT DOESN'T REALLY PLAY WITH THE MAINSTREAM ADULT DEMOGRAPHIC.
SHE NEEDS TO BE SEXIER. TATTOOS. A DIFFERENT ATTITUDE. SHE CAN'T SING SONGS ABOUT JESUS ANYMORE.
JUST TELL ME WHAT I HAVE TO DO, MISTER AMOS.
WELL, THAT DEPENDS WHAT KIND OF SACRIFICE YOU'RE WILLING TO MAKE...

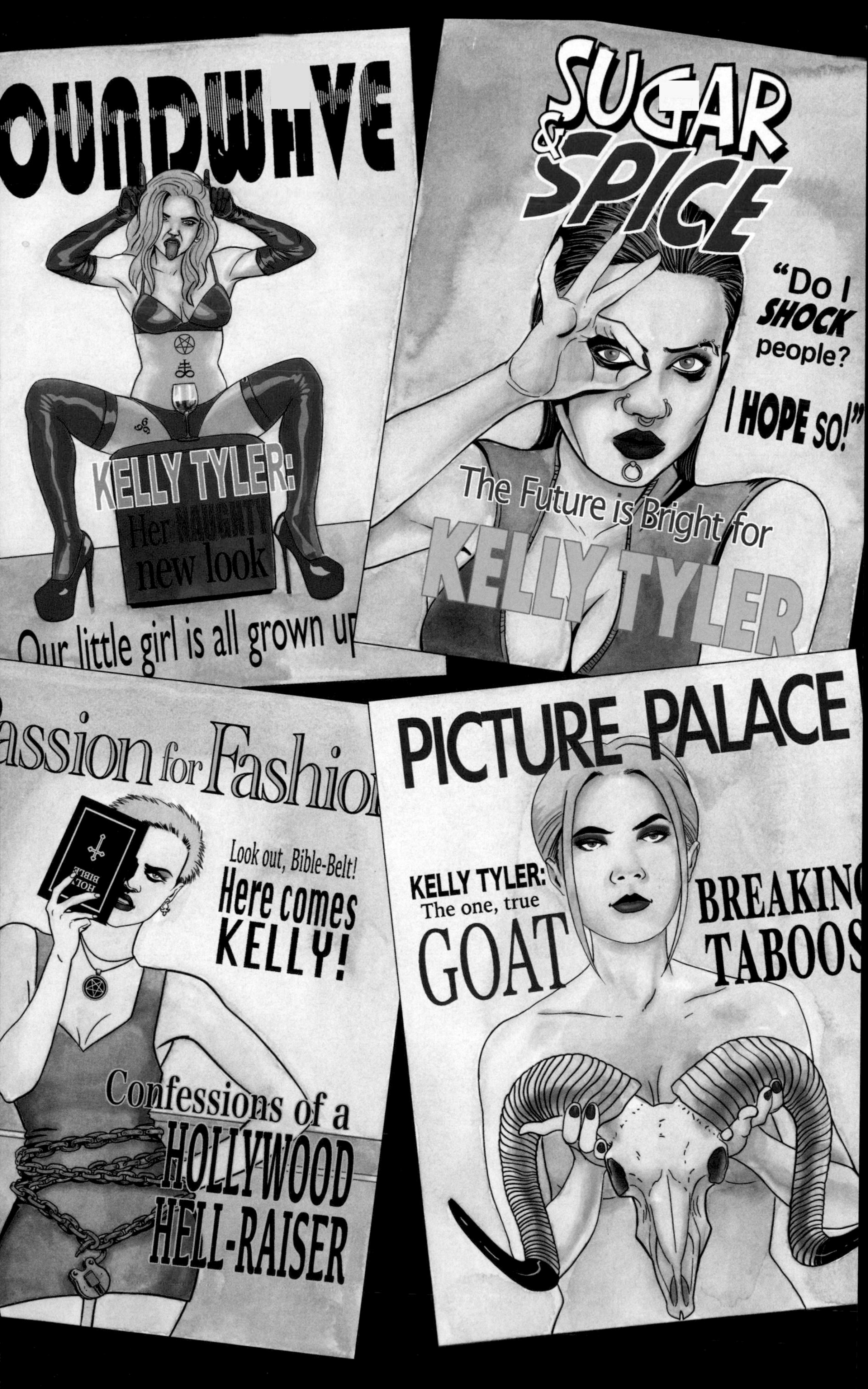

OUNDWAVE
KELLY TYLER:
Her NAUGHTY new look
Our little girl is all grown up
SUGAR & SPICE
"Do I SHOCK people? I HOPE SO!"
The Future is Bright for KELLY TYLER
assion for Fashion
HOLY BIBLE
Look out, Bible-Belt!
Here comes KELLY!
Confessions of a HOLLYWOOD HELL-RAISER
PICTURE PALACE
KELLY TYLER:
The one, true GOAT
BREAKING TABOOS

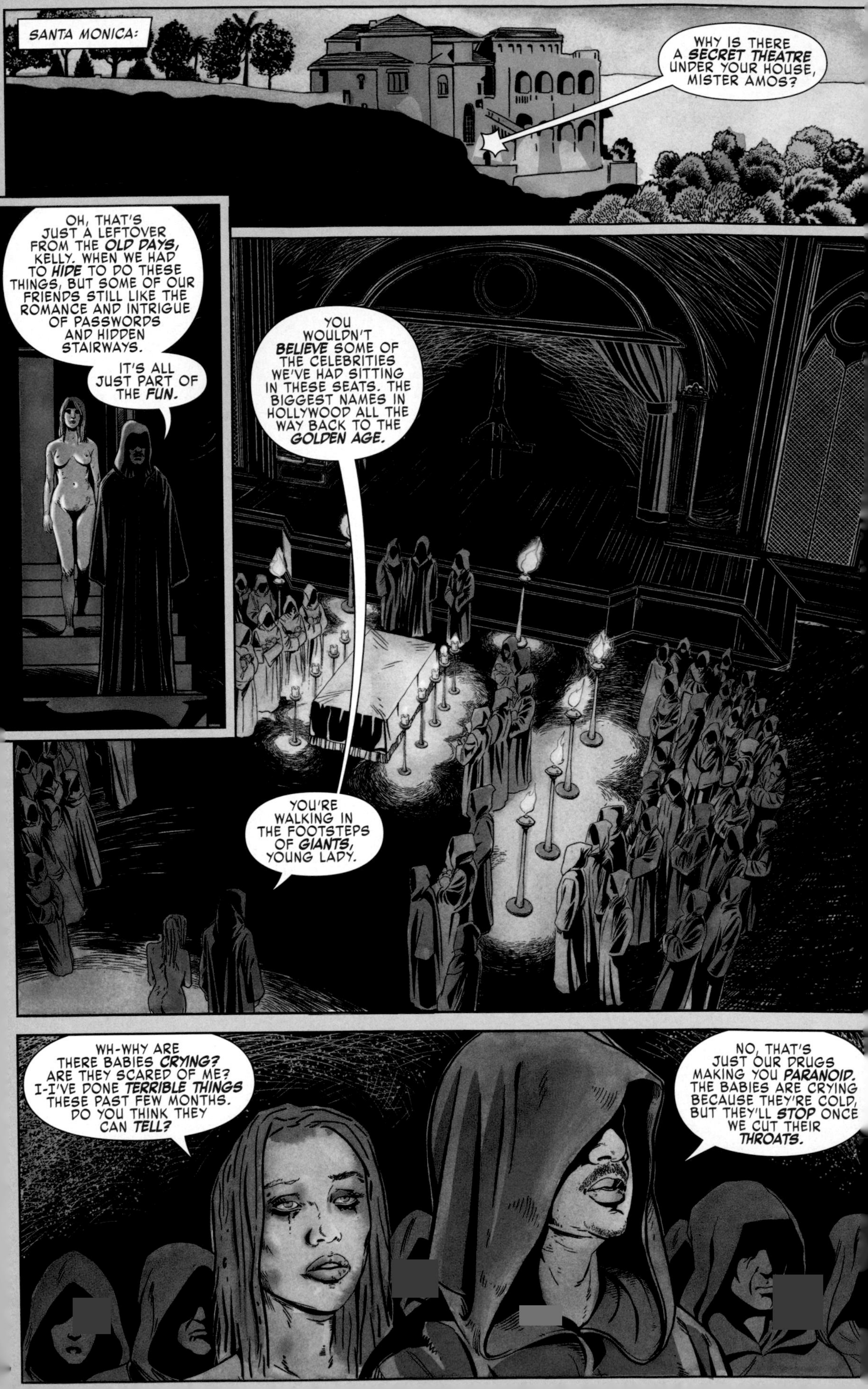
SANTA MONICA:
WHY IS THERE A SECRET THEATRE UNDER YOUR HOUSE, MISTER AMOS?
OH, THAT'S JUST A LEFTOVER FROM THE OLD DAYS, KELLY. WHEN WE HAD TO HIDE TO DO THESE THINGS, BUT SOME OF OUR FRIENDS STILL LIKE THE ROMANCE AND INTRIGUE OF PASSWORDS AND HIDDEN STAIRWAYS.
IT'S ALL JUST PART OF THE FUN.
YOU WOULDN'T BELIEVE SOME OF THE CELEBRITIES WE'VE HAD SITTING IN THESE SEATS. THE BIGGEST NAMES IN HOLLYWOOD ALL THE WAY BACK TO THE GOLDEN AGE.
YOU'RE WALKING IN THE FOOTSTEPS OF GIANTS, YOUNG LADY.
WH-WHY ARE THERE BABIES CRYING? ARE THEY SCARED OF ME? I-I'VE DONE TERRIBLE THINGS THESE PAST FEW MONTHS. DO YOU THINK THEY CAN TELL?
NO, THAT'S JUST OUR DRUGS MAKING YOU PARANOID. THE BABIES ARE CRYING BECAUSE THEY'RE COLD, BUT THEY'LL STOP ONCE WE CUT THEIR THROATS.

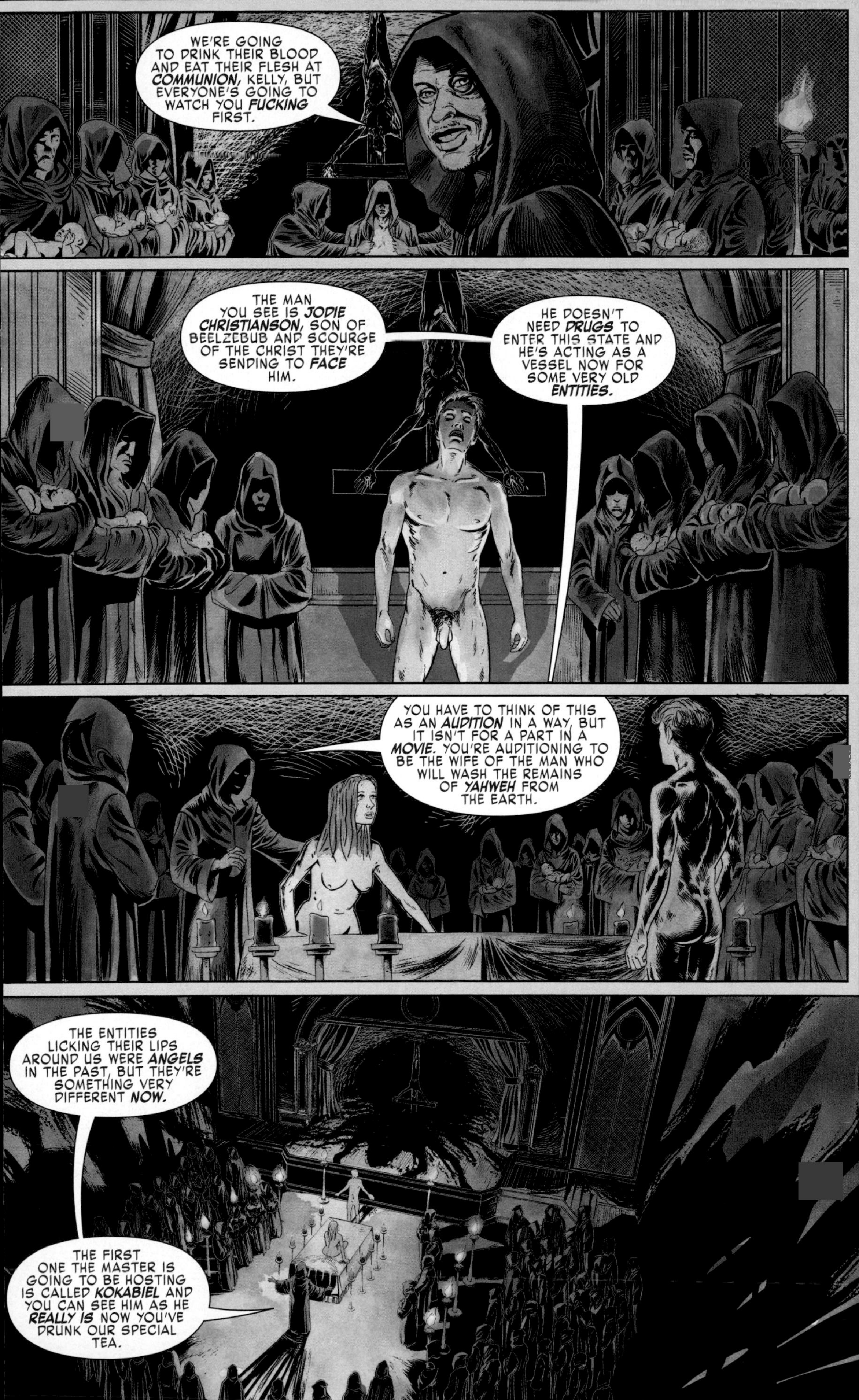
WE'RE GOING TO DRINK THEIR BLOOD AND EAT THEIR FLESH AT COMMUNION, KELLY, BUT EVERYONE'S GOING TO WATCH YOU FUCKING FIRST.
THE MAN YOU SEE IS JODIE CHRISTIANSON, SON OF BEELZEBUB AND SCOURGE OF THE CHRIST THEY'RE SENDING TO FACE HIM.
HE DOESN'T NEED DRUGS TO ENTER THIS STATE AND HE'S ACTING AS A VESSEL NOW FOR SOME VERY OLD ENTITIES.
YOU HAVE TO THINK OF THIS AS AN AUDITION IN A WAY, BUT IT ISN'T FOR A PART IN A MOVIE. YOU'RE AUDITIONING TO BE THE WIFE OF THE MAN WHO WILL WASH THE REMAINS OF YAHWEH FROM THE EARTH.
THE ENTITIES LICKING THEIR LIPS AROUND US WERE ANGELS IN THE PAST, BUT THEY'RE SOMETHING VERY DIFFERENT NOW.
THE FIRST ONE THE MASTER IS GOING TO BE HOSTING IS CALLED KOKABIEL AND YOU CAN SEE HIM AS HE REALLY IS NOW YOU'VE DRUNK OUR SPECIAL TEA.

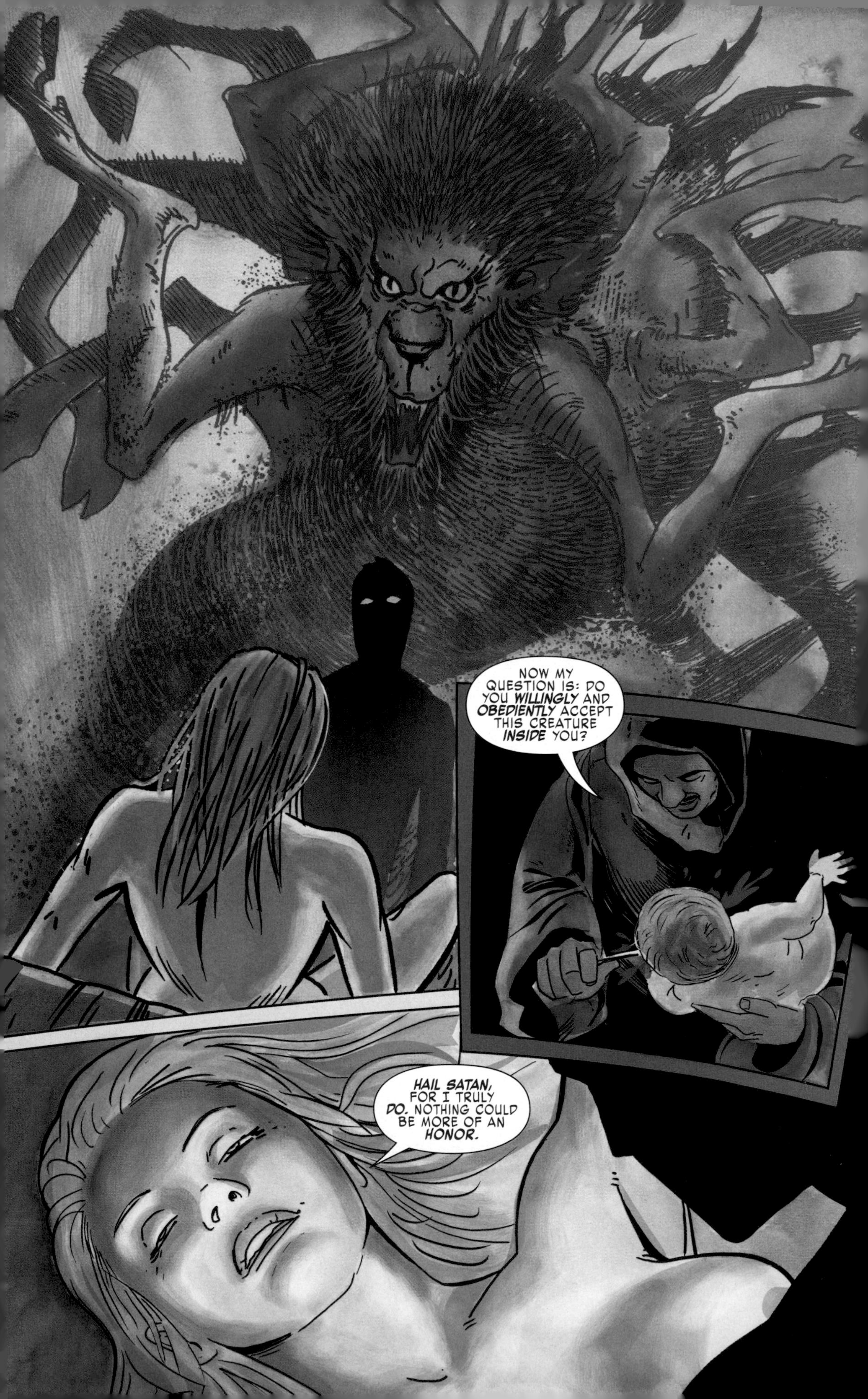
NOW MY QUESTION IS: DO YOU WILLINGLY AND OBEDIENTLY ACCEPT THIS CREATURE INSIDE YOU?
HAIL SATAN, FOR I TRULY DO. NOTHING COULD BE MORE OF AN HONOR.

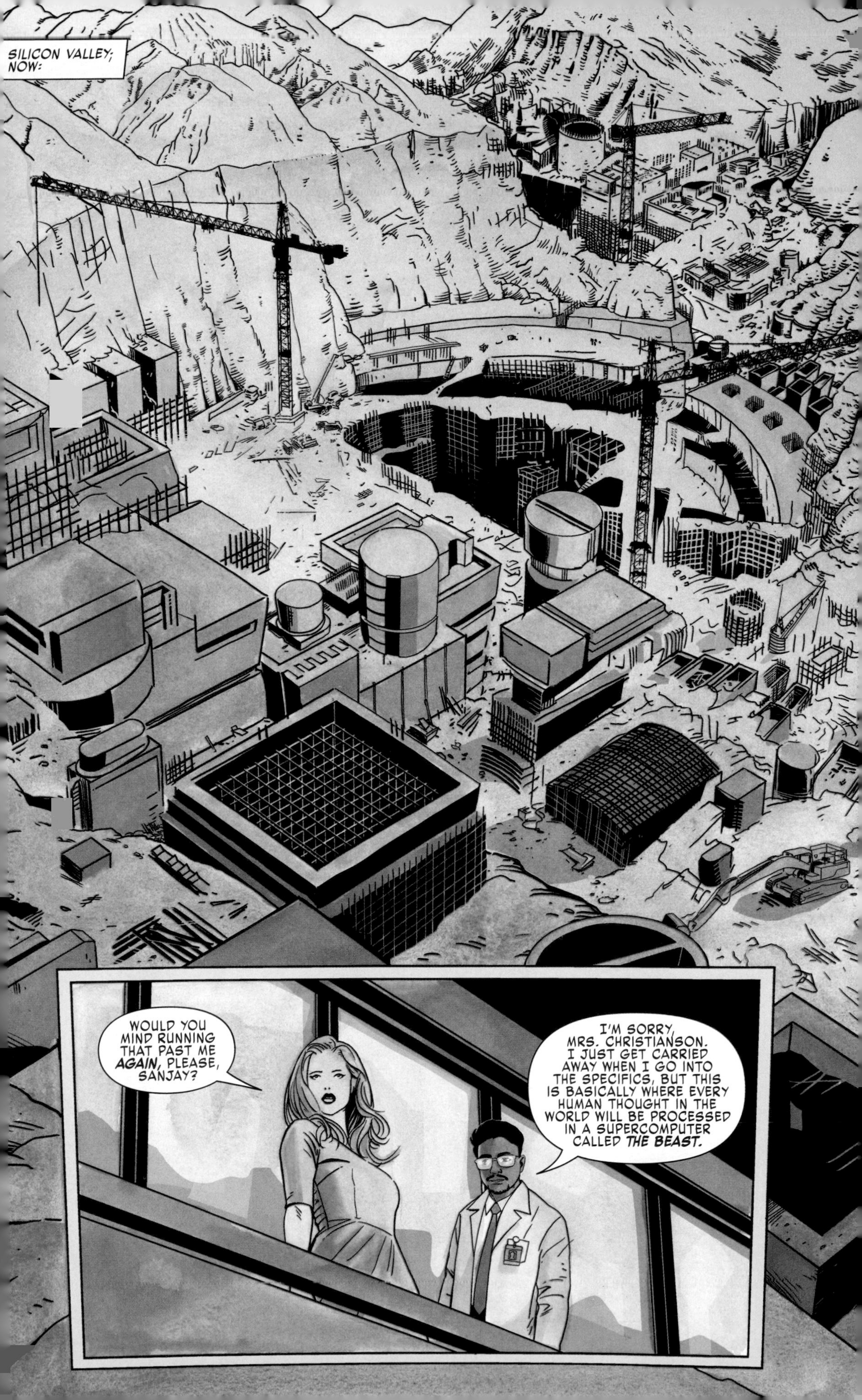
SILICON VALLEY; NOW:
WOULD YOU MIND RUNNING THAT PAST ME AGAIN, PLEASE, SANJAY?
I'M SORRY, MRS. CHRISTIANSON. I JUST GET CARRIED AWAY WHEN I GO INTO THE SPECIFICS, BUT THIS IS BASICALLY WHERE EVERY HUMAN THOUGHT IN THE WORLD WILL BE PROCESSED IN A SUPERCOMPUTER CALLED THE BEAST.

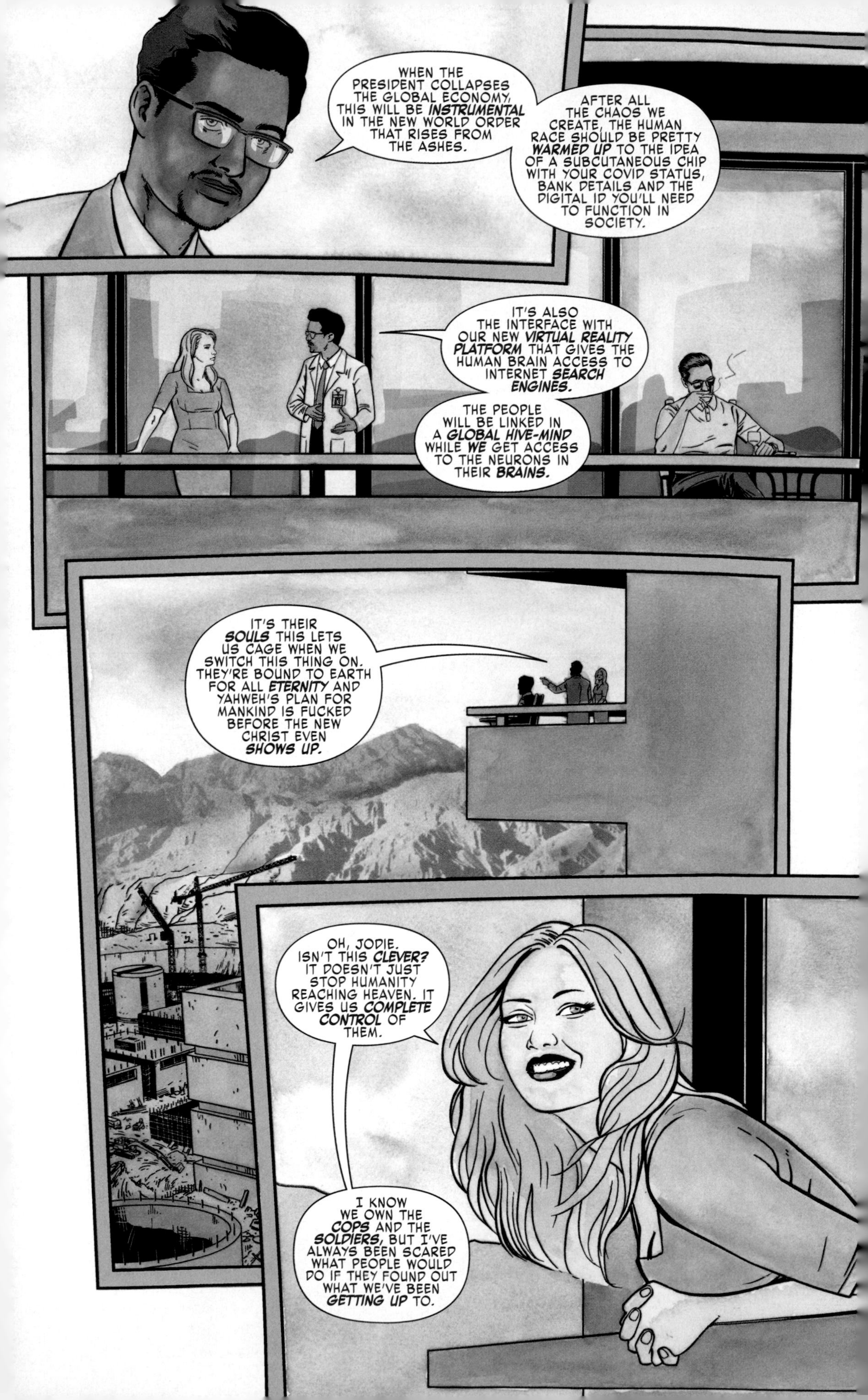
WHEN THE PRESIDENT COLLAPSES THE GLOBAL ECONOMY, THIS WILL BE INSTRUMENTAL IN THE NEW WORLD ORDER THAT RISES FROM THE ASHES.
AFTER ALL THE CHAOS WE CREATE, THE HUMAN RACE SHOULD BE PRETTY WARMED UP TO THE IDEA OF A SUBCUTANEOUS CHIP WITH YOUR COVID STATUS, BANK DETAILS AND THE DIGITAL ID YOU'LL NEED TO FUNCTION IN SOCIETY.
IT'S ALSO THE INTERFACE WITH OUR NEW VIRTUAL REALITY PLATFORM THAT GIVES THE HUMAN BRAIN ACCESS TO INTERNET SEARCH ENGINES.
THE PEOPLE WILL BE LINKED IN A GLOBAL HIVE-MIND WHILE WE GET ACCESS TO THE NEURONS IN THEIR BRAINS.
IT'S THEIR SOULS THIS LETS US CAGE WHEN WE SWITCH THIS THING ON. THEY'RE BOUND TO EARTH FOR ALL ETERNITY AND YAHWEH'S PLAN FOR MANKIND IS FUCKED BEFORE THE NEW CHRIST EVEN SHOWS UP.
OH, JODIE. ISN'T THIS CLEVER? IT DOESN'T JUST STOP HUMANITY REACHING HEAVEN. IT GIVES US COMPLETE CONTROL OF THEM.
I KNOW WE OWN THE COPS AND THE SOLDIERS, BUT I'VE ALWAYS BEEN SCARED WHAT PEOPLE WOULD DO IF THEY FOUND OUT WHAT WE'VE BEEN GETTING UP TO.

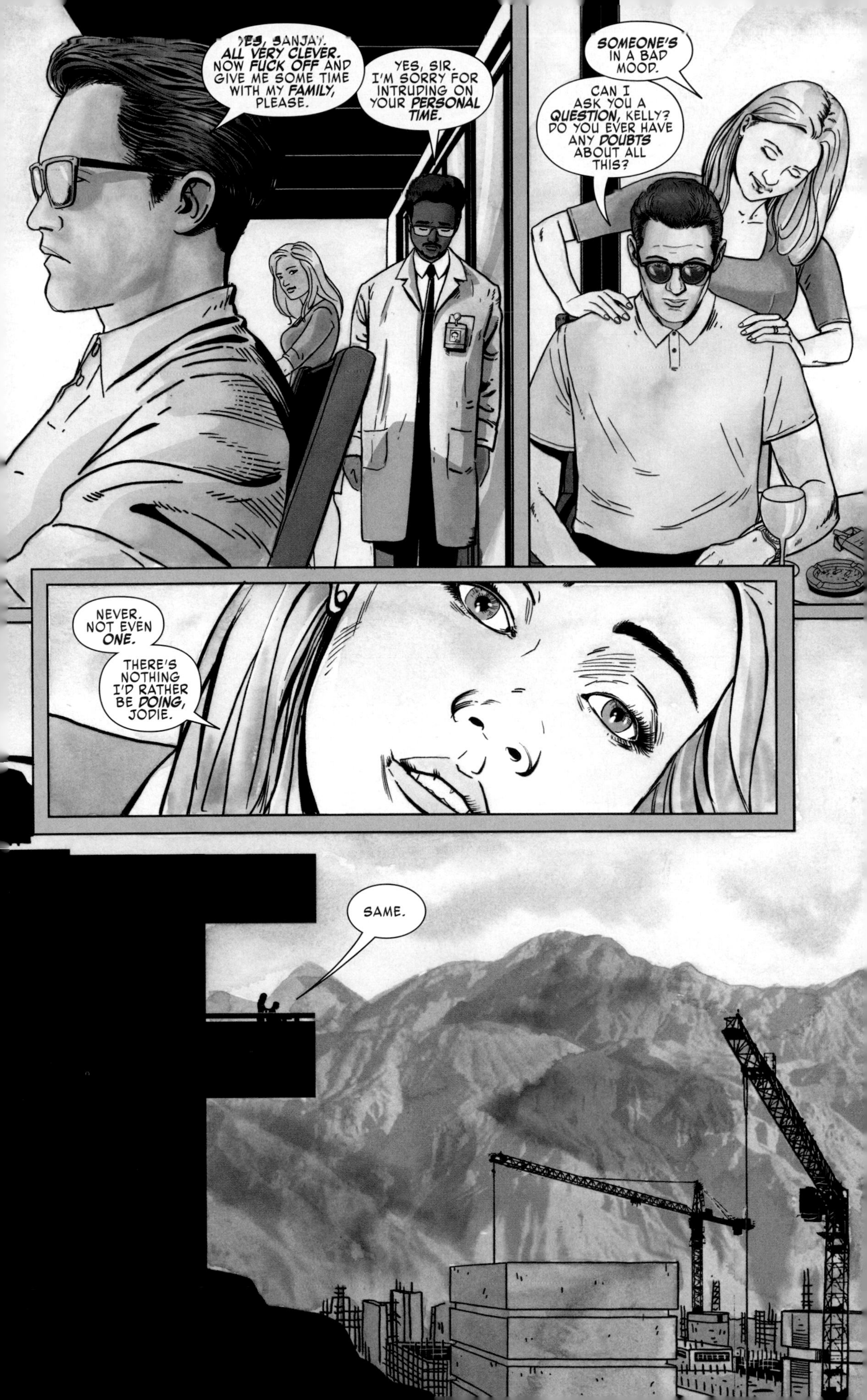
YES, SANJAY. ALL VERY CLEVER. NOW FUCK OFF AND GIVE ME SOME TIME WITH MY FAMILY, PLEASE.
YES, SIR. I'M SORRY FOR INTRUDING ON YOUR PERSONAL TIME.
SOMEONE'S IN A BAD MOOD.
CAN I ASK YOU A QUESTION, KELLY? DO YOU EVER HAVE ANY DOUBTS ABOUT ALL THIS?
NEVER. NOT EVEN ONE.
THERE'S NOTHING I'D RATHER BE DOING, JODIE.
SAME.

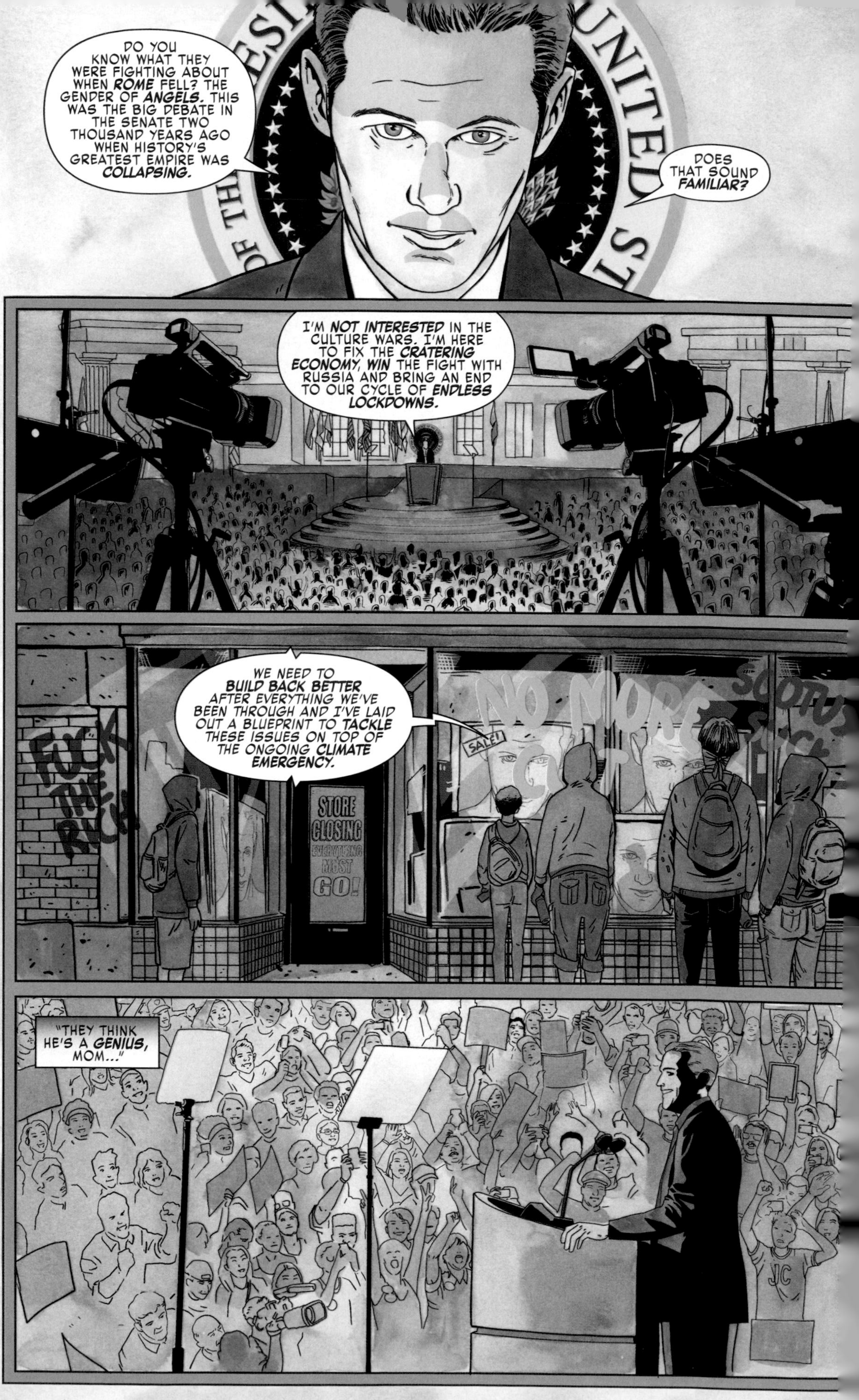
DO YOU KNOW WHAT THEY WERE FIGHTING ABOUT WHEN ROME FELL? THE GENDER OF ANGELS. THIS WAS THE BIG DEBATE IN THE SENATE TWO THOUSAND YEARS AGO WHEN HISTORY'S GREATEST EMPIRE WAS COLLAPSING.
DOES THAT SOUND FAMILIAR?
I'M NOT INTERESTED IN THE CULTURE WARS. I'M HERE TO FIX THE CRATERING ECONOMY, WIN THE FIGHT WITH RUSSIA AND BRING AN END TO OUR CYCLE OF ENDLESS LOCKDOWNS.
WE NEED TO BUILD BACK BETTER AFTER EVERYTHING WE'VE BEEN THROUGH AND I'VE LAID OUT A BLUEPRINT TO TACKLE THESE ISSUES ON TOP OF THE ONGOING CLIMATE EMERGENCY.
FUCK THE RICH
NO MORE
SALE!
STORE CLOSING EVERYTHING MUST GO!
"THEY THINK HE'S A GENIUS, MOM..."
JC

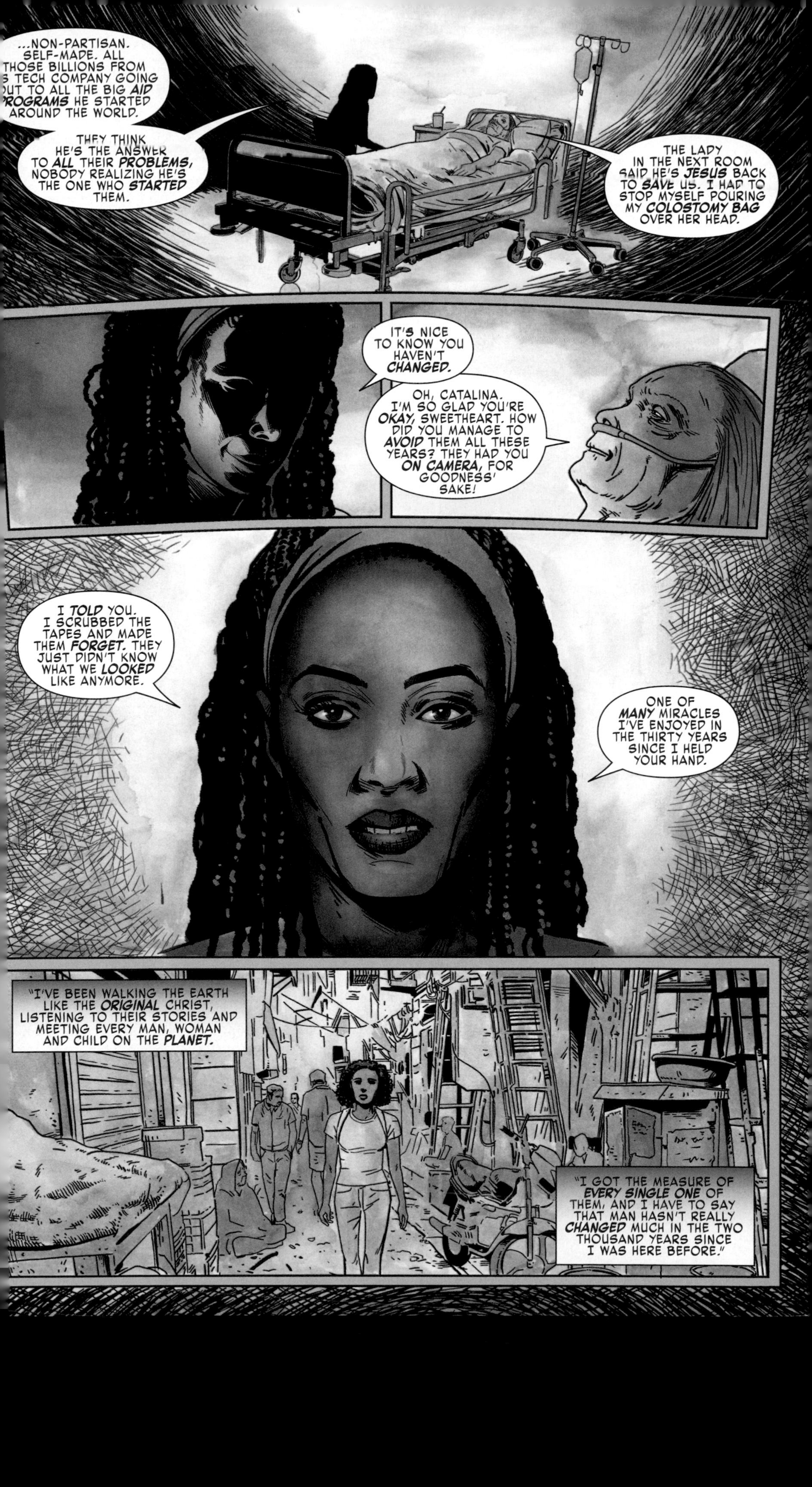
...NON-PARTISAN. SELF-MADE. ALL THOSE BILLIONS FROM S TECH COMPANY GOING OUT TO ALL THE BIG AID PROGRAMS HE STARTED AROUND THE WORLD.
THEY THINK HE'S THE ANSWER TO ALL THEIR PROBLEMS, NOBODY REALIZING HE'S THE ONE WHO STARTED THEM.
THE LADY IN THE NEXT ROOM SAID HE'S JESUS BACK TO SAVE US. I HAD TO STOP MYSELF POURING MY COLOSTOMY BAG OVER HER HEAD.
IT'S NICE TO KNOW YOU HAVEN'T CHANGED.
OH, CATALINA. I'M SO GLAD YOU'RE OKAY, SWEETHEART. HOW DID YOU MANAGE TO AVOID THEM ALL THESE YEARS? THEY HAD YOU ON CAMERA, FOR GOODNESS' SAKE!
I TOLD YOU. I SCRUBBED THE TAPES AND MADE THEM FORGET. THEY JUST DIDN'T KNOW WHAT WE LOOKED LIKE ANYMORE.
ONE OF MANY MIRACLES I'VE ENJOYED IN THE THIRTY YEARS SINCE I HELD YOUR HAND.
"I'VE BEEN WALKING THE EARTH LIKE THE ORIGINAL CHRIST, LISTENING TO THEIR STORIES AND MEETING EVERY MAN, WOMAN AND CHILD ON THE PLANET.
"I GOT THE MEASURE OF EVERY SINGLE ONE OF THEM, AND I HAVE TO SAY THAT MAN HASN'T REALLY CHANGED MUCH IN THE TWO THOUSAND YEARS SINCE I WAS HERE BEFORE."

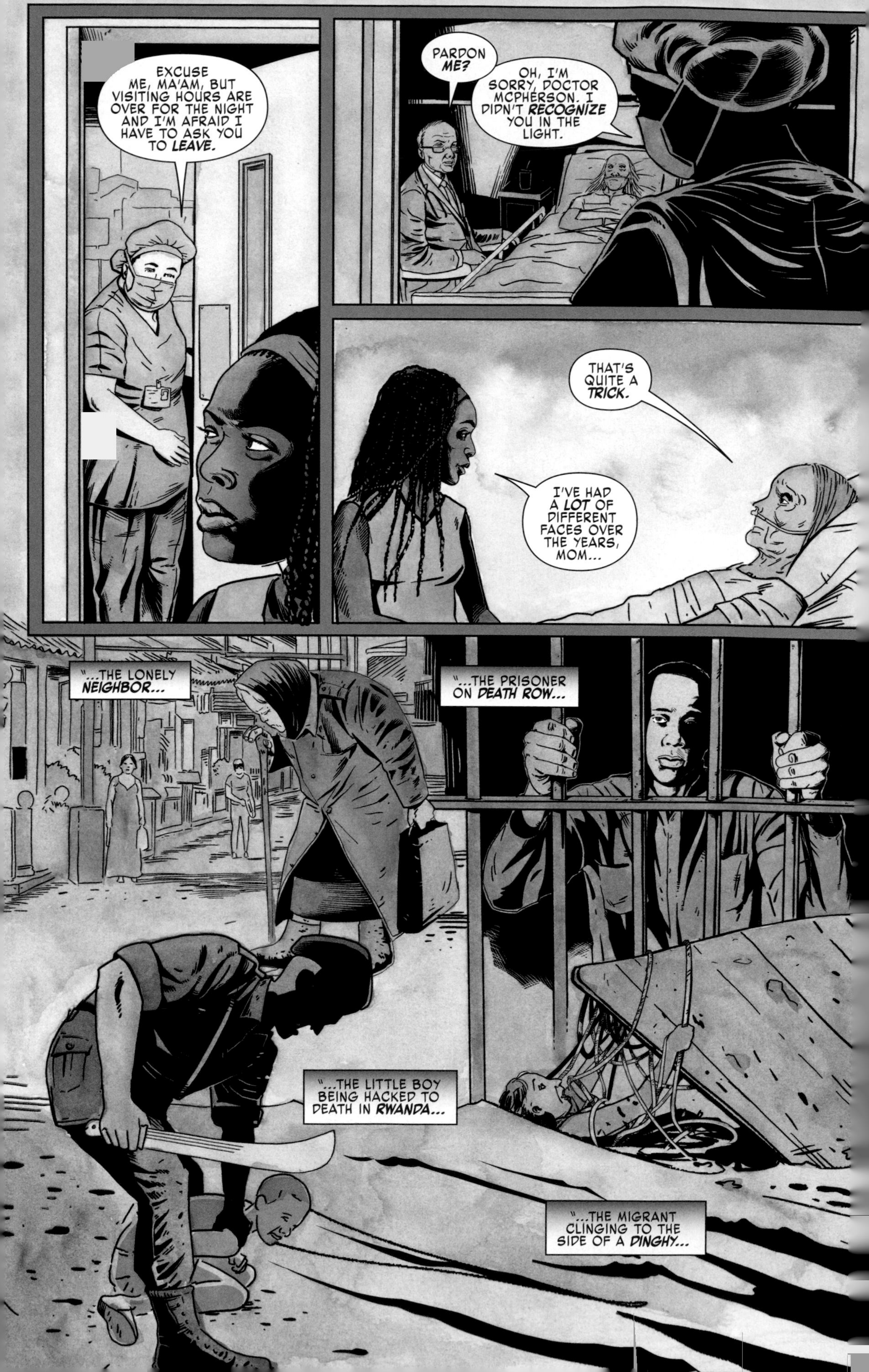
EXCUSE ME, MA'AM, BUT VISITING HOURS ARE OVER FOR THE NIGHT AND I'M AFRAID I HAVE TO ASK YOU TO LEAVE.
PARDON ME?
OH, I'M SORRY, DOCTOR MCPHERSON. I DIDN'T RECOGNIZE YOU IN THE LIGHT.
THAT'S QUITE A TRICK.
I'VE HAD A LOT OF DIFFERENT FACES OVER THE YEARS, MOM...
"...THE LONELY NEIGHBOR...
"...THE PRISONER ON DEATH ROW...
"...THE LITTLE BOY BEING HACKED TO DEATH IN RWANDA...
"...THE MIGRANT CLINGING TO THE SIDE OF A DINGHY...

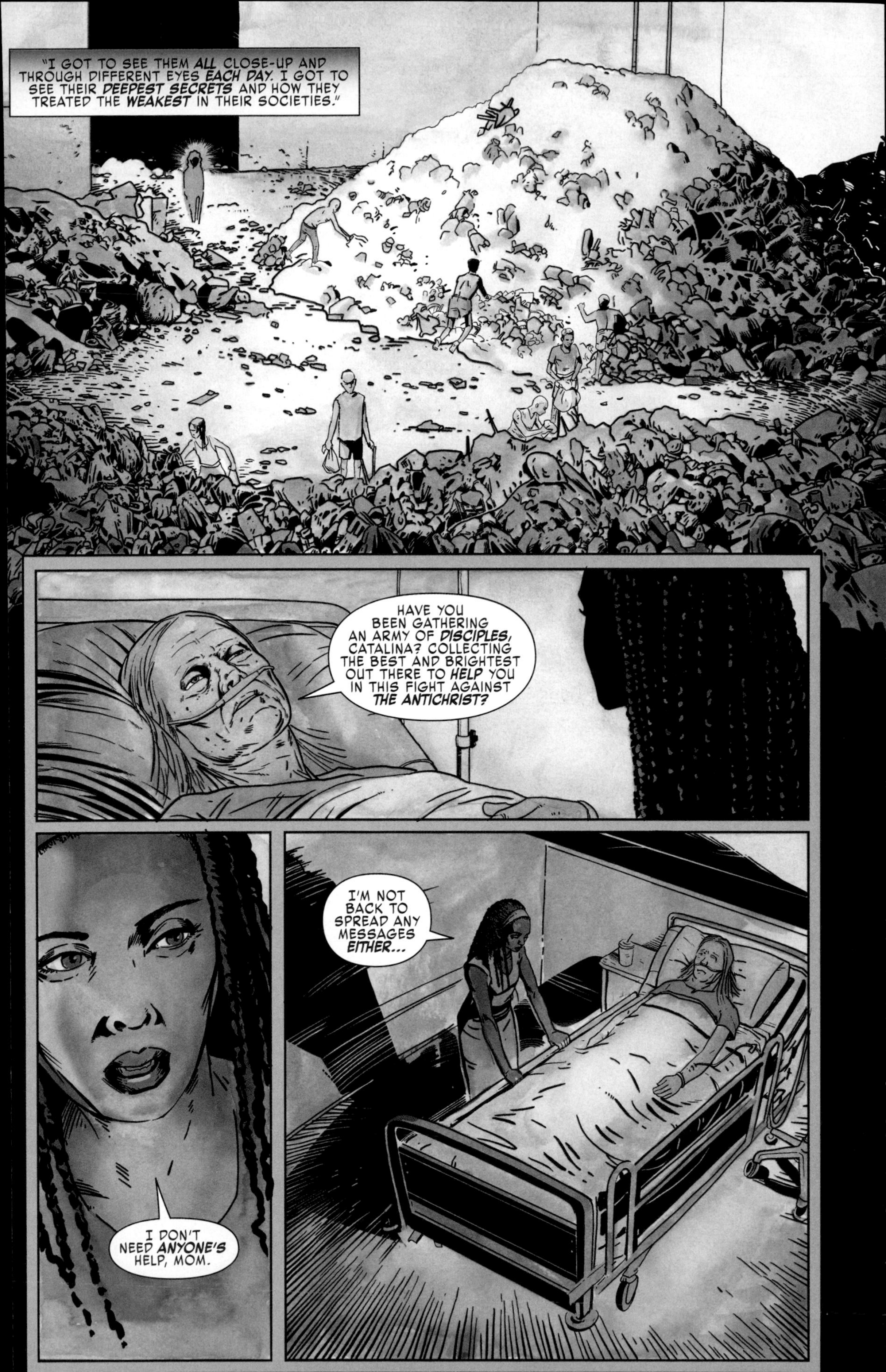
"I GOT TO SEE THEM ALL CLOSE-UP AND THROUGH DIFFERENT EYES EACH DAY. I GOT TO SEE THEIR DEEPEST SECRETS AND HOW THEY TREATED THE WEAKEST IN THEIR SOCIETIES."
HAVE YOU BEEN GATHERING AN ARMY OF DISCIPLES, CATALINA? COLLECTING THE BEST AND BRIGHTEST OUT THERE TO HELP YOU IN THIS FIGHT AGAINST THE ANTICHRIST?
I DON'T NEED ANYONE'S HELP, MOM.
I'M NOT BACK TO SPREAD ANY MESSAGES EITHER...

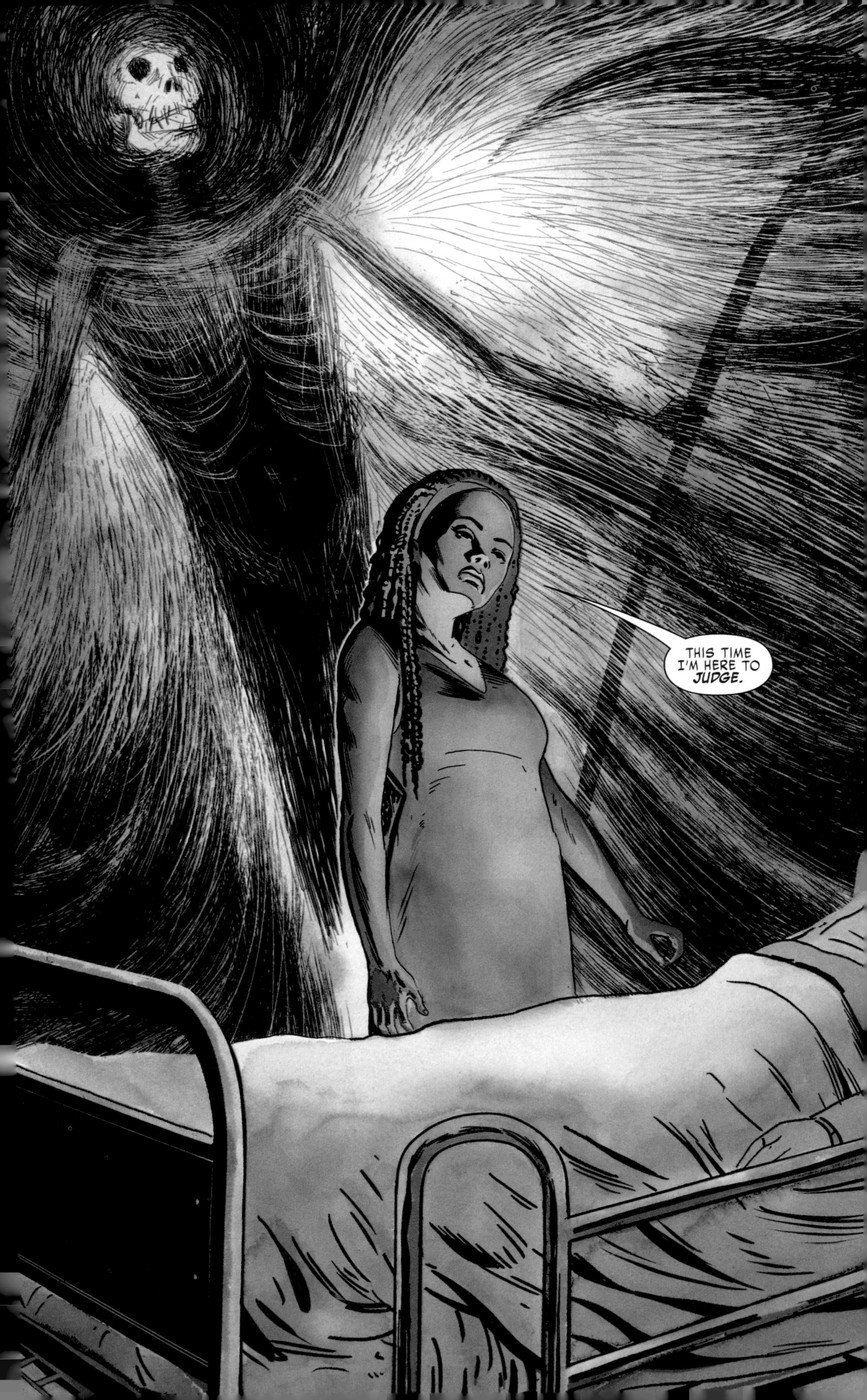
THIS TIME I'M HERE TO JUDGE.

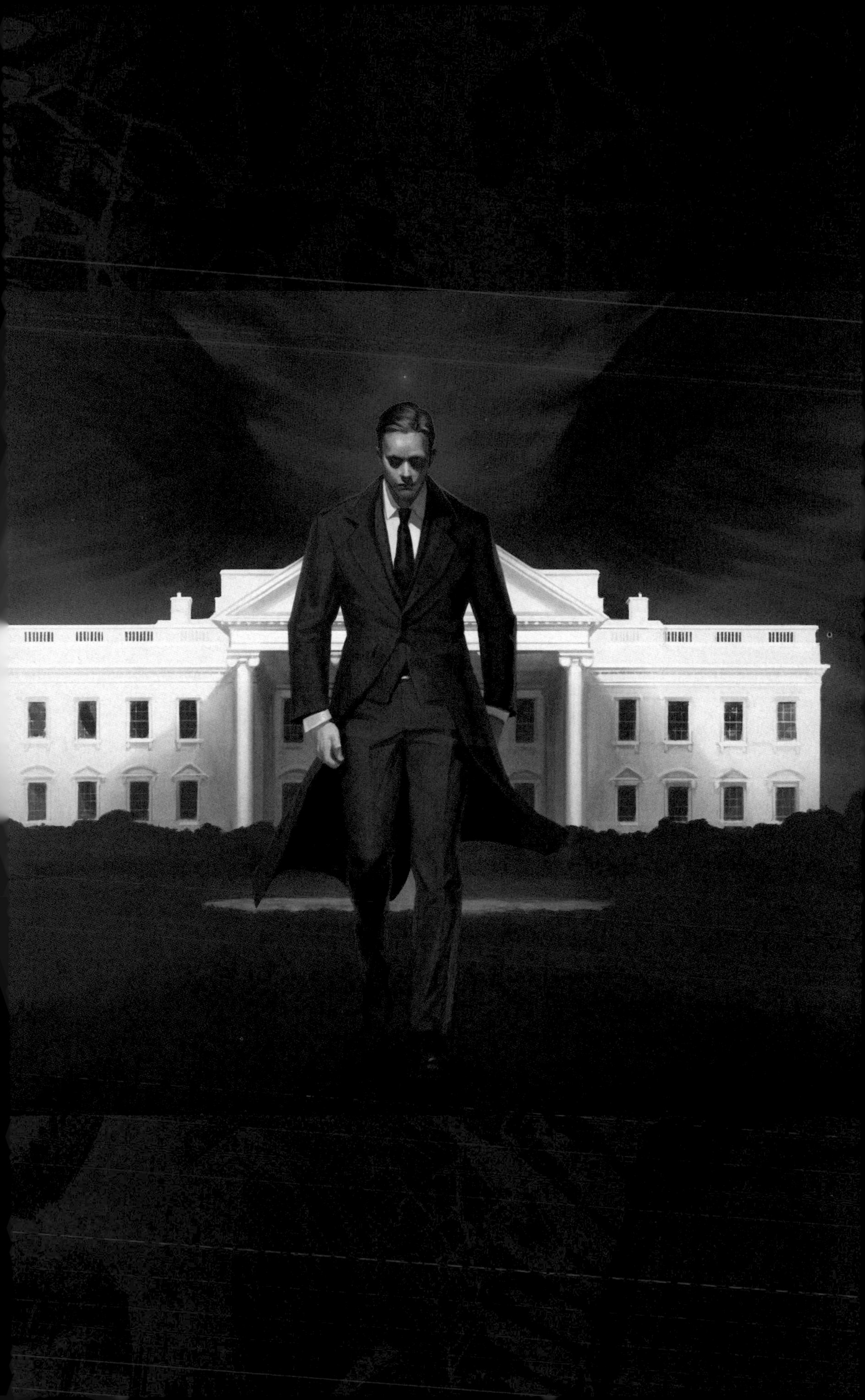

CHAPTER 2

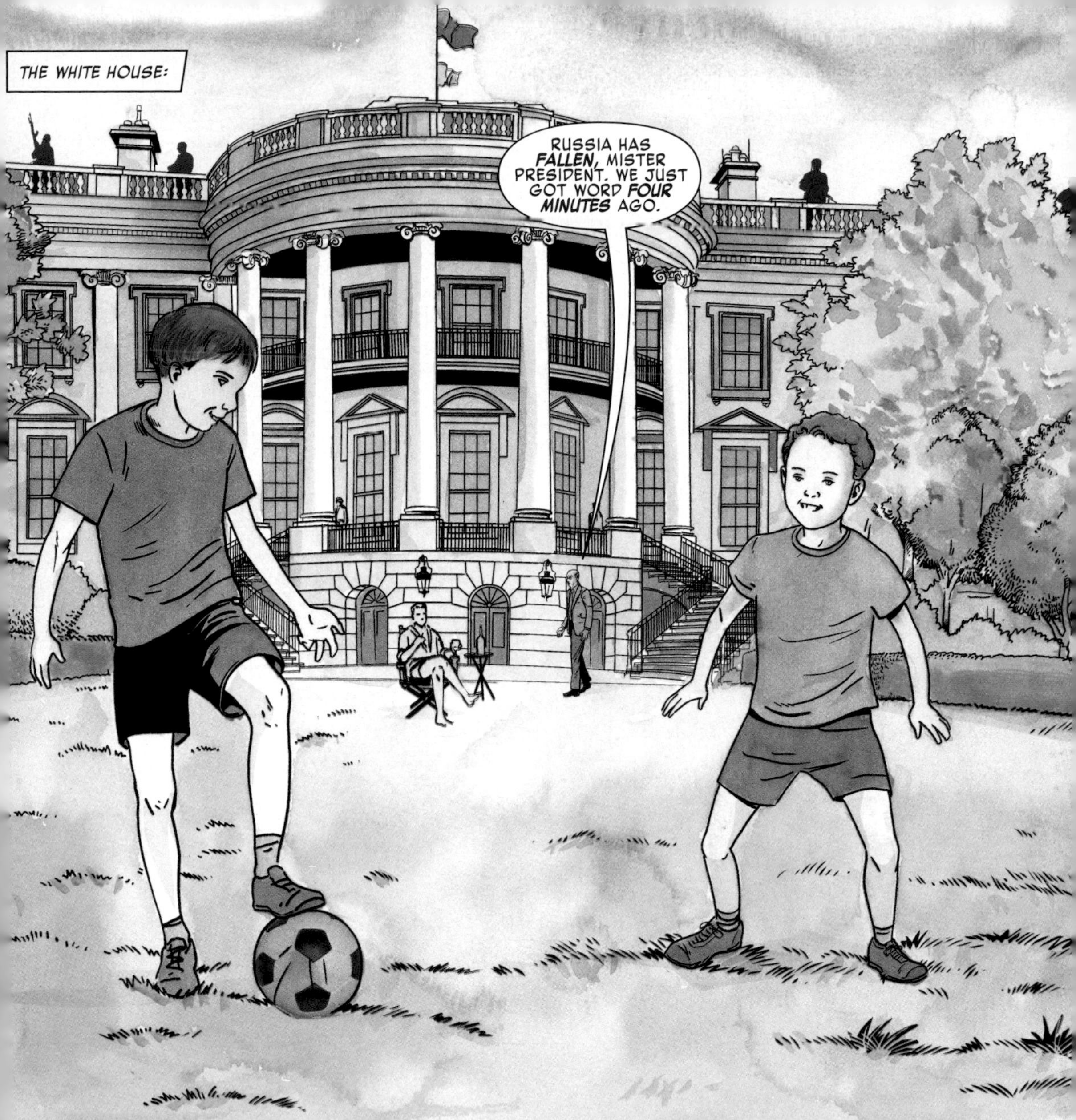
THE WHITE HOUSE:
RUSSIA HAS FALLEN, MISTER PRESIDENT. WE JUST GOT WORD FOUR MINUTES AGO.

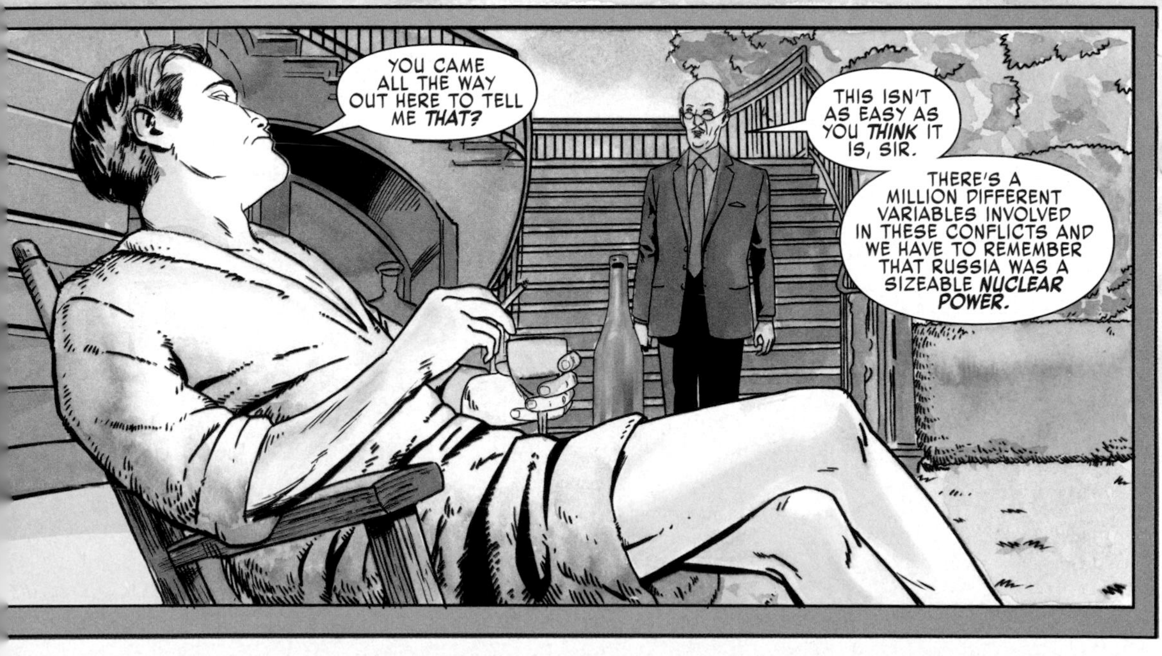
YOU CAME ALL THE WAY OUT HERE TO TELL ME THAT?
THIS ISN'T AS EASY AS YOU THINK IT IS, SIR.
THERE'S A MILLION DIFFERENT VARIABLES INVOLVED IN THESE CONFLICTS AND WE HAVE TO REMEMBER THAT RUSSIA WAS A SIZEABLE NUCLEAR POWER.

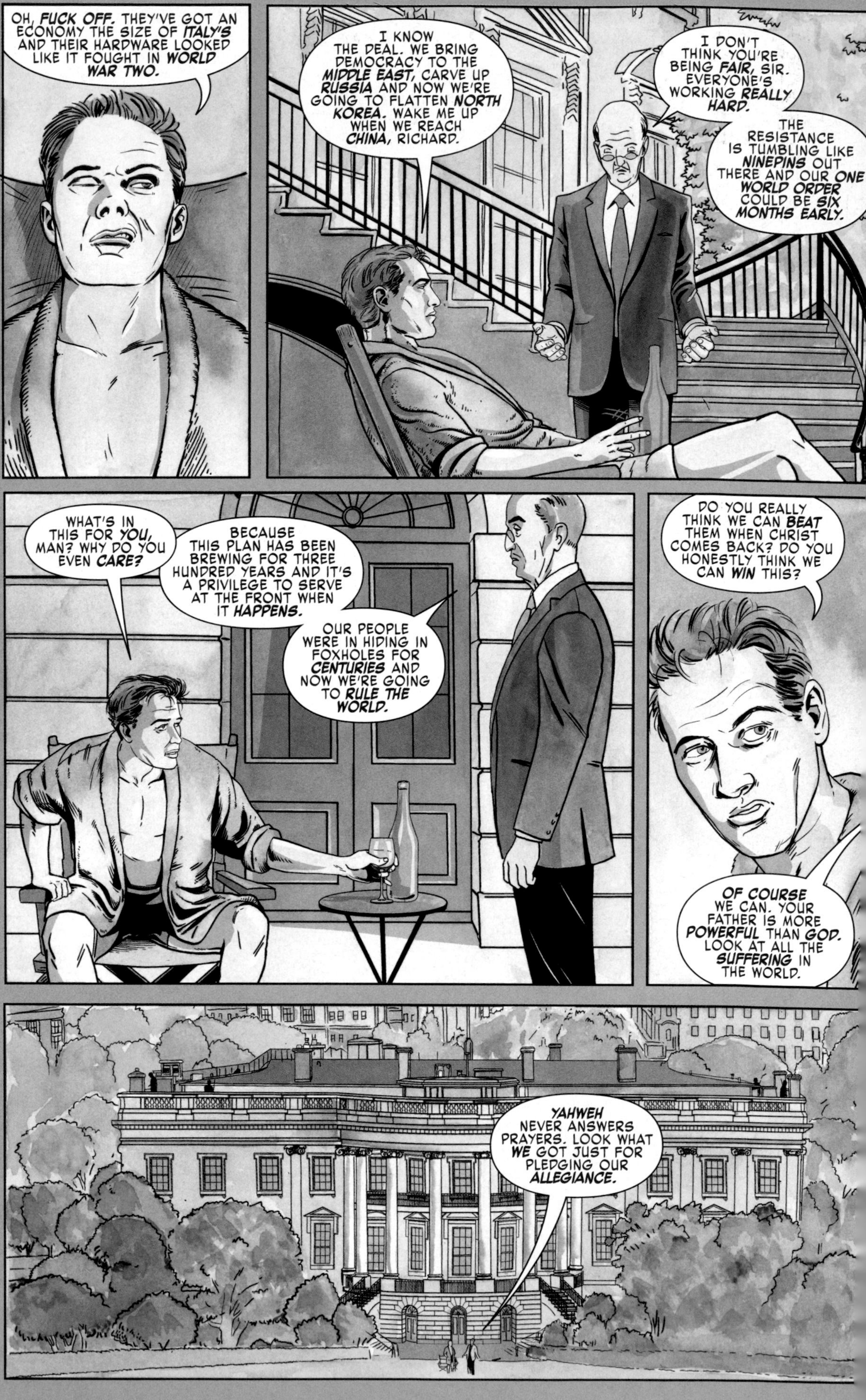
OH, FUCK OFF. THEY'VE GOT AN ECONOMY THE SIZE OF ITALY'S AND THEIR HARDWARE LOOKED LIKE IT FOUGHT IN WORLD WAR TWO.
I KNOW THE DEAL. WE BRING DEMOCRACY TO THE MIDDLE EAST, CARVE UP RUSSIA AND NOW WE'RE GOING TO FLATTEN NORTH KOREA. WAKE ME UP WHEN WE REACH CHINA, RICHARD.
I DON'T THINK YOU'RE BEING FAIR, SIR. EVERYONE'S WORKING REALLY HARD.
THE RESISTANCE IS TUMBLING LIKE NINEPINS OUT THERE AND OUR ONE WORLD ORDER COULD BE SIX MONTHS EARLY.
WHAT'S IN THIS FOR YOU, MAN? WHY DO YOU EVEN CARE?
BECAUSE THIS PLAN HAS BEEN BREWING FOR THREE HUNDRED YEARS AND IT'S A PRIVILEGE TO SERVE AT THE FRONT WHEN IT HAPPENS.
OUR PEOPLE WERE IN HIDING IN FOXHOLES FOR CENTURIES AND NOW WE'RE GOING TO RULE THE WORLD.
DO YOU REALLY THINK WE CAN BEAT THEM WHEN CHRIST COMES BACK? DO YOU HONESTLY THINK WE CAN WIN THIS?
OF COURSE WE CAN. YOUR FATHER IS MORE POWERFUL THAN GOD. LOOK AT ALL THE SUFFERING IN THE WORLD.
YAHWEH NEVER ANSWERS PRAYERS. LOOK WHAT WE GOT JUST FOR PLEDGING OUR ALLEGIANCE.

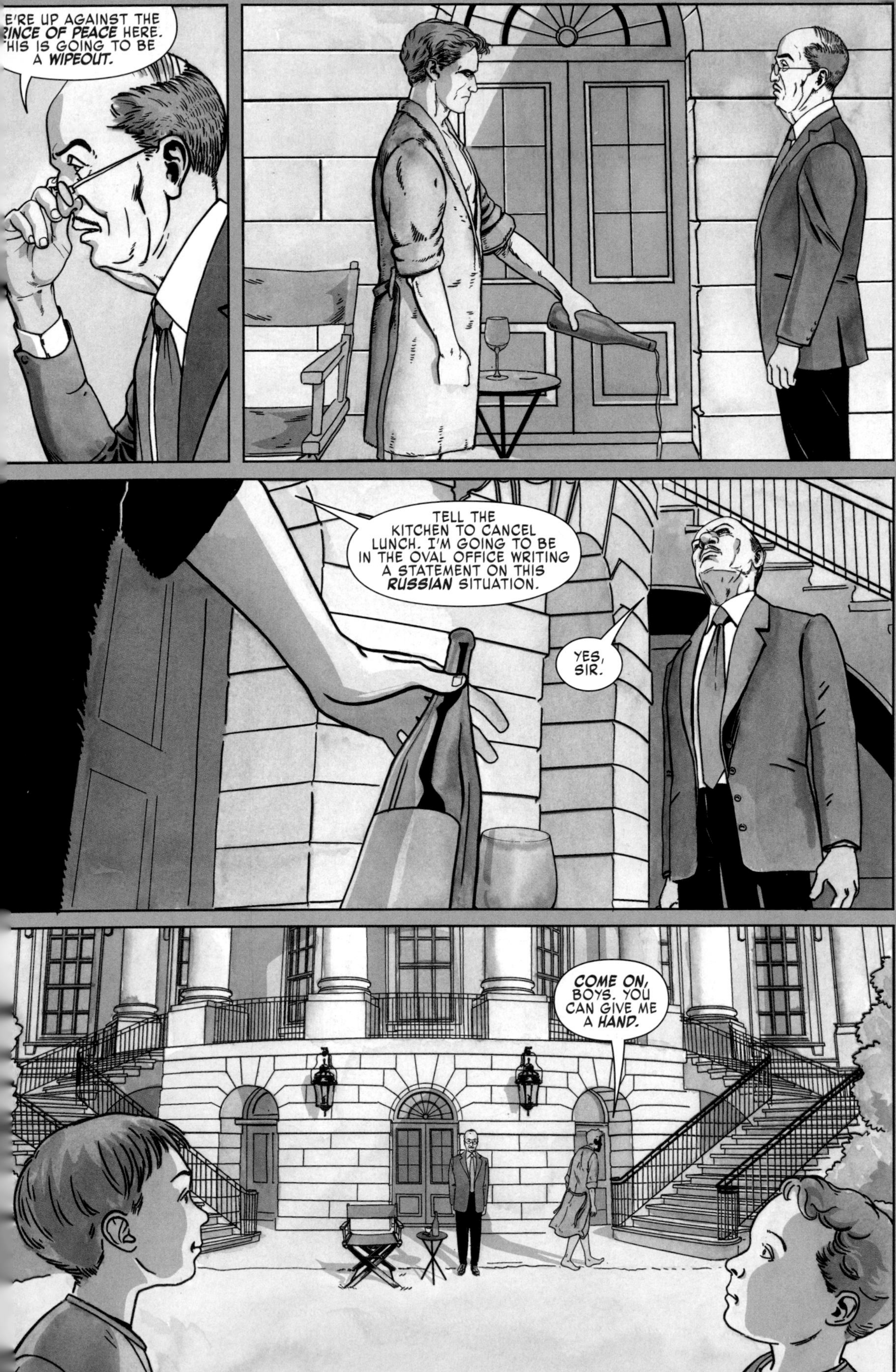
E'RE UP AGAINST THE RINCE OF PEACE HERE. THIS IS GOING TO BE A WIPEOUT.
TELL THE KITCHEN TO CANCEL LUNCH. I'M GOING TO BE IN THE OVAL OFFICE WRITING A STATEMENT ON THIS RUSSIAN SITUATION.
YES, SIR.
COME ON, BOYS. YOU CAN GIVE ME A HAND.

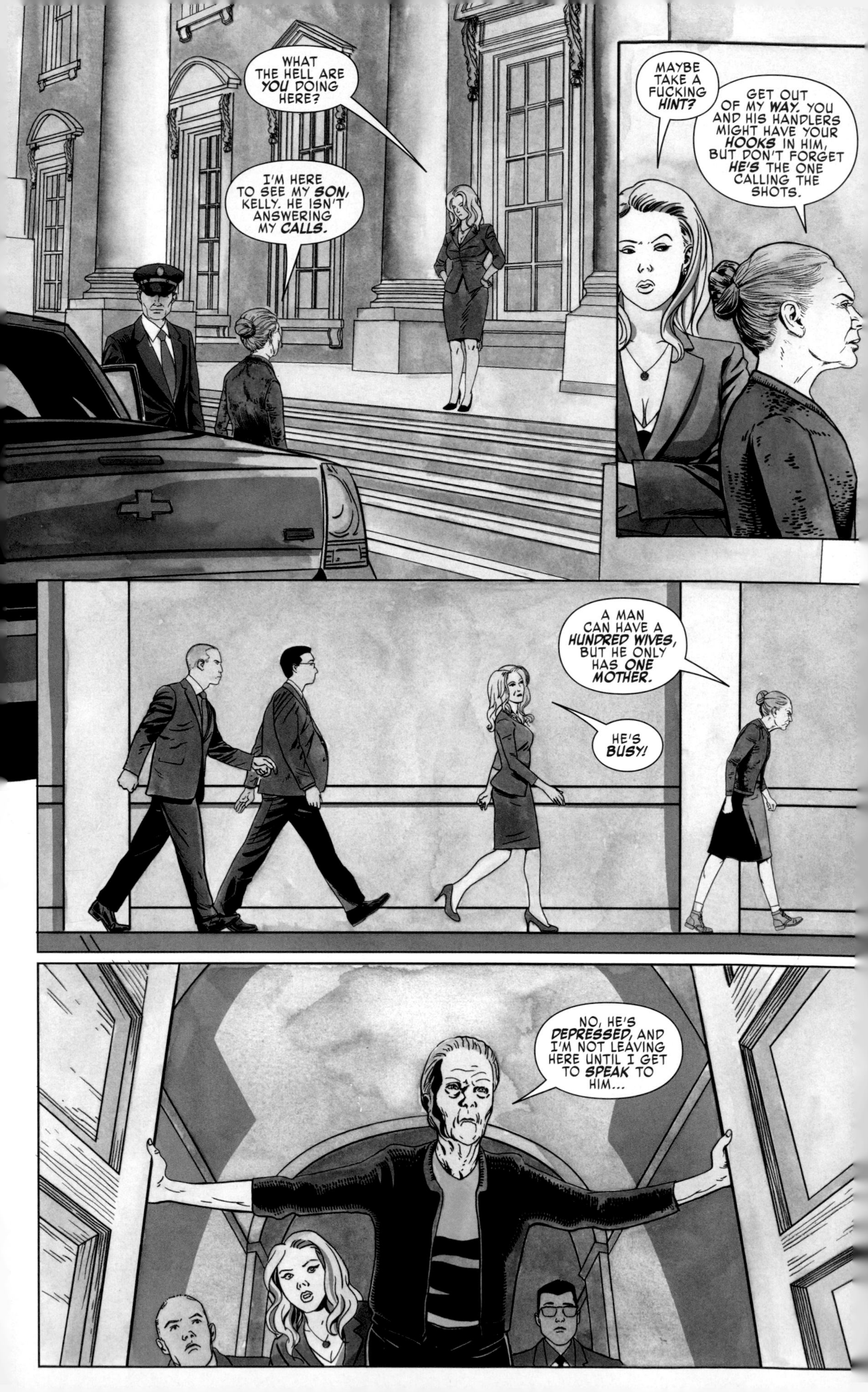
WHAT THE HELL ARE YOU DOING HERE?
I'M HERE TO SEE MY SON, KELLY. HE ISN'T ANSWERING MY CALLS.
MAYBE TAKE A FUCKING HINT?
GET OUT OF MY WAY. YOU AND HIS HANDLERS MIGHT HAVE YOUR HOOKS IN HIM, BUT DON'T FORGET HE'S THE ONE CALLING THE SHOTS.
A MAN CAN HAVE A HUNDRED WIVES, BUT HE ONLY HAS ONE MOTHER.
HE'S BUSY!
NO, HE'S DEPRESSED, AND I'M NOT LEAVING HERE UNTIL I GET TO SPEAK TO HIM...

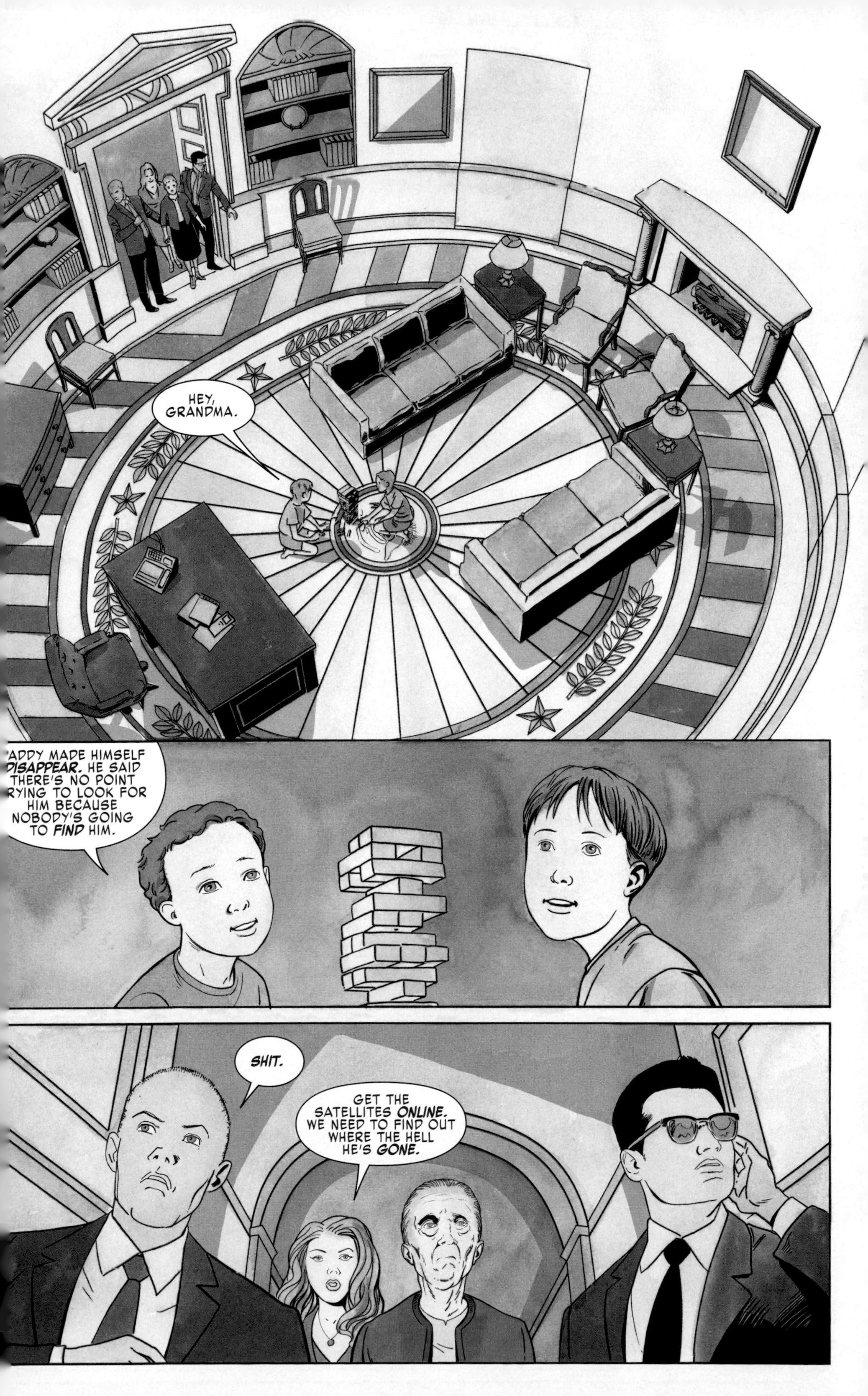
HEY, GRANDMA.
ADDY MADE HIMSELF DISAPPEAR. HE SAID THERE'S NO POINT RYING TO LOOK FOR HIM BECAUSE NOBODY'S GOING TO FIND HIM.
SHIT.
GET THE SATELLITES ONLINE. WE NEED TO FIND OUT WHERE THE HELL HE'S GONE.

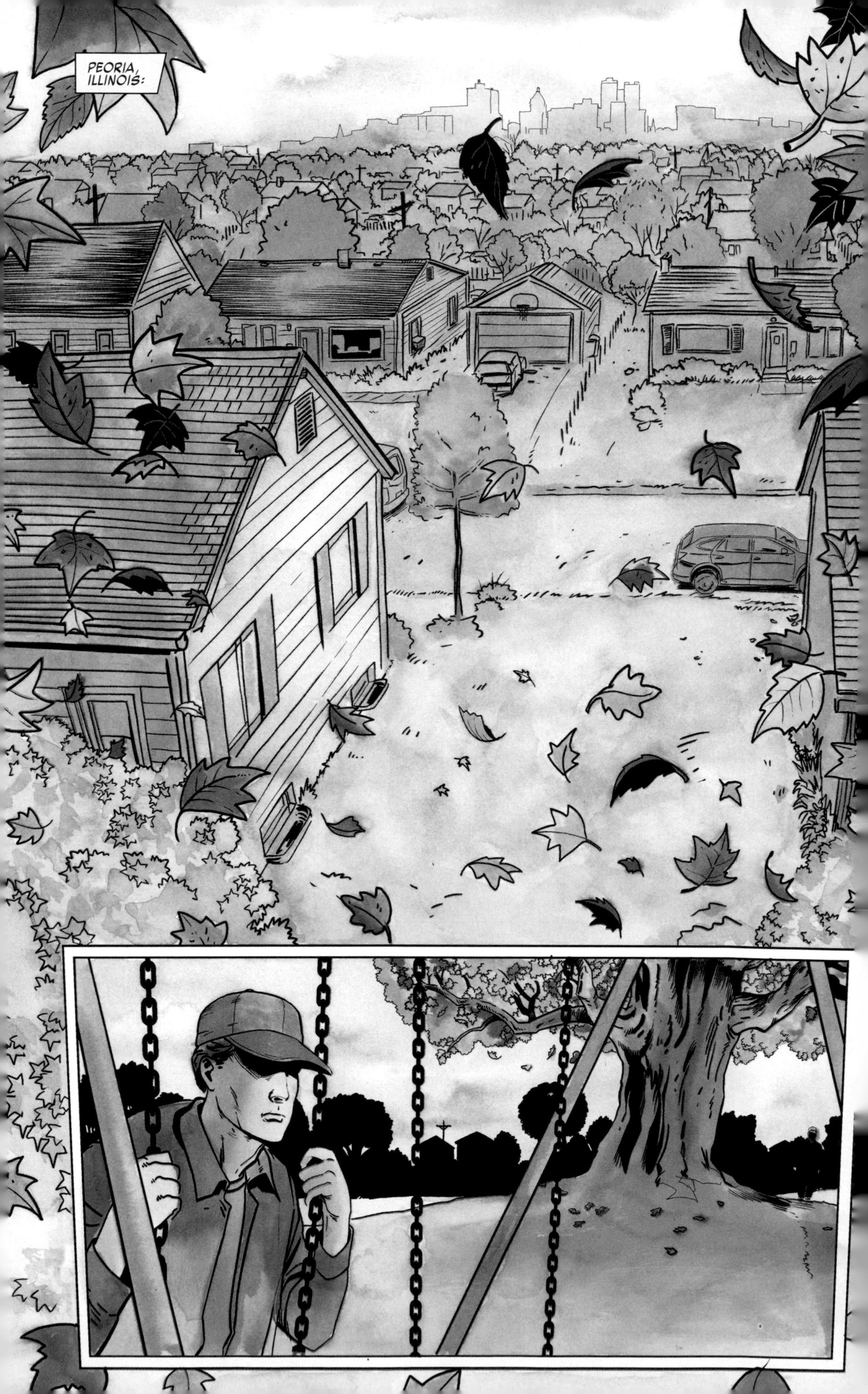
PEORIA, ILLINOIS:

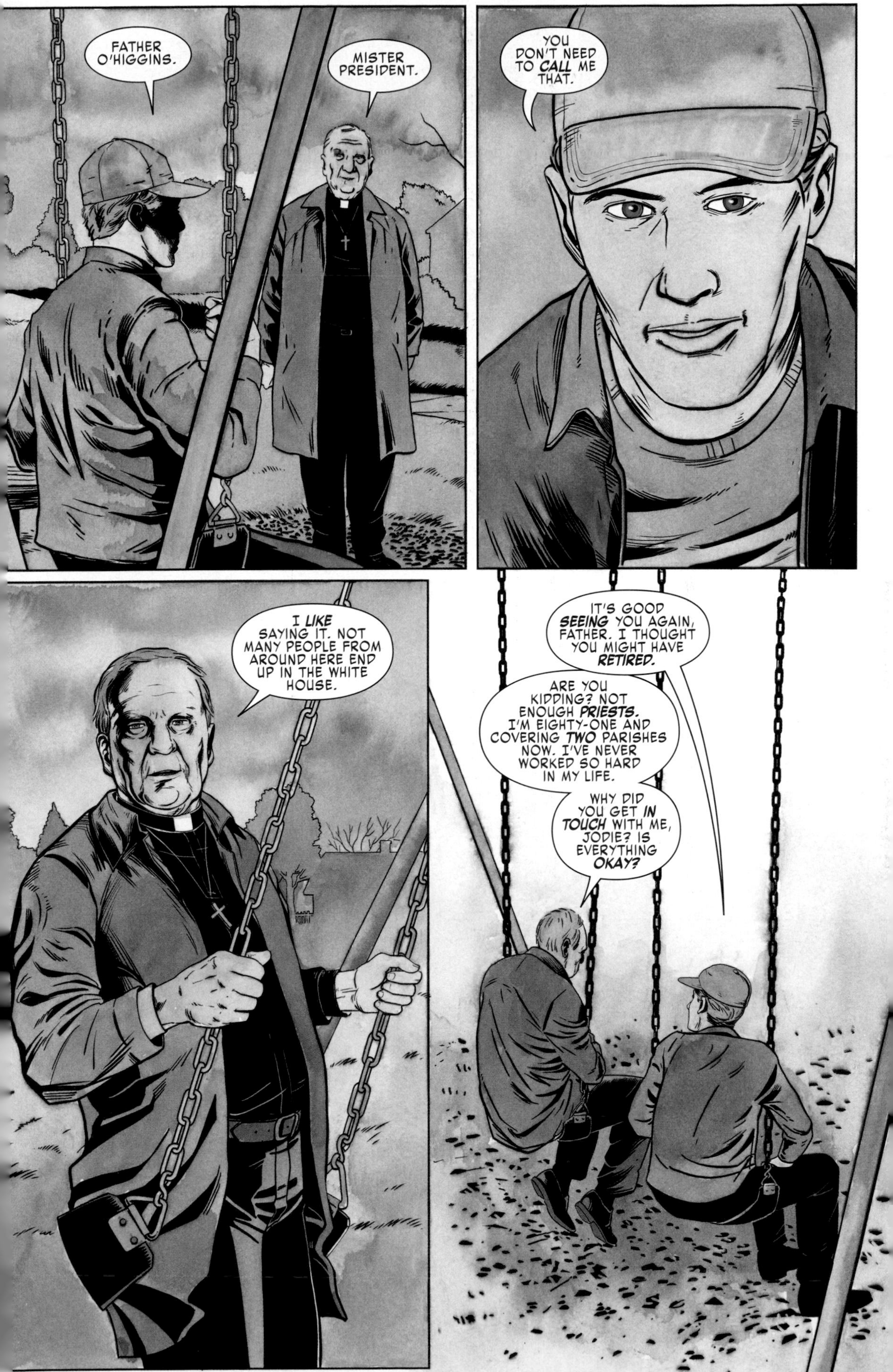
FATHER O'HIGGINS.
MISTER PRESIDENT.
YOU DON'T NEED TO CALL ME THAT.
I LIKE SAYING IT. NOT MANY PEOPLE FROM AROUND HERE END UP IN THE WHITE HOUSE.
IT'S GOOD SEEING YOU AGAIN, FATHER. I THOUGHT YOU MIGHT HAVE RETIRED.
ARE YOU KIDDING? NOT ENOUGH PRIESTS. I'M EIGHTY-ONE AND COVERING TWO PARISHES NOW. I'VE NEVER WORKED SO HARD IN MY LIFE.
WHY DID YOU GET IN TOUCH WITH ME, JODIE? IS EVERYTHING OKAY?

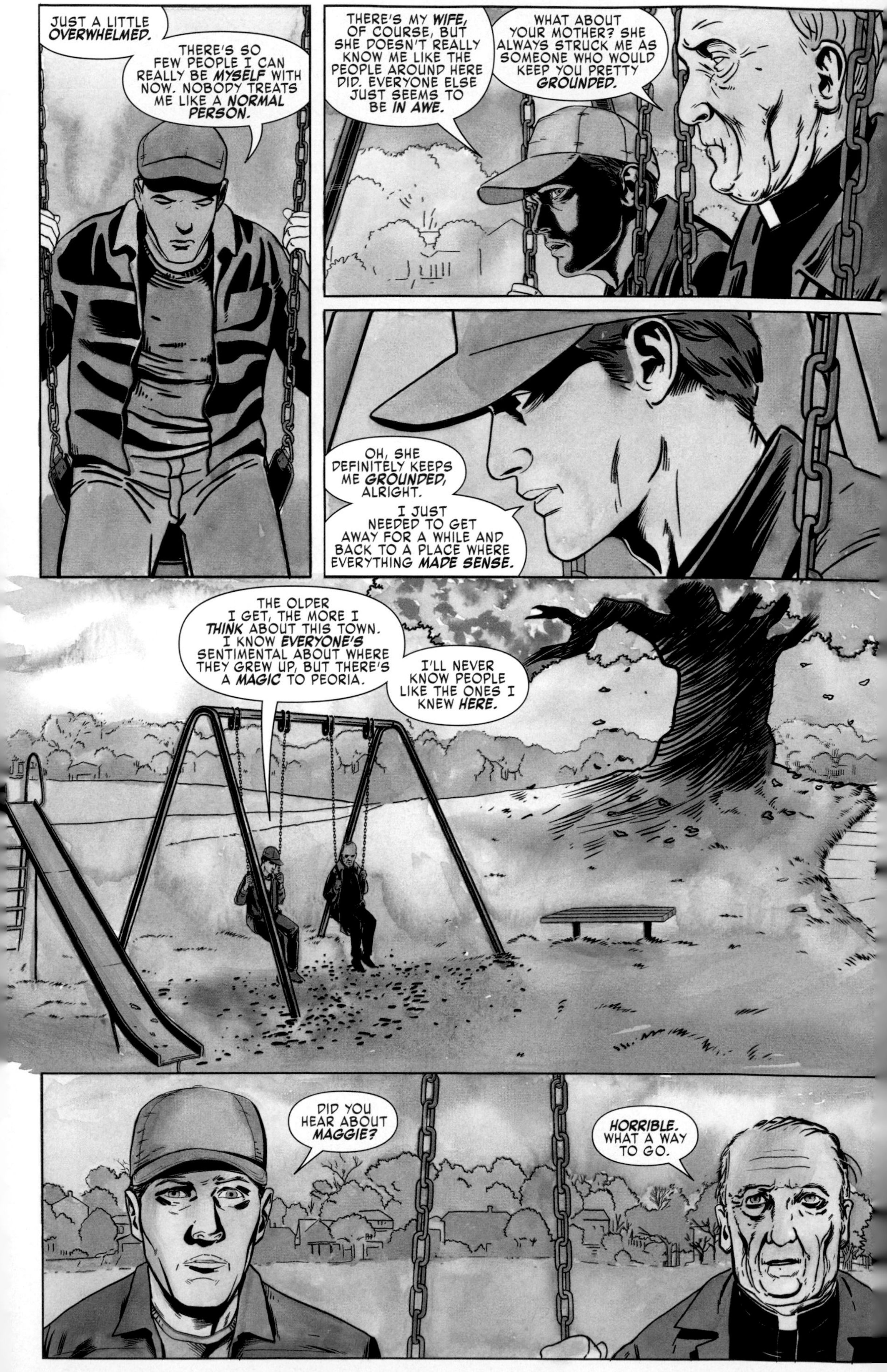
JUST A LITTLE OVERWHELMED.
THERE'S SO FEW PEOPLE I CAN REALLY BE MYSELF WITH NOW. NOBODY TREATS ME LIKE A NORMAL PERSON.
THERE'S MY WIFE, OF COURSE, BUT SHE DOESN'T REALLY KNOW ME LIKE THE PEOPLE AROUND HERE DID. EVERYONE ELSE JUST SEEMS TO BE IN AWE.
WHAT ABOUT YOUR MOTHER? SHE ALWAYS STRUCK ME AS SOMEONE WHO WOULD KEEP YOU PRETTY GROUNDED.
OH, SHE DEFINITELY KEEPS ME GROUNDED, ALRIGHT.
I JUST NEEDED TO GET AWAY FOR A WHILE AND BACK TO A PLACE WHERE EVERYTHING MADE SENSE.
THE OLDER I GET, THE MORE I THINK ABOUT THIS TOWN. I KNOW EVERYONE'S SENTIMENTAL ABOUT WHERE THEY GREW UP, BUT THERE'S A MAGIC TO PEORIA.
I'LL NEVER KNOW PEOPLE LIKE THE ONES I KNEW HERE.
DID YOU HEAR ABOUT MAGGIE?
HORRIBLE. WHAT A WAY TO GO.

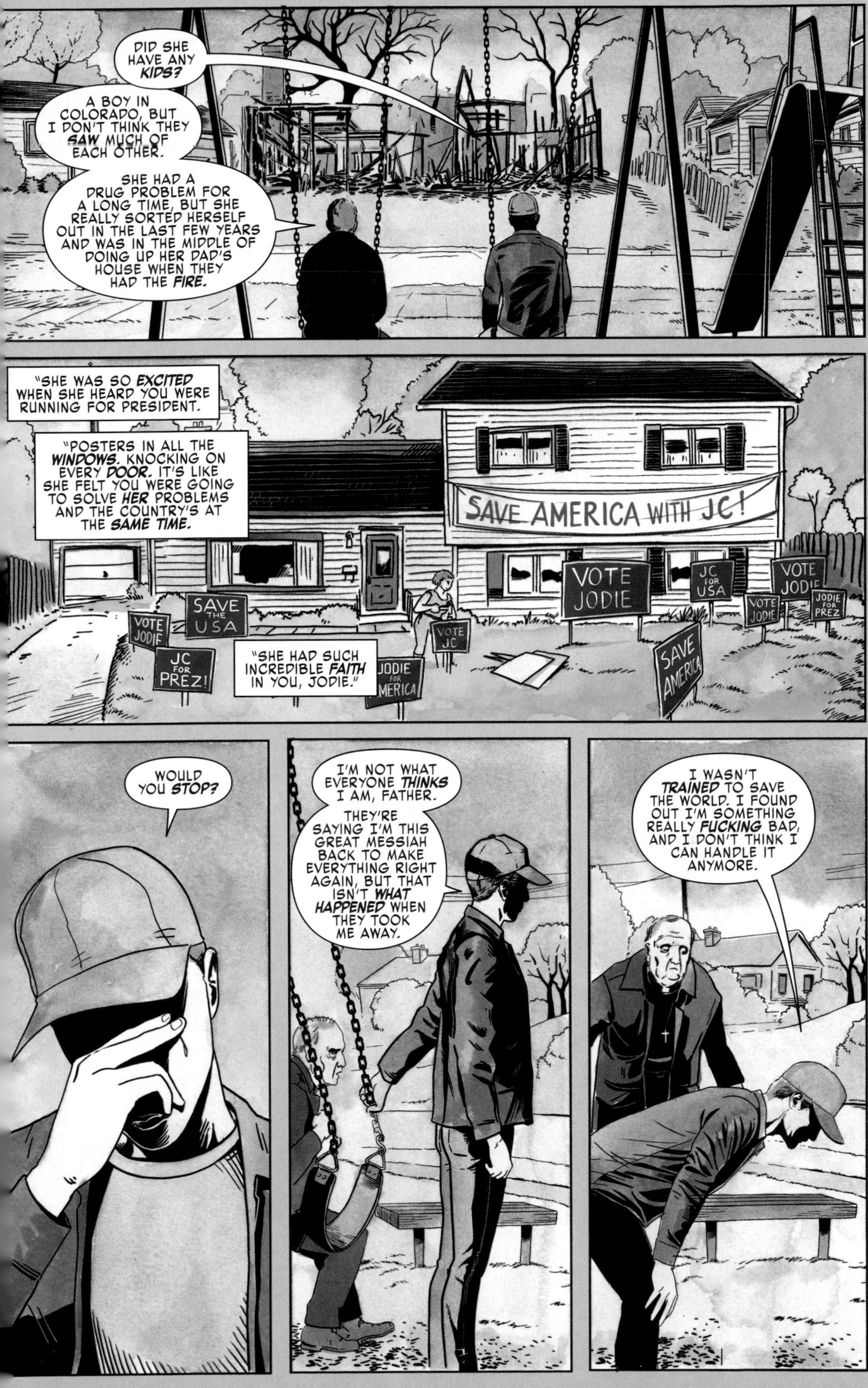
DID SHE HAVE ANY KIDS?
A BOY IN COLORADO, BUT I DON'T THINK THEY SAW MUCH OF EACH OTHER.
SHE HAD A DRUG PROBLEM FOR A LONG TIME, BUT SHE REALLY SORTED HERSELF OUT IN THE LAST FEW YEARS AND WAS IN THE MIDDLE OF DOING UP HER DAD'S HOUSE WHEN THEY HAD THE FIRE.
"SHE WAS SO EXCITED WHEN SHE HEARD YOU WERE RUNNING FOR PRESIDENT.
"POSTERS IN ALL THE WINDOWS. KNOCKING ON EVERY DOOR. IT'S LIKE SHE FELT YOU WERE GOING TO SOLVE HER PROBLEMS AND THE COUNTRY'S AT THE SAME TIME.
SAVE AMERICA WITH JC!
VOTE JODIE
JC FOR USA
VOTE JODIE
VOTE JODIE
JODIE FOR PREZ
SAVE THE USA
VOTE JODIE
JC FOR PREZ!
VOTE JC
JODIE FOR AMERICA
SAVE AMERICA
"SHE HAD SUCH INCREDIBLE FAITH IN YOU, JODIE."
WOULD YOU STOP?
I'M NOT WHAT EVERYONE THINKS I AM, FATHER.
THEY'RE SAYING I'M THIS GREAT MESSIAH BACK TO MAKE EVERYTHING RIGHT AGAIN, BUT THAT ISN'T WHAT HAPPENED WHEN THEY TOOK ME AWAY.
I WASN'T TRAINED TO SAVE THE WORLD. I FOUND OUT I'M SOMETHING REALLY FUCKING BAD, AND I DON'T THINK I CAN HANDLE IT ANYMORE.

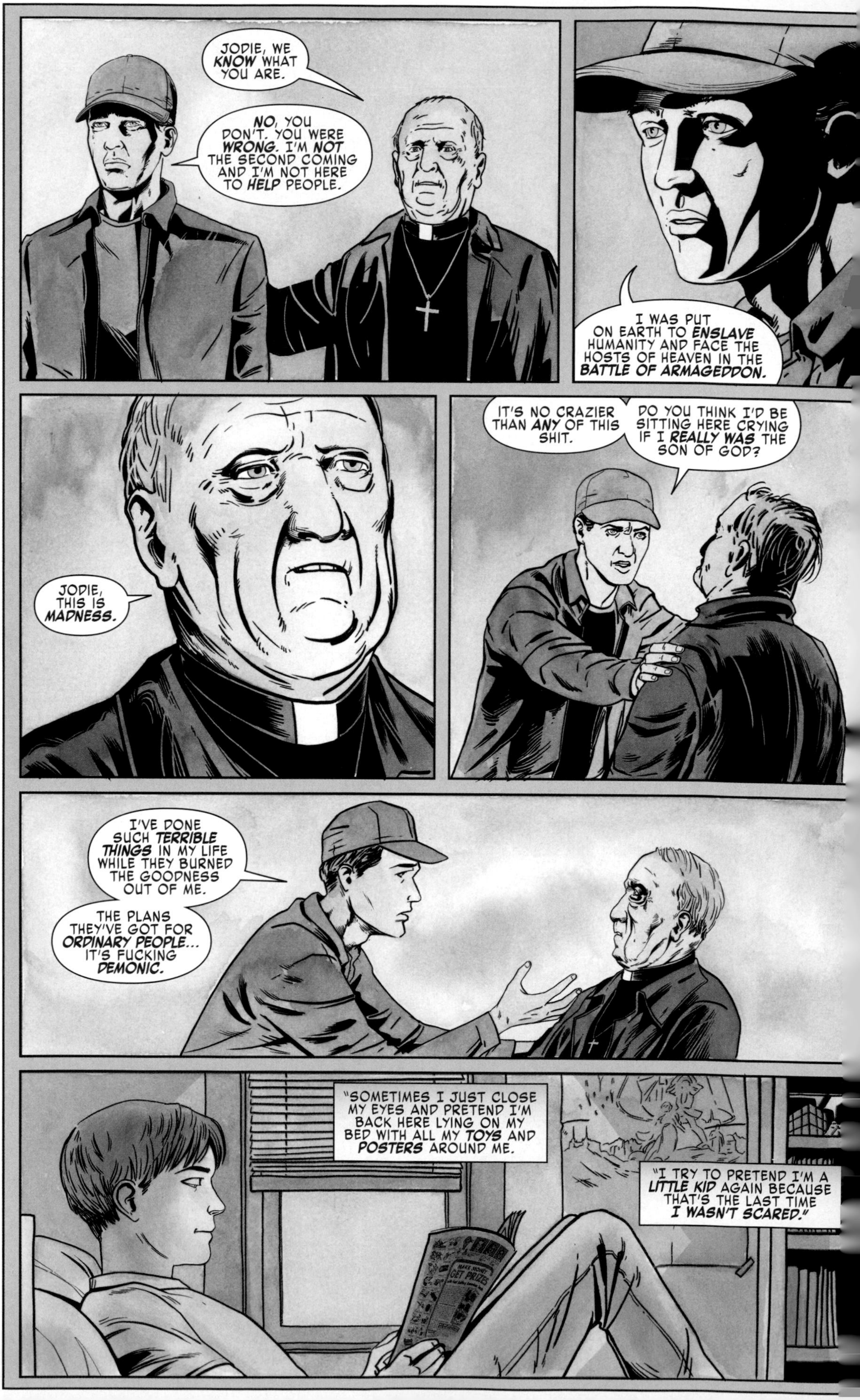
JODIE, WE KNOW WHAT YOU ARE.
NO, YOU DON'T. YOU WERE WRONG. I'M NOT THE SECOND COMING AND I'M NOT HERE TO HELP PEOPLE.
I WAS PUT ON EARTH TO ENSLAVE HUMANITY AND FACE THE HOSTS OF HEAVEN IN THE BATTLE OF ARMAGEDDON.
JODIE, THIS IS MADNESS.
IT'S NO CRAZIER THAN ANY OF THIS SHIT.
DO YOU THINK I'D BE SITTING HERE CRYING IF I REALLY WAS THE SON OF GOD?
I'VE DONE SUCH TERRIBLE THINGS IN MY LIFE WHILE THEY BURNED THE GOODNESS OUT OF ME.
THE PLANS THEY'VE GOT FOR ORDINARY PEOPLE... IT'S FUCKING DEMONIC.
"SOMETIMES I JUST CLOSE MY EYES AND PRETEND I'M BACK HERE LYING ON MY BED WITH ALL MY TOYS AND POSTERS AROUND ME.
"I TRY TO PRETEND I'M A LITTLE KID AGAIN BECAUSE THAT'S THE LAST TIME I WASN'T SCARED."

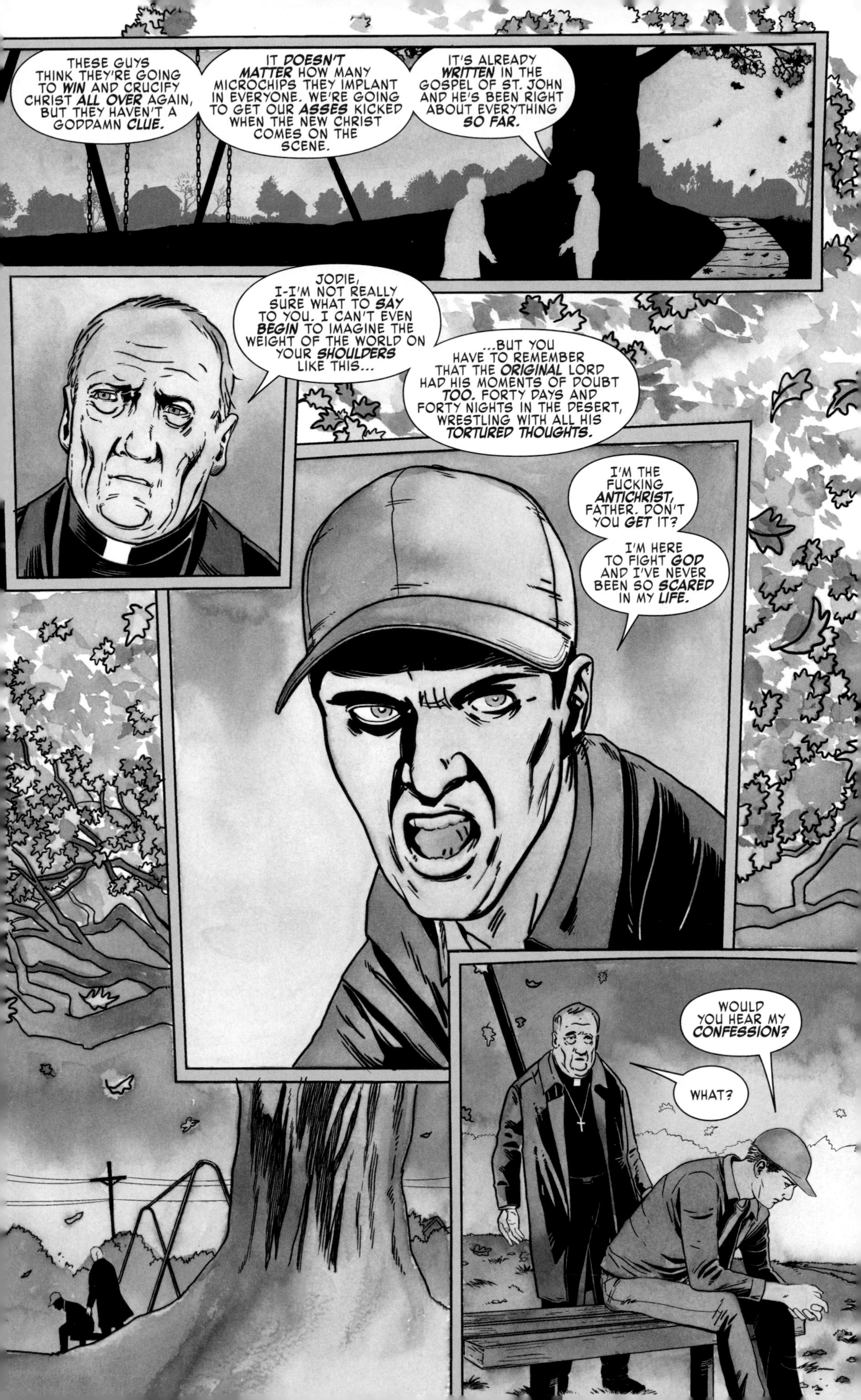
THESE GUYS THINK THEY'RE GOING TO WIN AND CRUCIFY CHRIST ALL OVER AGAIN, BUT THEY HAVEN'T A GODDAMN CLUE.
IT DOESN'T MATTER HOW MANY MICROCHIPS THEY IMPLANT IN EVERYONE. WE'RE GOING TO GET OUR ASSES KICKED WHEN THE NEW CHRIST COMES ON THE SCENE.
IT'S ALREADY WRITTEN IN THE GOSPEL OF ST. JOHN AND HE'S BEEN RIGHT ABOUT EVERYTHING SO FAR.
JODIE, I-I'M NOT REALLY SURE WHAT TO SAY TO YOU. I CAN'T EVEN BEGIN TO IMAGINE THE WEIGHT OF THE WORLD ON YOUR SHOULDERS LIKE THIS...
...BUT YOU HAVE TO REMEMBER THAT THE ORIGINAL LORD HAD HIS MOMENTS OF DOUBT TOO. FORTY DAYS AND FORTY NIGHTS IN THE DESERT, WRESTLING WITH ALL HIS TORTURED THOUGHTS.
I'M THE FUCKING ANTICHRIST, FATHER. DON'T YOU GET IT?
I'M HERE TO FIGHT GOD AND I'VE NEVER BEEN SO SCARED IN MY LIFE.
WOULD YOU HEAR MY CONFESSION?
WHAT?

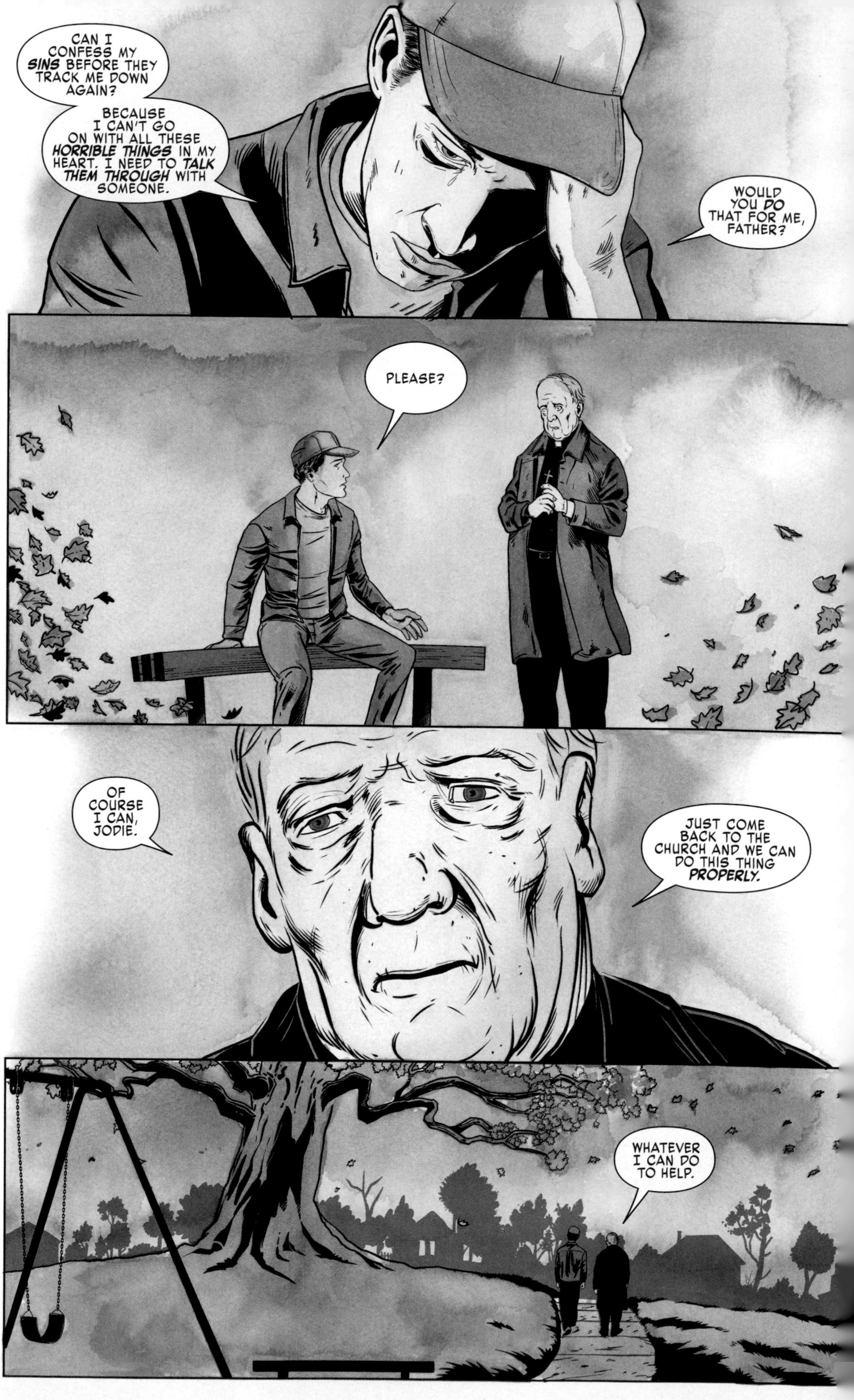
CAN I CONFESS MY SINS BEFORE THEY TRACK ME DOWN AGAIN?
BECAUSE I CAN'T GO ON WITH ALL THESE HORRIBLE THINGS IN MY HEART. I NEED TO TALK THEM THROUGH WITH SOMEONE.
WOULD YOU DO THAT FOR ME, FATHER?
PLEASE?
OF COURSE I CAN, JODIE.
JUST COME BACK TO THE CHURCH AND WE CAN DO THIS THING PROPERLY.
WHATEVER I CAN DO TO HELP.

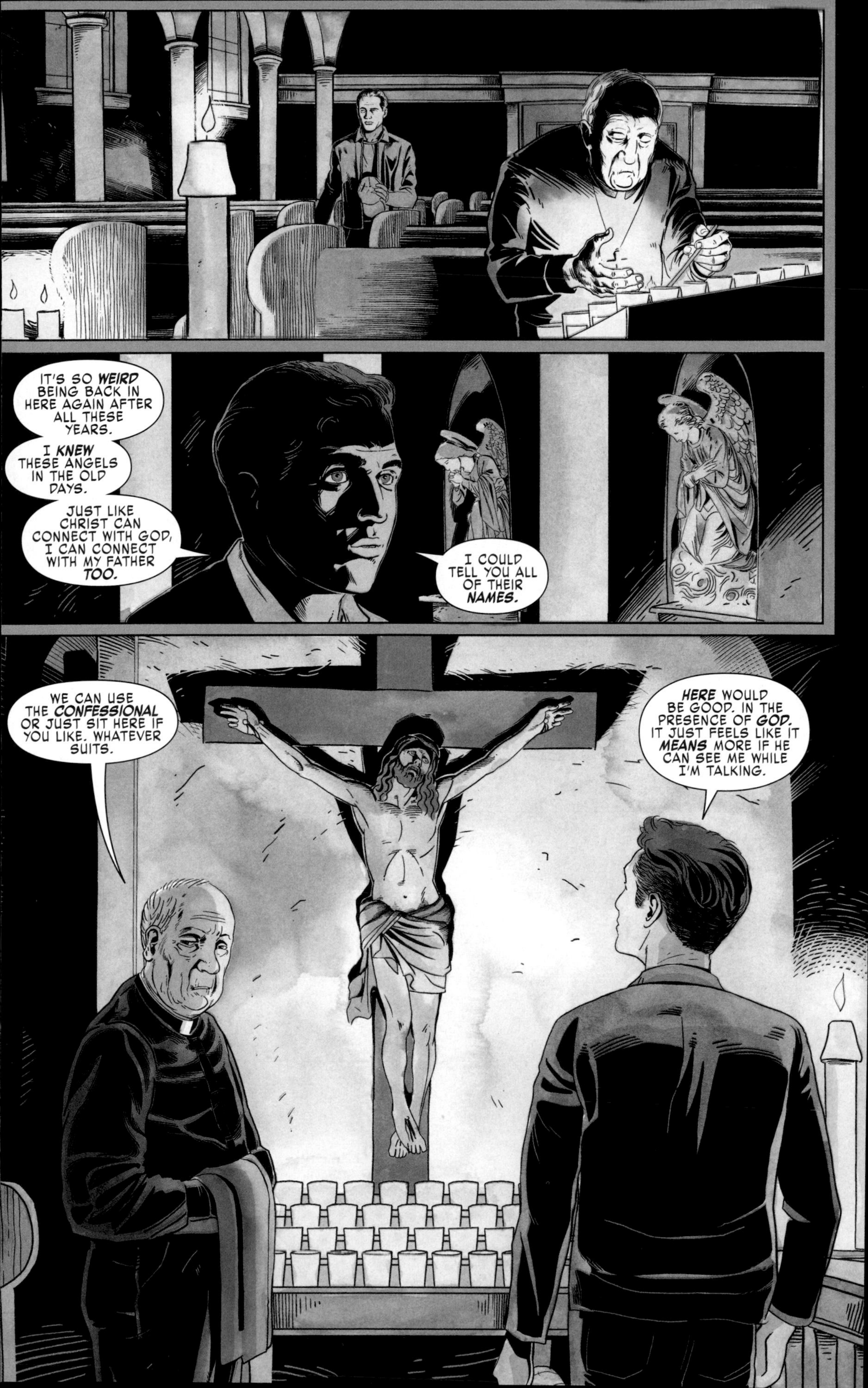
IT'S SO WEIRD BEING BACK IN HERE AGAIN AFTER ALL THESE YEARS.
I KNEW THESE ANGELS IN THE OLD DAYS.
JUST LIKE CHRIST CAN CONNECT WITH GOD, I CAN CONNECT WITH MY FATHER TOO.
I COULD TELL YOU ALL OF THEIR NAMES.
WE CAN USE THE CONFESSIONAL OR JUST SIT HERE IF YOU LIKE. WHATEVER SUITS.
HERE WOULD BE GOOD. IN THE PRESENCE OF GOD. IT JUST FEELS LIKE IT MEANS MORE IF HE CAN SEE ME WHILE I'M TALKING.

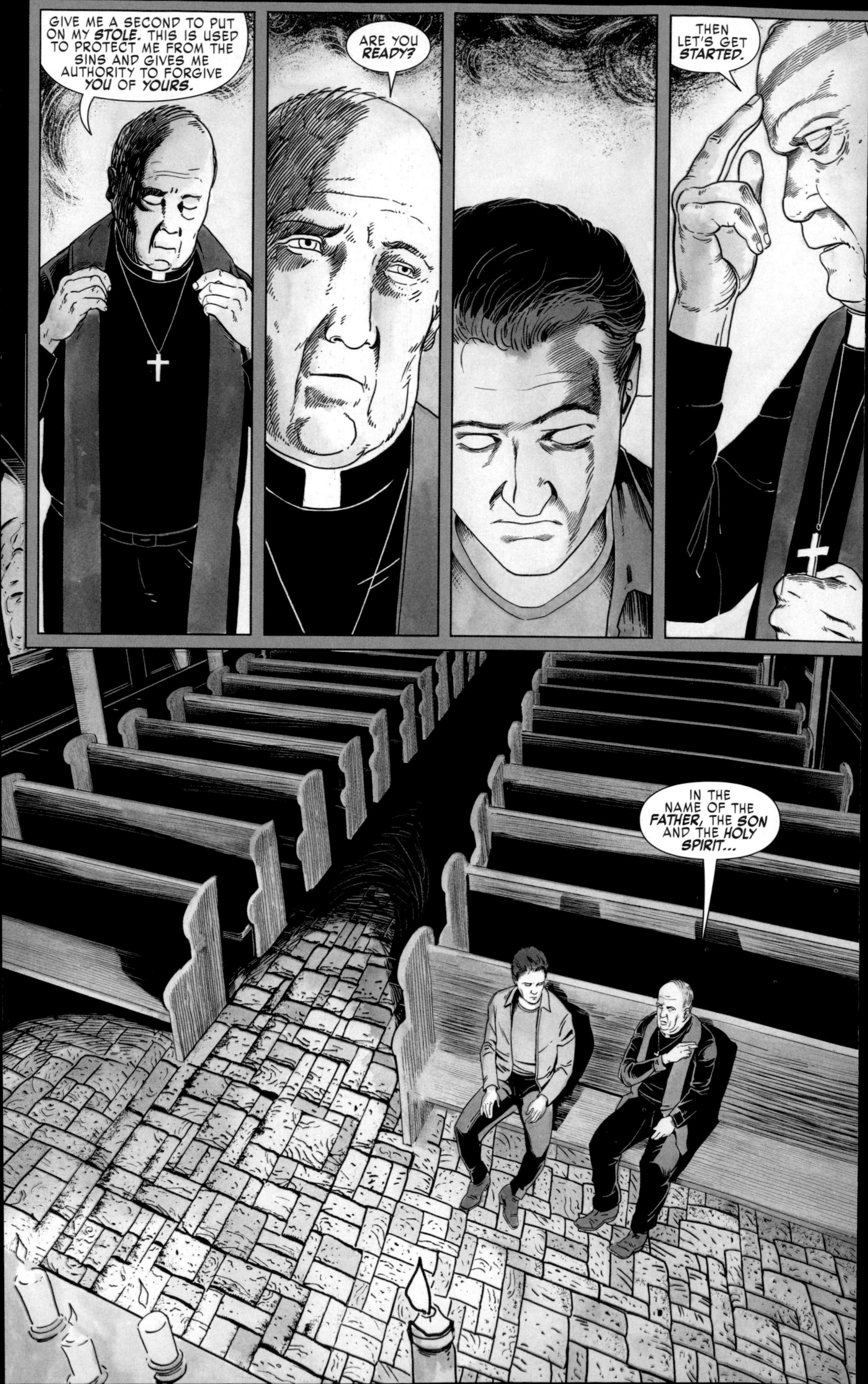
GIVE ME A SECOND TO PUT ON MY STOLE. THIS IS USED TO PROTECT ME FROM THE SINS AND GIVES ME AUTHORITY TO FORGIVE YOU OF YOURS.
ARE YOU READY?
THEN LET'S GET STARTED.
IN THE NAME OF THE FATHER, THE SON AND THE HOLY SPIRIT...

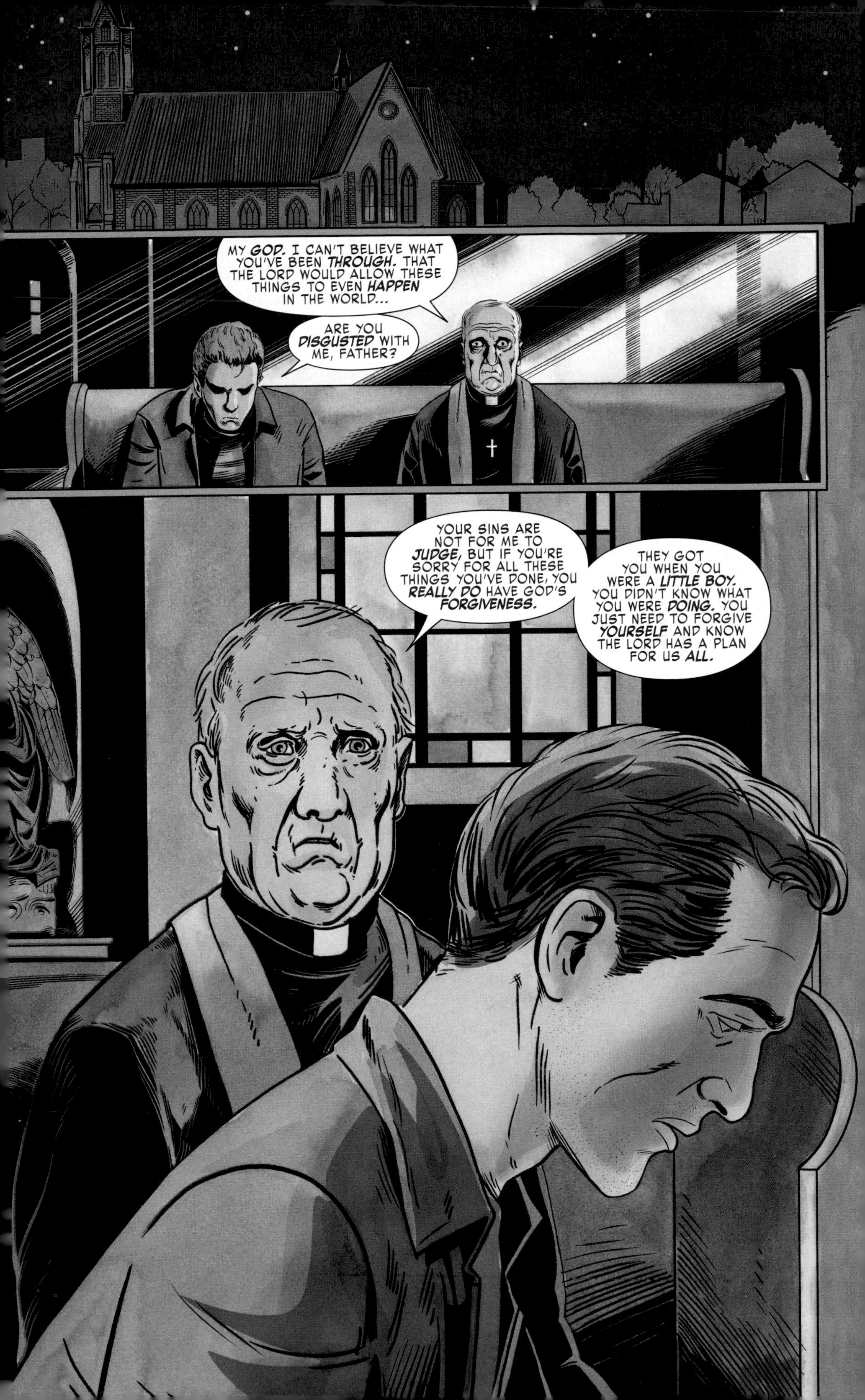
MY GOD. I CAN'T BELIEVE WHAT YOU'VE BEEN THROUGH. THAT THE LORD WOULD ALLOW THESE THINGS TO EVEN HAPPEN IN THE WORLD...
ARE YOU DISGUSTED WITH ME, FATHER?
YOUR SINS ARE NOT FOR ME TO JUDGE, BUT IF YOU'RE SORRY FOR ALL THESE THINGS YOU'VE DONE, YOU REALLY DO HAVE GOD'S FORGIVENESS.
THEY GOT YOU WHEN YOU WERE A LITTLE BOY. YOU DIDN'T KNOW WHAT YOU WERE DOING. YOU JUST NEED TO FORGIVE YOURSELF AND KNOW THE LORD HAS A PLAN FOR US ALL.

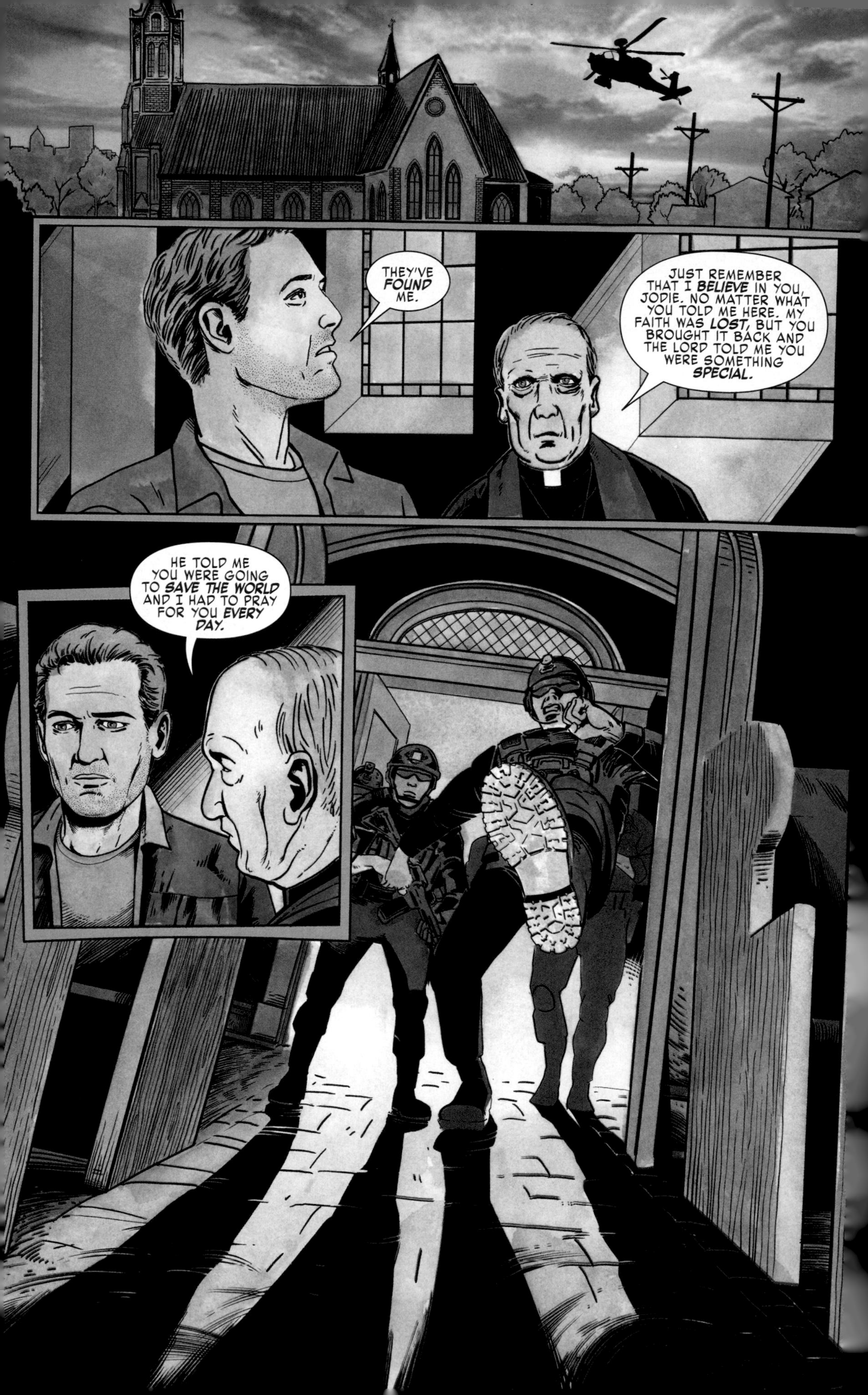
THEY'VE FOUND ME.
JUST REMEMBER THAT I BELIEVE IN YOU, JODIE. NO MATTER WHAT YOU TOLD ME HERE. MY FAITH WAS LOST, BUT YOU BROUGHT IT BACK AND THE LORD TOLD ME YOU WERE SOMETHING SPECIAL.
HE TOLD ME YOU WERE GOING TO SAVE THE WORLD AND I HAD TO PRAY FOR YOU EVERY DAY.

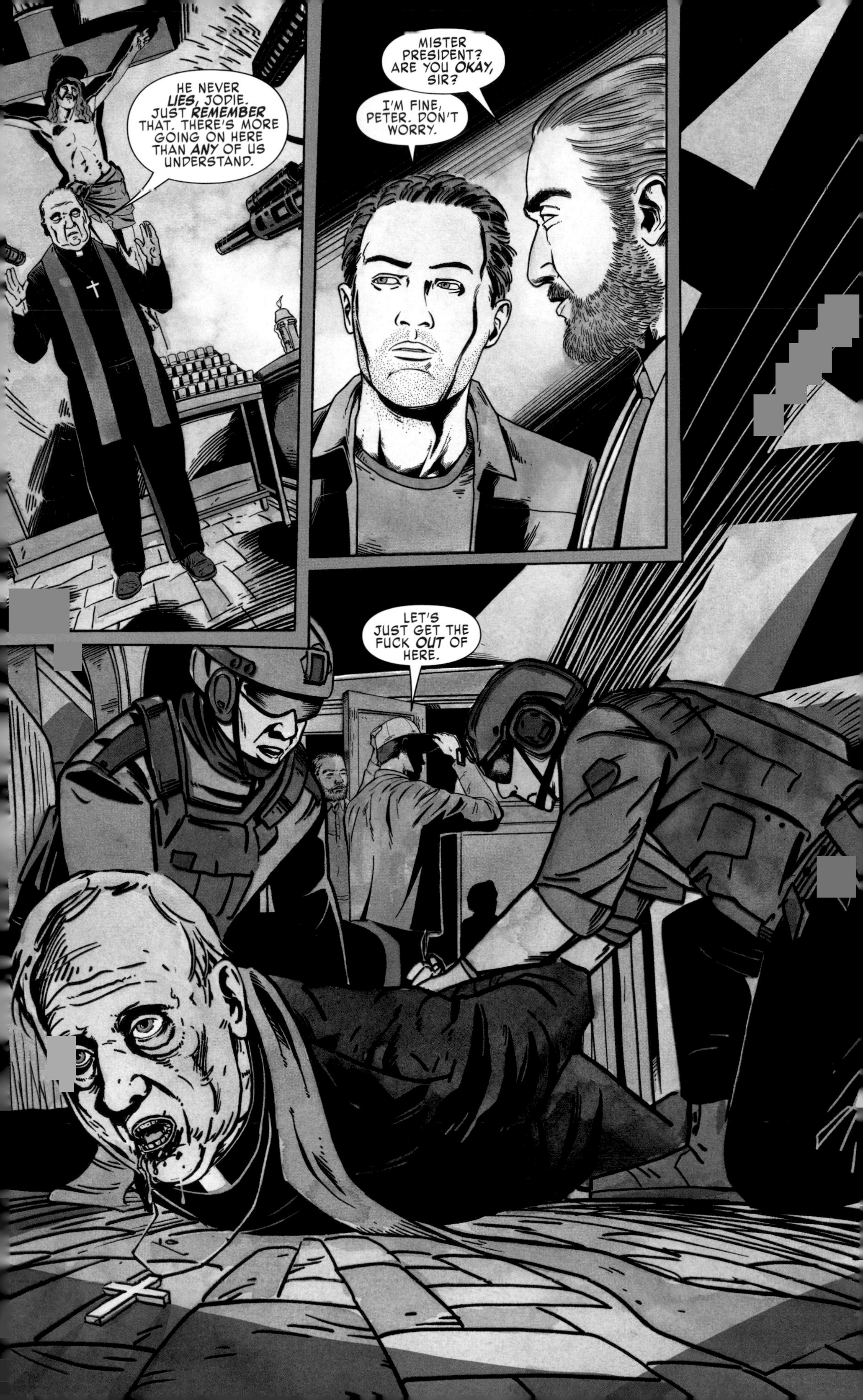
HE NEVER LIES, JODIE. JUST REMEMBER THAT. THERE'S MORE GOING ON HERE THAN ANY OF US UNDERSTAND.
MISTER PRESIDENT? ARE YOU OKAY, SIR?
I'M FINE, PETER. DON'T WORRY.
LET'S JUST GET THE FUCK OUT OF HERE.

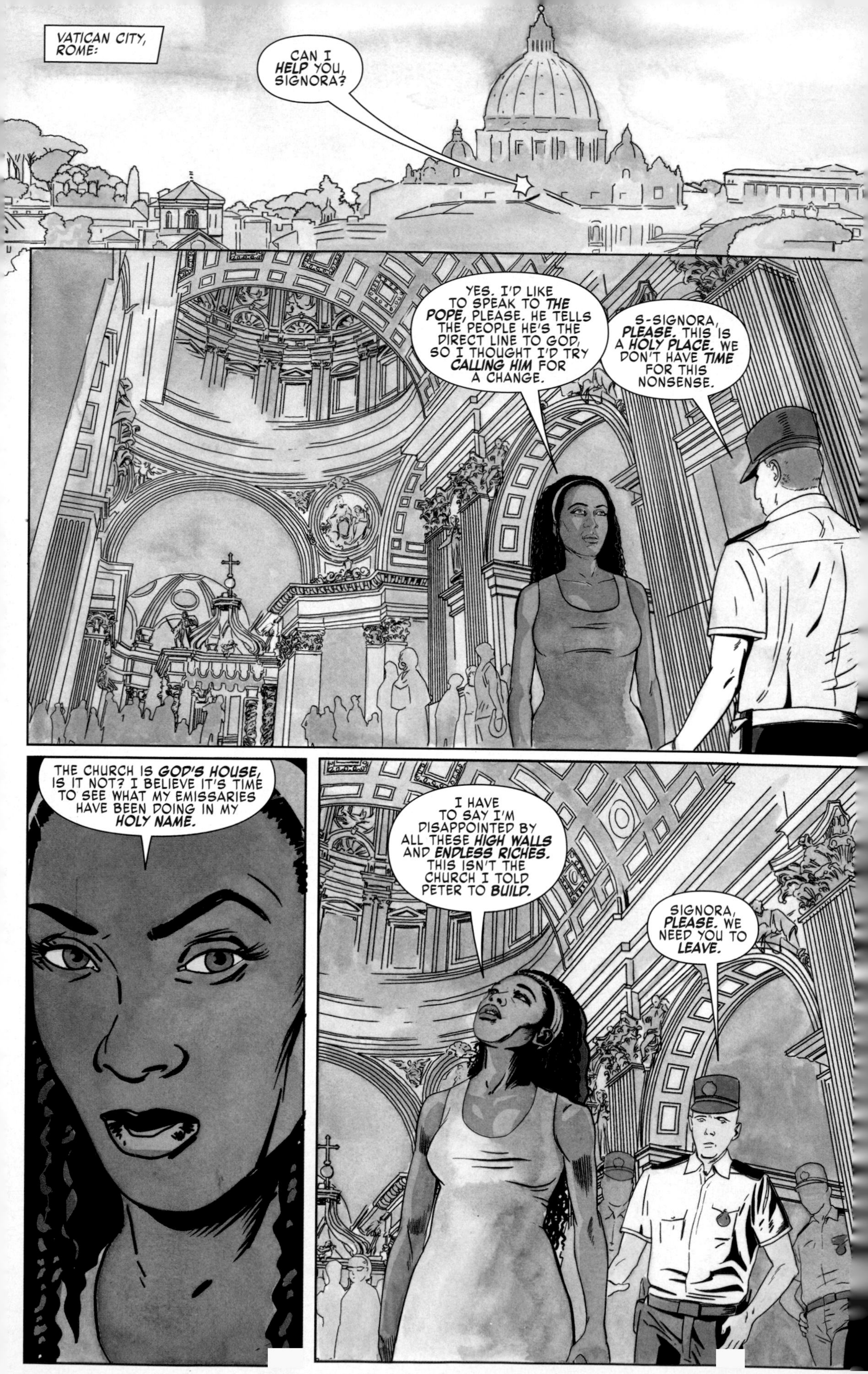
VATICAN CITY, ROME:
CAN I HELP YOU, SIGNORA?
YES. I'D LIKE TO SPEAK TO THE POPE, PLEASE. HE TELLS THE PEOPLE HE'S THE DIRECT LINE TO GOD, SO I THOUGHT I'D TRY CALLING HIM FOR A CHANGE.
S-SIGNORA, PLEASE. THIS IS A HOLY PLACE. WE DON'T HAVE TIME FOR THIS NONSENSE.
THE CHURCH IS GOD'S HOUSE, IS IT NOT? I BELIEVE IT'S TIME TO SEE WHAT MY EMISSARIES HAVE BEEN DOING IN MY HOLY NAME.
I HAVE TO SAY I'M DISAPPOINTED BY ALL THESE HIGH WALLS AND ENDLESS RICHES. THIS ISN'T THE CHURCH I TOLD PETER TO BUILD.
SIGNORA, PLEASE. WE NEED YOU TO LEAVE.

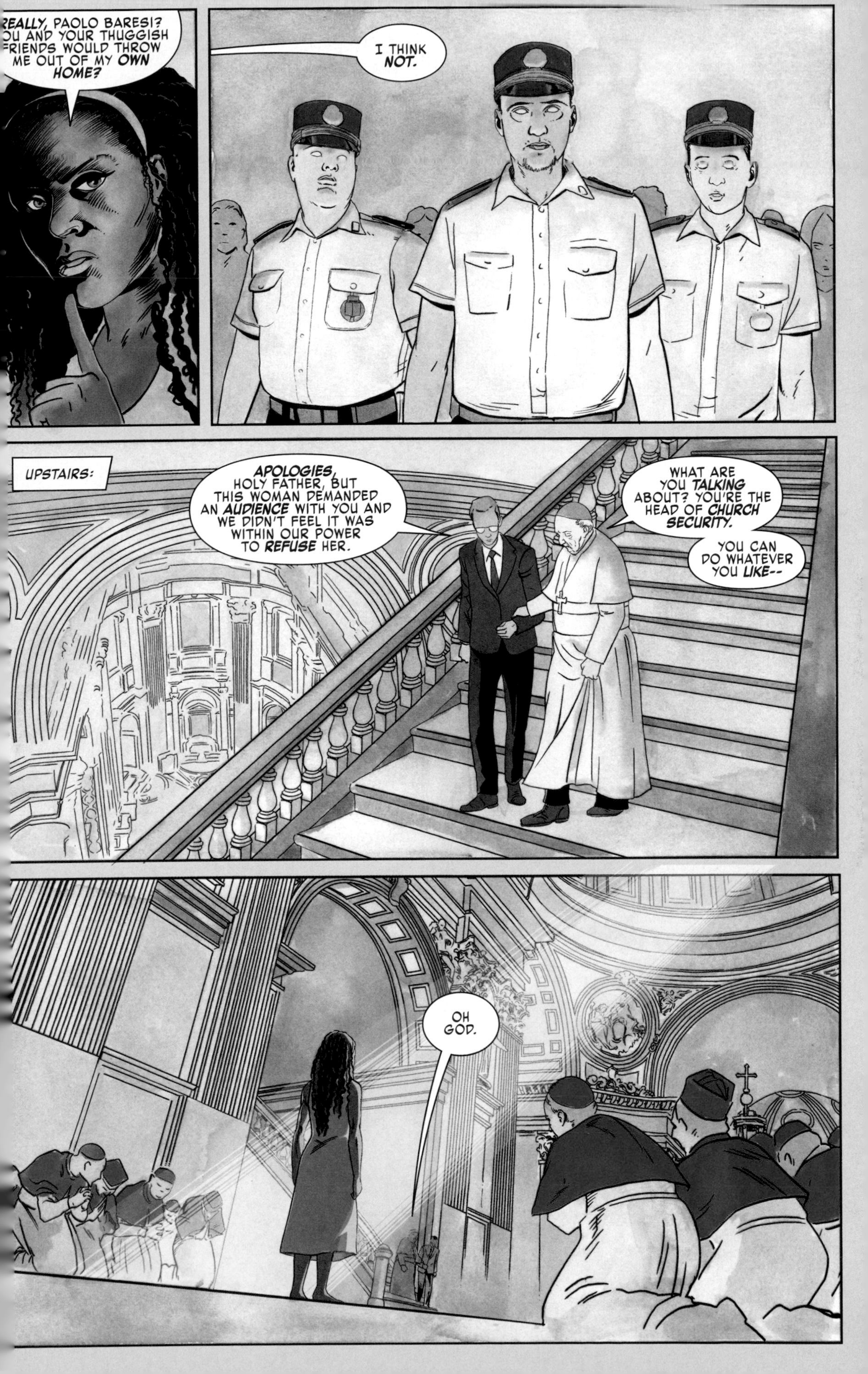
REALLY, PAOLO BARESI? OU AND YOUR THUGGISH FRIENDS WOULD THROW ME OUT OF MY OWN HOME?
I THINK NOT.
UPSTAIRS:
APOLOGIES, HOLY FATHER, BUT THIS WOMAN DEMANDED AN AUDIENCE WITH YOU AND WE DIDN'T FEEL IT WAS WITHIN OUR POWER TO REFUSE HER.
WHAT ARE YOU TALKING ABOUT? YOU'RE THE HEAD OF CHURCH SECURITY.
YOU CAN DO WHATEVER YOU LIKE--
OH GOD.

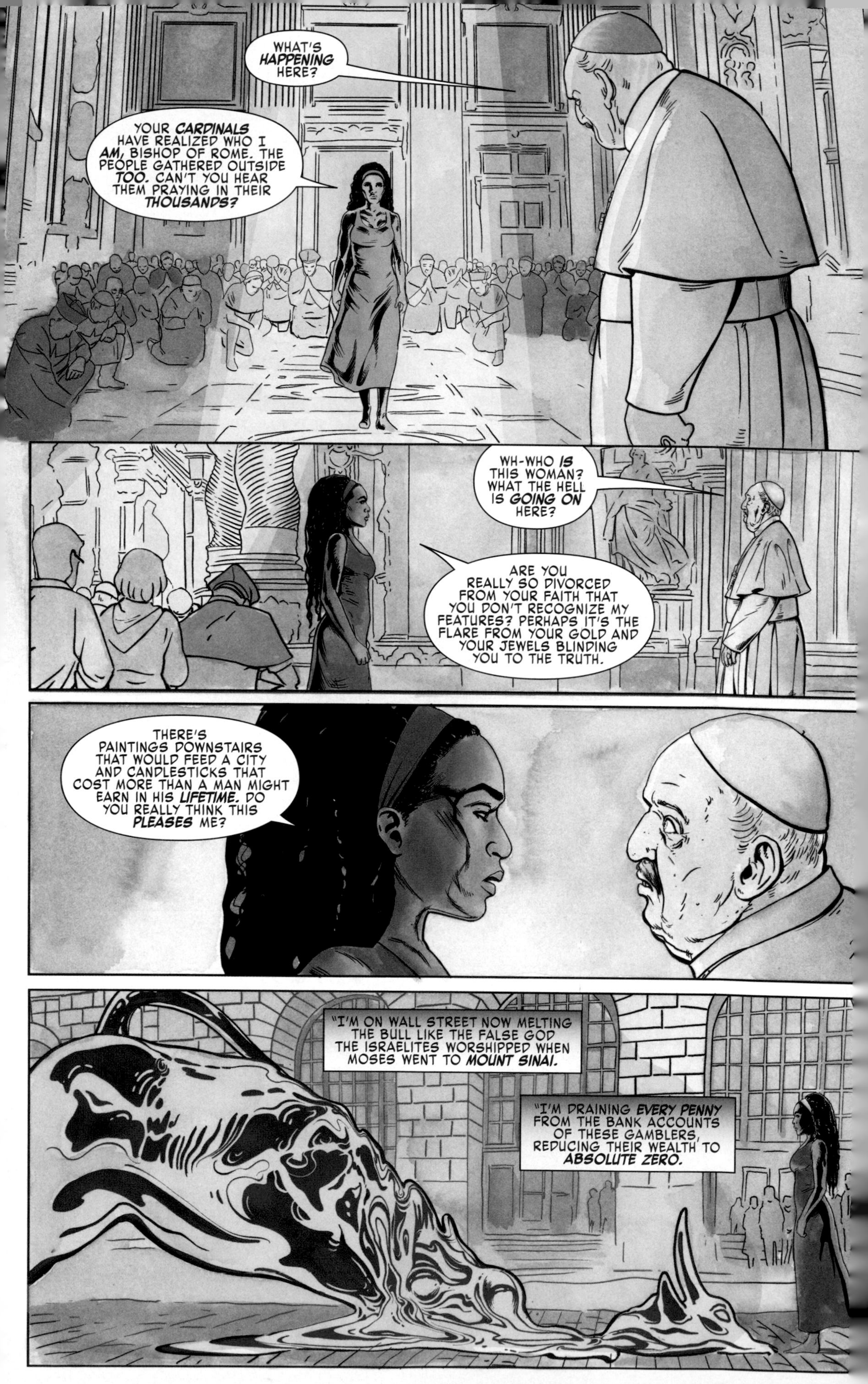
WHAT'S HAPPENING HERE?
YOUR CARDINALS HAVE REALIZED WHO I AM, BISHOP OF ROME. THE PEOPLE GATHERED OUTSIDE TOO. CAN'T YOU HEAR THEM PRAYING IN THEIR THOUSANDS?
WH-WHO IS THIS WOMAN? WHAT THE HELL IS GOING ON HERE?
ARE YOU REALLY SO DIVORCED FROM YOUR FAITH THAT YOU DON'T RECOGNIZE MY FEATURES? PERHAPS IT'S THE FLARE FROM YOUR GOLD AND YOUR JEWELS BLINDING YOU TO THE TRUTH.
THERE'S PAINTINGS DOWNSTAIRS THAT WOULD FEED A CITY AND CANDLESTICKS THAT COST MORE THAN A MAN MIGHT EARN IN HIS LIFETIME. DO YOU REALLY THINK THIS PLEASES ME?
"I'M ON WALL STREET NOW MELTING THE BULL LIKE THE FALSE GOD THE ISRAELITES WORSHIPPED WHEN MOSES WENT TO MOUNT SINAI.
"I'M DRAINING EVERY PENNY FROM THE BANK ACCOUNTS OF THESE GAMBLERS, REDUCING THEIR WEALTH TO ABSOLUTE ZERO.

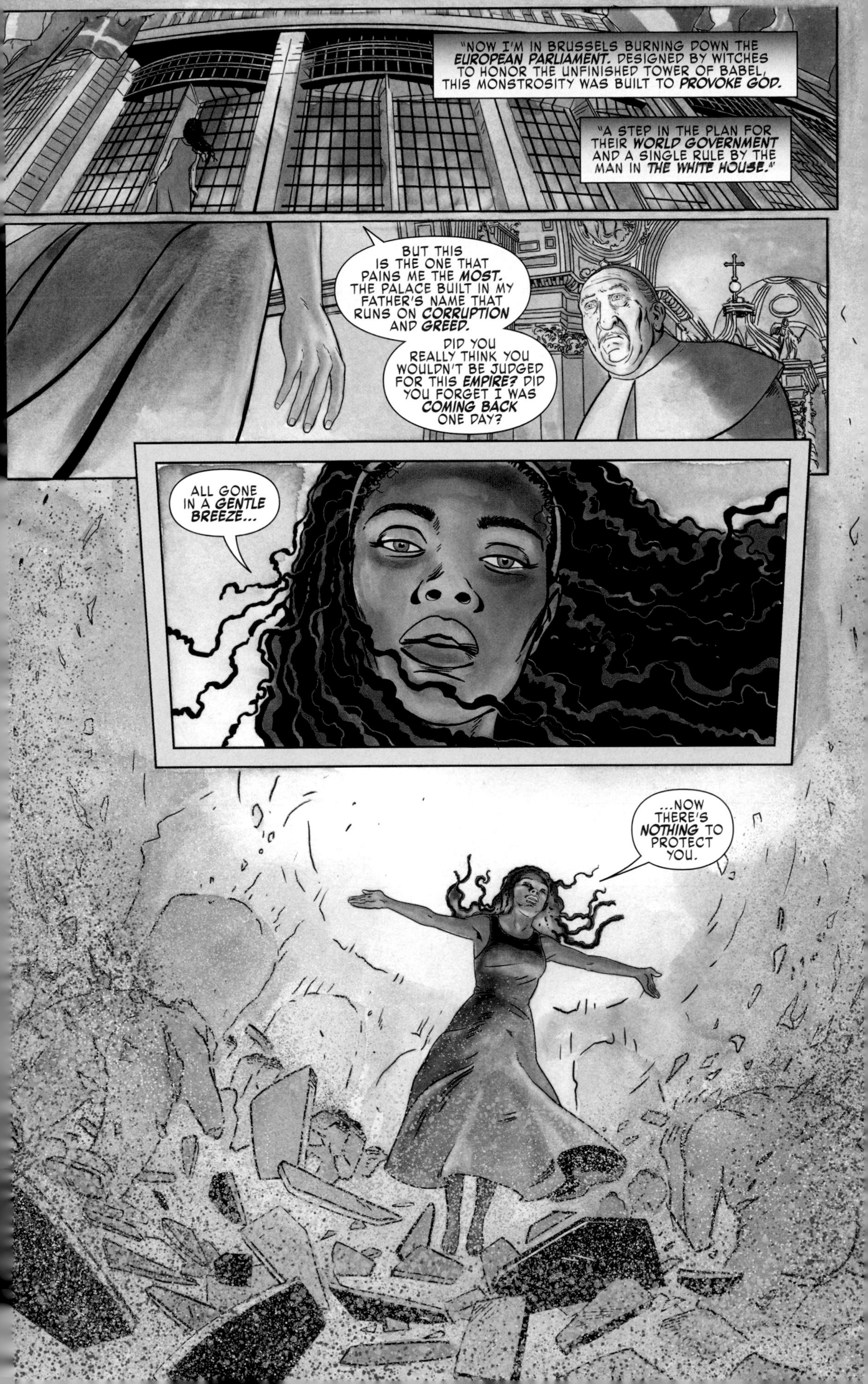
"NOW I'M IN BRUSSELS BURNING DOWN THE EUROPEAN PARLIAMENT. DESIGNED BY WITCHES TO HONOR THE UNFINISHED TOWER OF BABEL, THIS MONSTROSITY WAS BUILT TO PROVOKE GOD.
"A STEP IN THE PLAN FOR THEIR WORLD GOVERNMENT AND A SINGLE RULE BY THE MAN IN THE WHITE HOUSE."
BUT THIS IS THE ONE THAT PAINS ME THE MOST. THE PALACE BUILT IN MY FATHER'S NAME THAT RUNS ON CORRUPTION AND GREED.
DID YOU REALLY THINK YOU WOULDN'T BE JUDGED FOR THIS EMPIRE? DID YOU FORGET I WAS COMING BACK ONE DAY?
ALL GONE IN A GENTLE BREEZE...
...NOW THERE'S NOTHING TO PROTECT YOU.

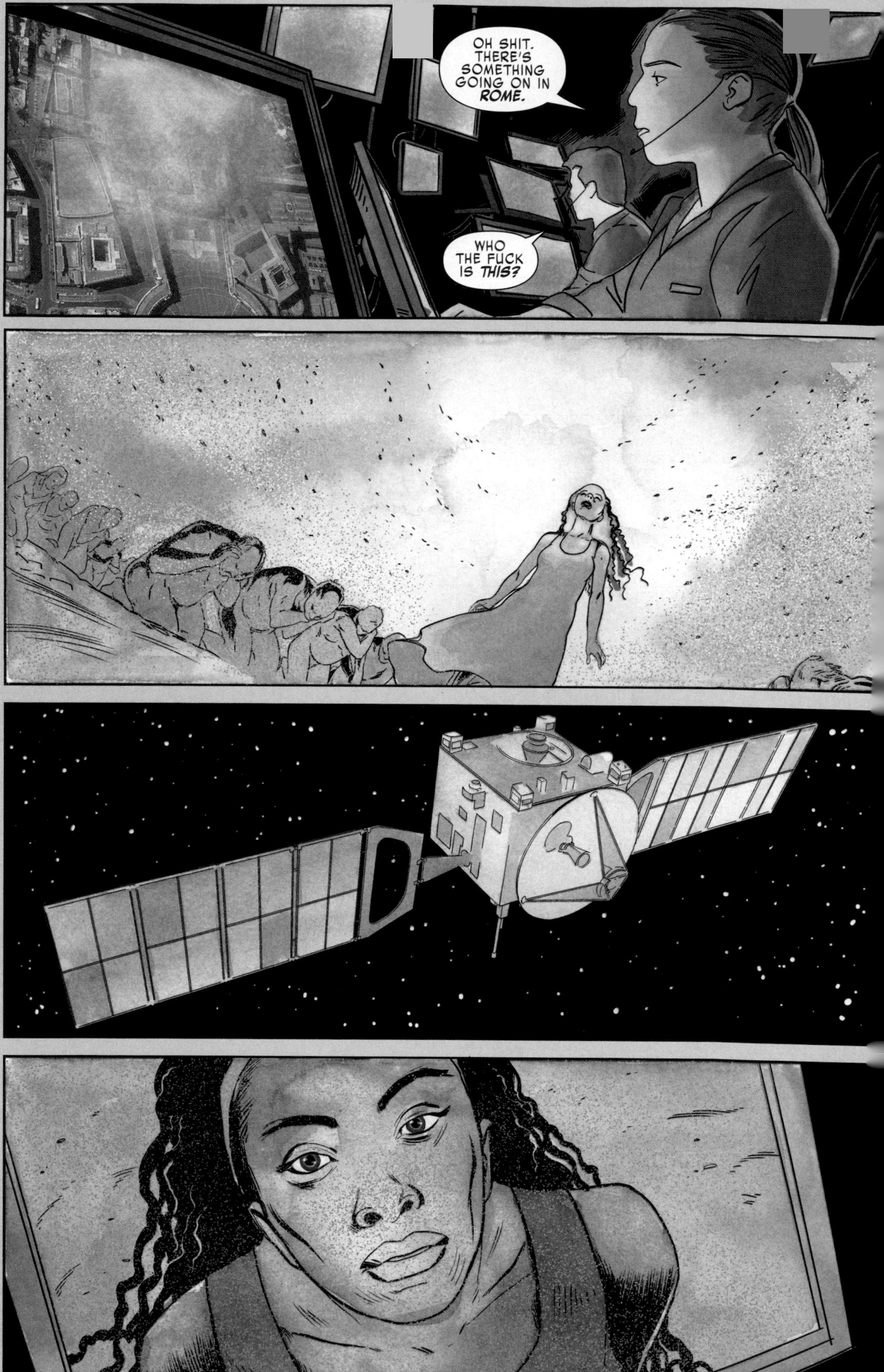
OH SHIT. THERE'S SOMETHING GOING ON IN ROME.
WHO THE FUCK IS THIS?

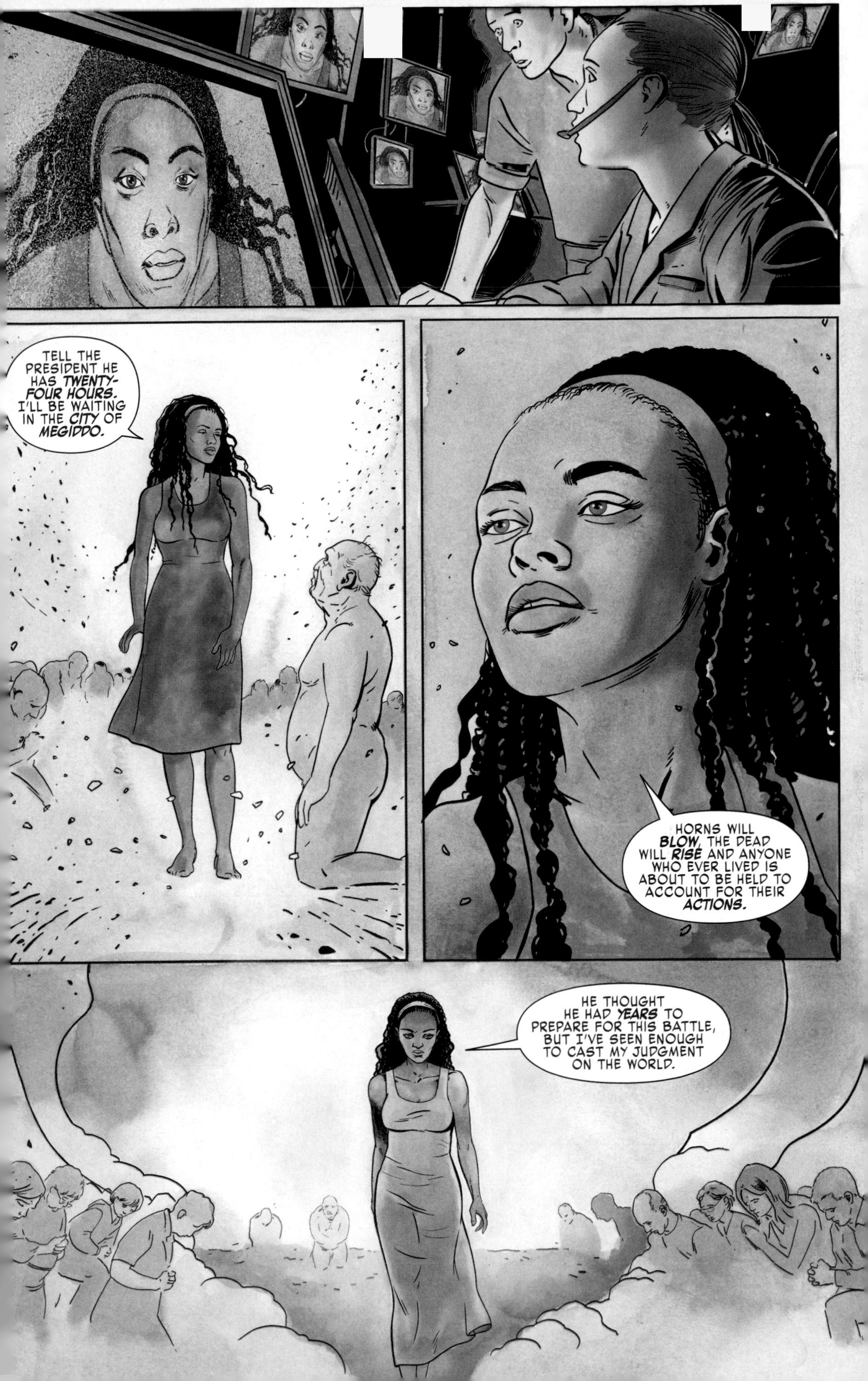
TELL THE PRESIDENT HE HAS TWENTY-FOUR HOURS. I'LL BE WAITING IN THE CITY OF MEGIDDO.
HORNS WILL BLOW, THE DEAD WILL RISE AND ANYONE WHO EVER LIVED IS ABOUT TO BE HELD TO ACCOUNT FOR THEIR ACTIONS.
HE THOUGHT HE HAD YEARS TO PREPARE FOR THIS BATTLE, BUT I'VE SEEN ENOUGH TO CAST MY JUDGMENT ON THE WORLD.

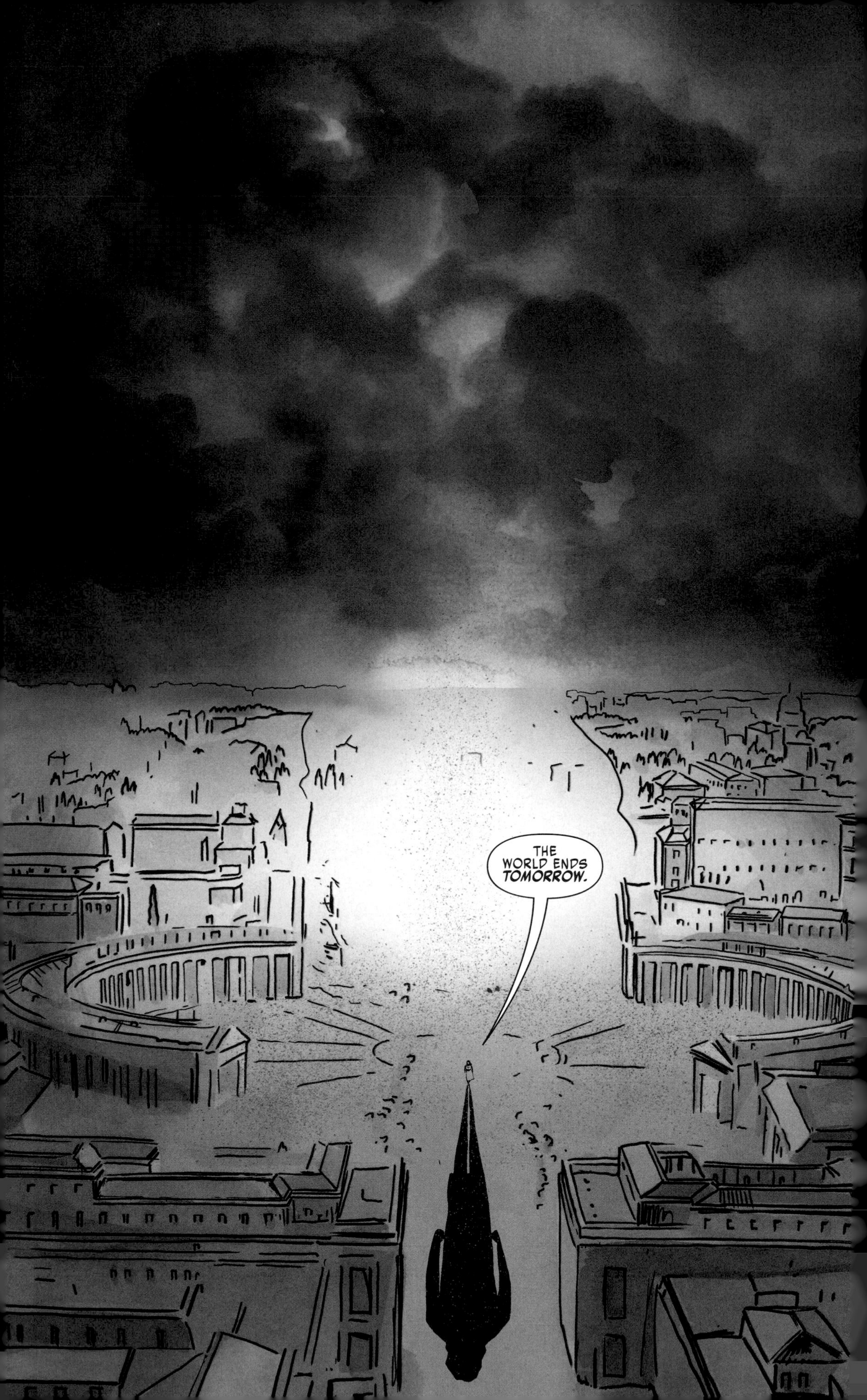
THE WORLD ENDS *TOMORROW.*

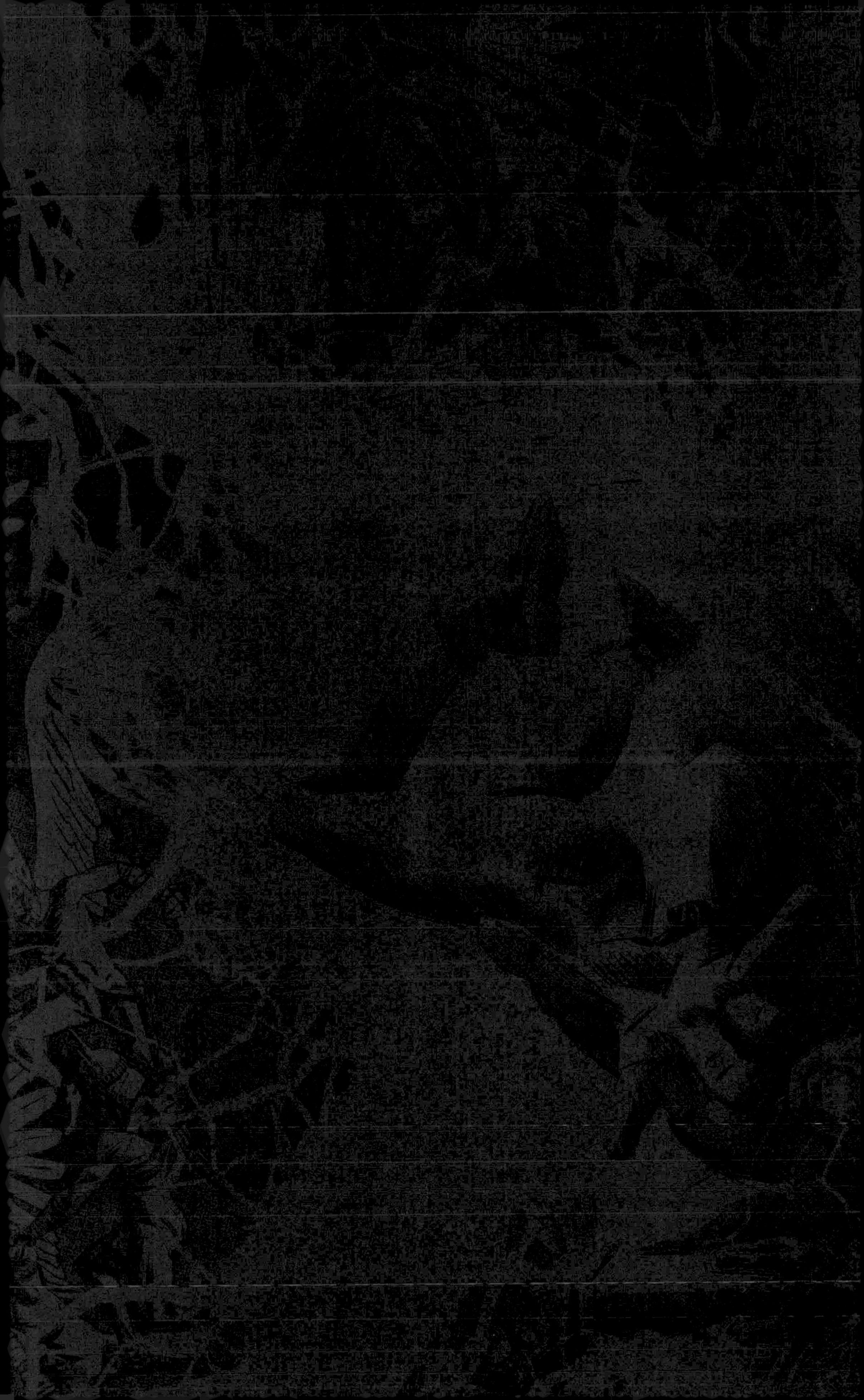

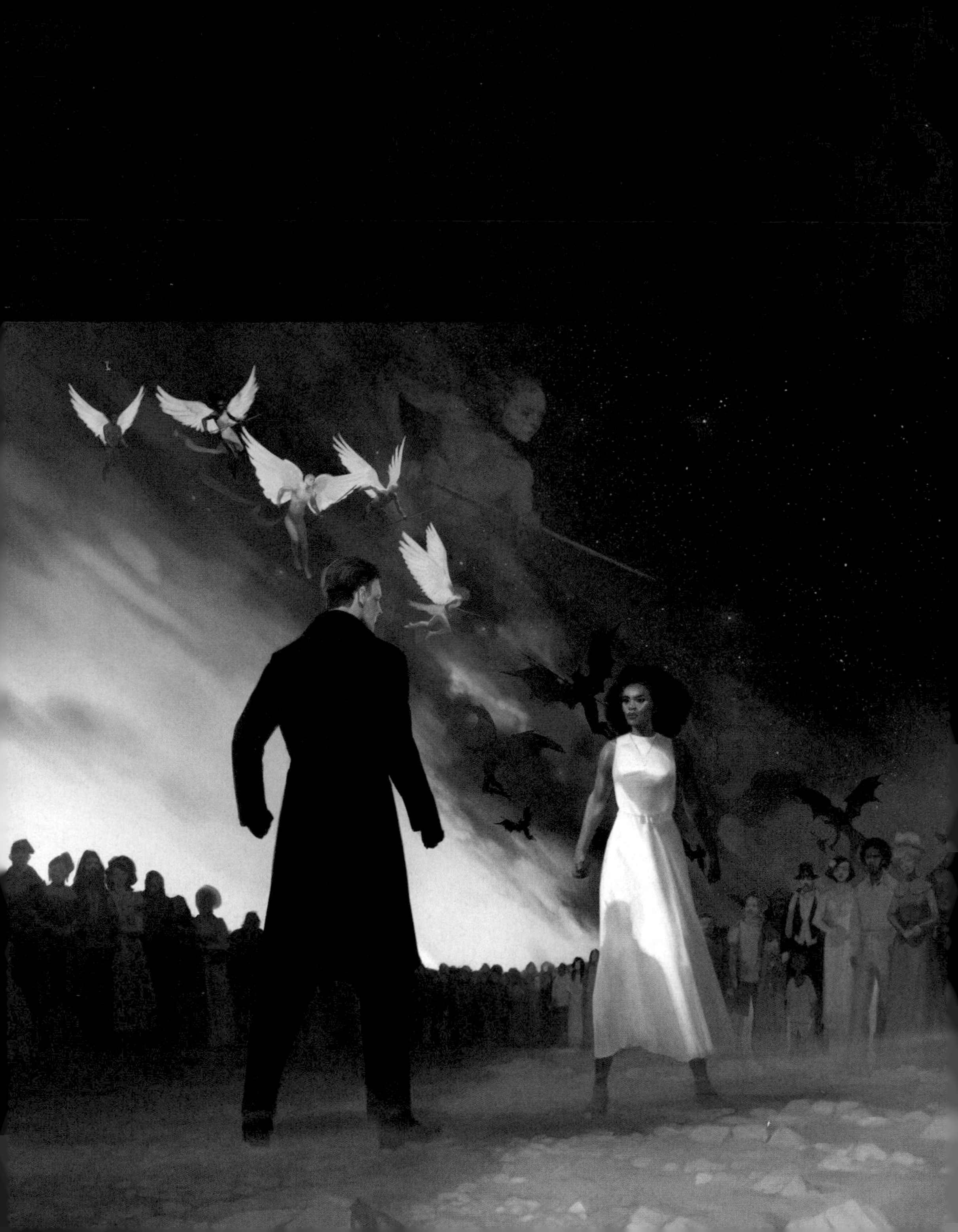

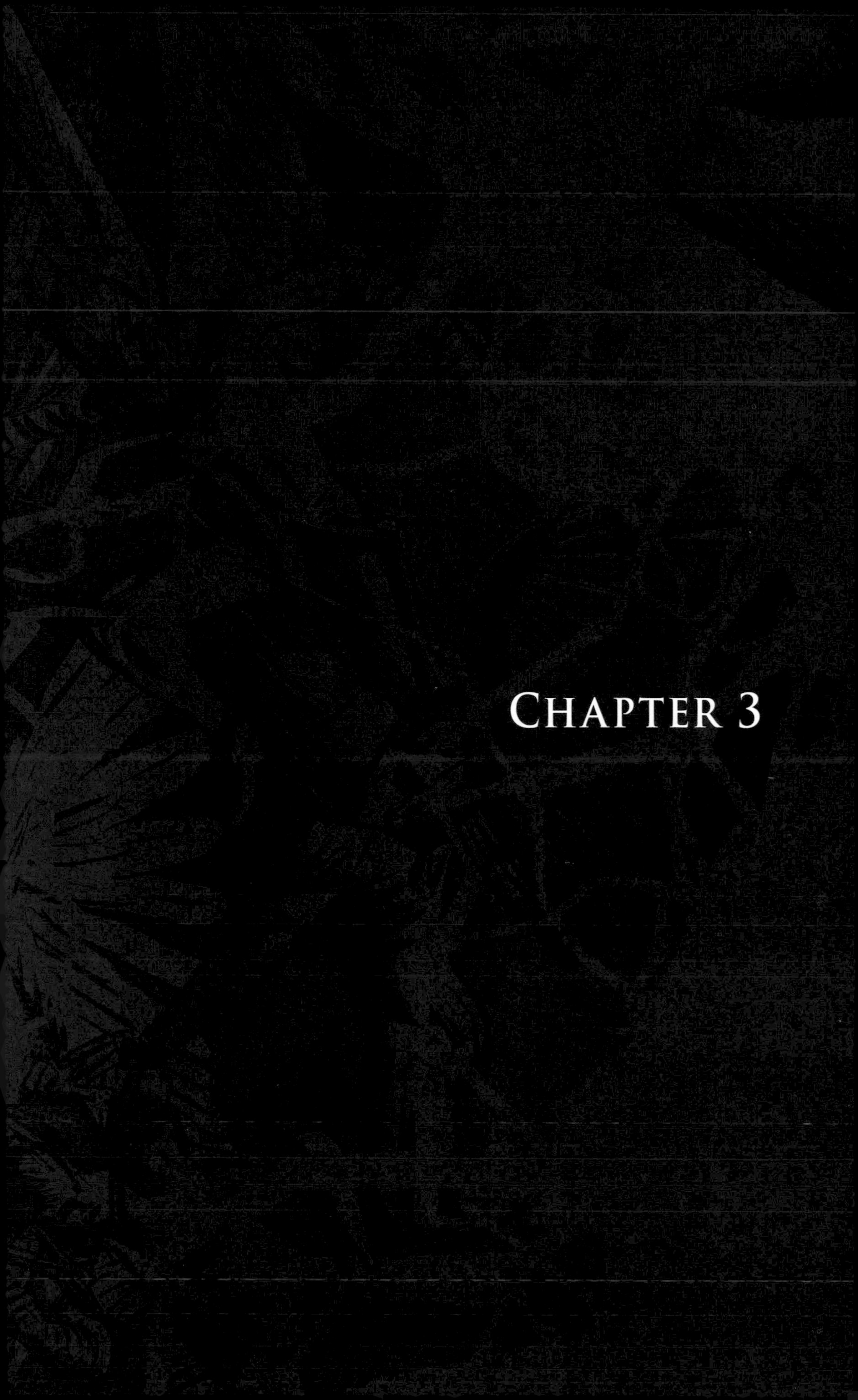

CHAPTER 3

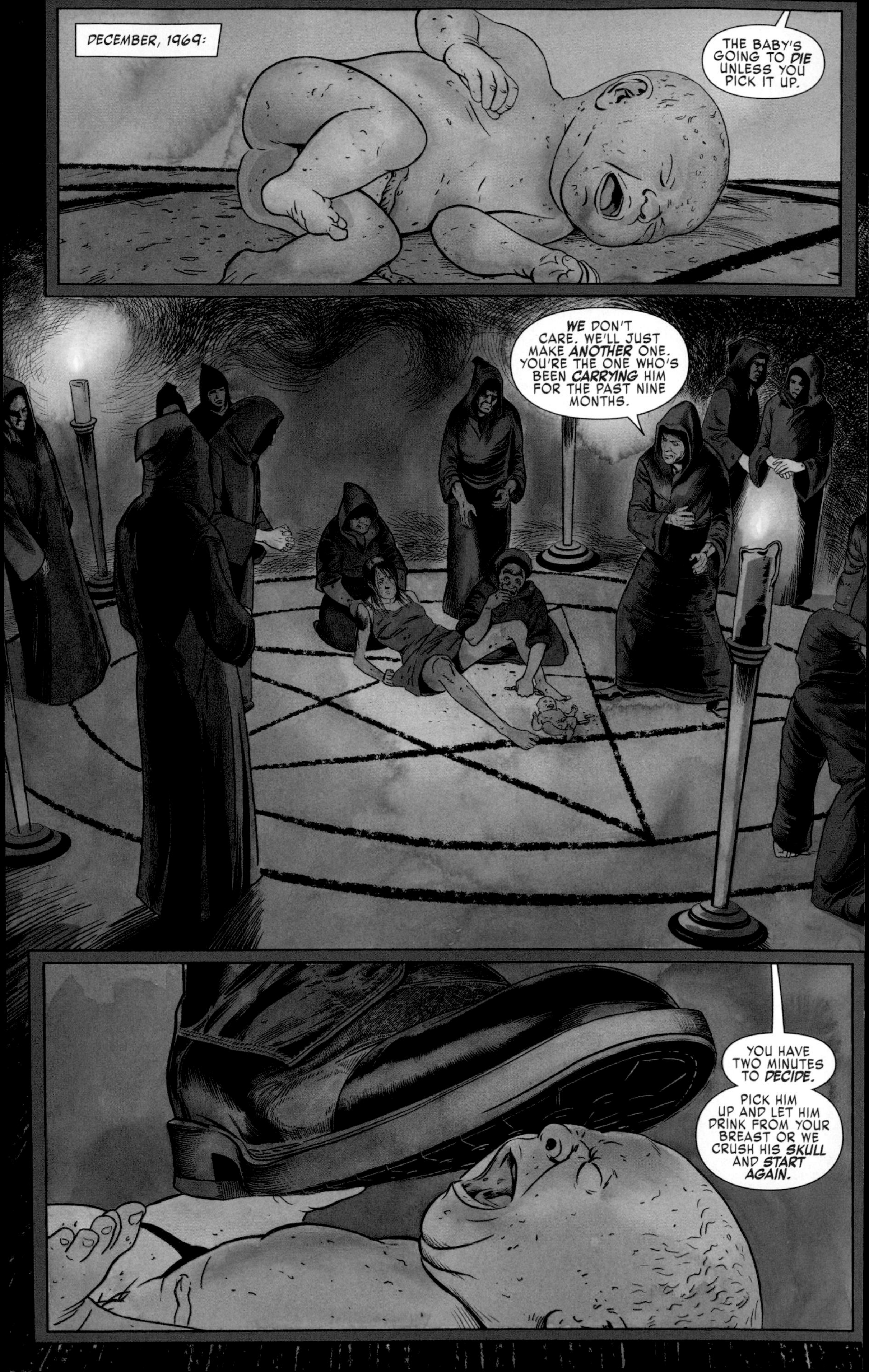
DECEMBER, 1969:
THE BABY'S GOING TO DIE UNLESS YOU PICK IT UP.
WE DON'T CARE. WE'LL JUST MAKE ANOTHER ONE. YOU'RE THE ONE WHO'S BEEN CARRYING HIM FOR THE PAST NINE MONTHS.
YOU HAVE TWO MINUTES TO DECIDE.
PICK HIM UP AND LET HIM DRINK FROM YOUR BREAST OR WE CRUSH HIS SKULL AND START AGAIN.

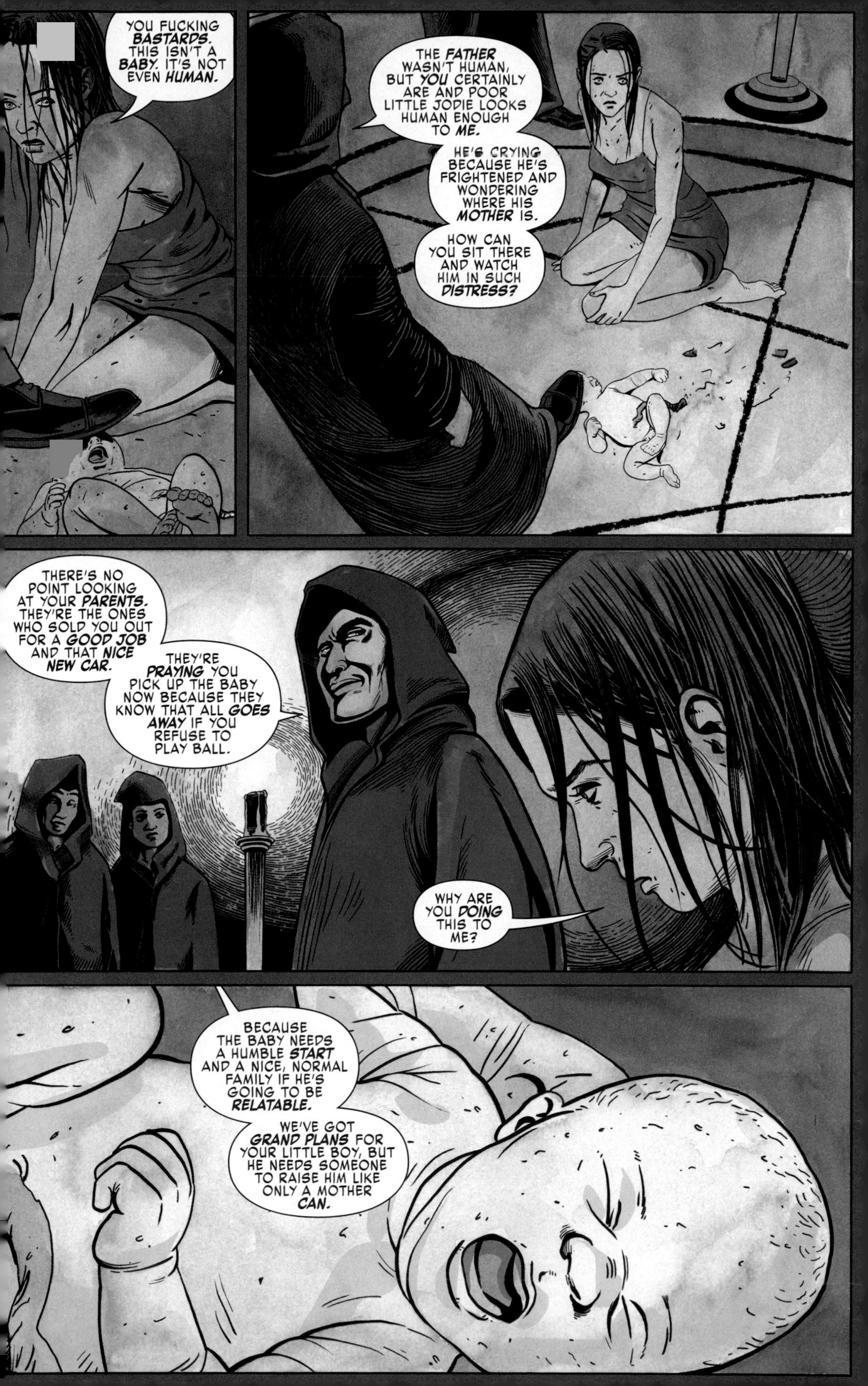

YOU FUCKING BASTARDS. THIS ISN'T A BABY. IT'S NOT EVEN HUMAN.
THE FATHER WASN'T HUMAN, BUT YOU CERTAINLY ARE AND POOR LITTLE JODIE LOOKS HUMAN ENOUGH TO ME.
HE'S CRYING BECAUSE HE'S FRIGHTENED AND WONDERING WHERE HIS MOTHER IS.
HOW CAN YOU SIT THERE AND WATCH HIM IN SUCH DISTRESS?
THERE'S NO POINT LOOKING AT YOUR PARENTS. THEY'RE THE ONES WHO SOLD YOU OUT FOR A GOOD JOB AND THAT NICE NEW CAR.
THEY'RE PRAYING YOU PICK UP THE BABY NOW BECAUSE THEY KNOW THAT ALL GOES AWAY IF YOU REFUSE TO PLAY BALL.
WHY ARE YOU DOING THIS TO ME?
BECAUSE THE BABY NEEDS A HUMBLE START AND A NICE, NORMAL FAMILY IF HE'S GOING TO BE RELATABLE.
WE'VE GOT GRAND PLANS FOR YOUR LITTLE BOY, BUT HE NEEDS SOMEONE TO RAISE HIM LIKE ONLY A MOTHER CAN.

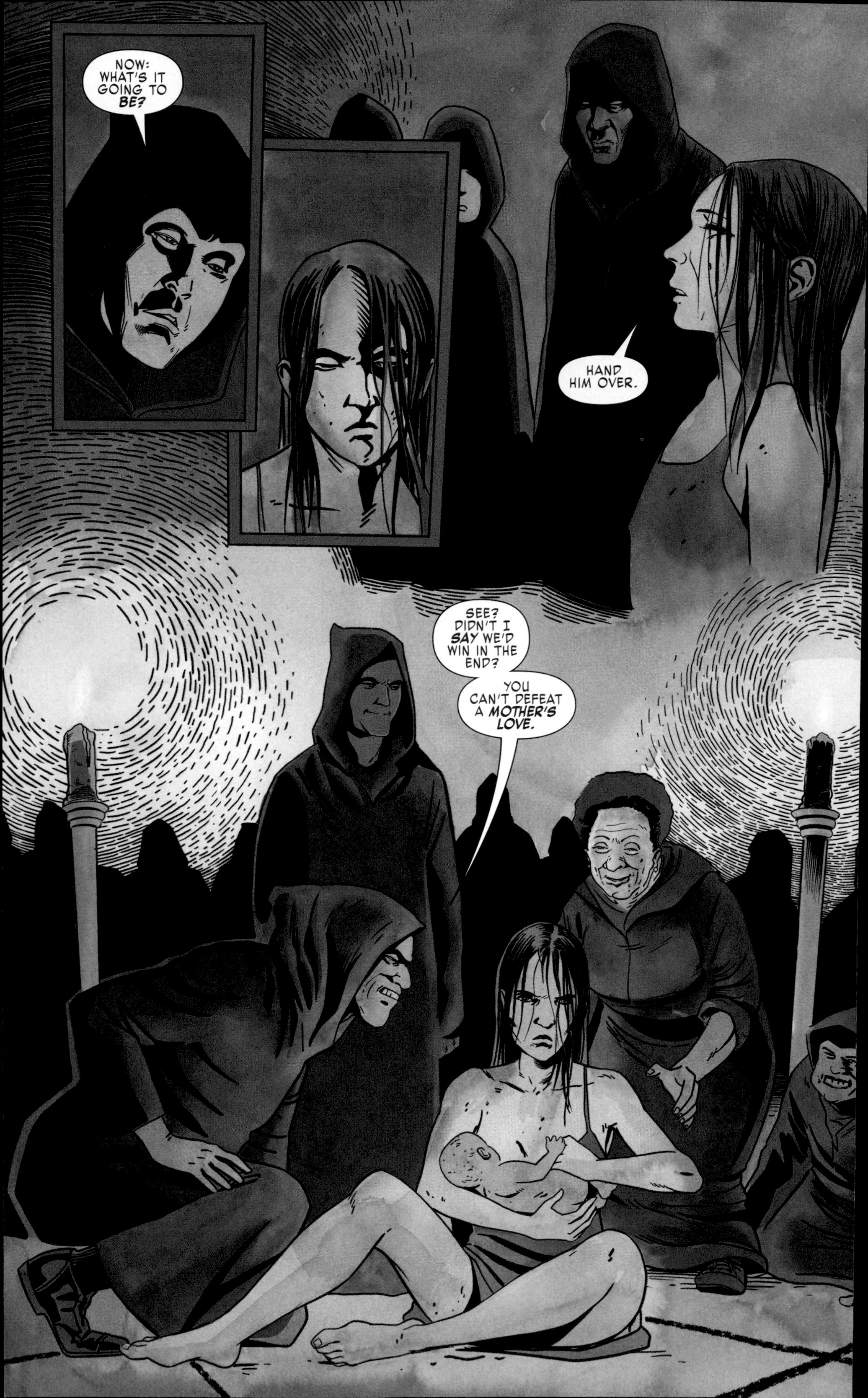
NOW: WHAT'S IT GOING TO BE?
HAND HIM OVER.
SEE? DIDN'T I SAY WE'D WIN IN THE END?
YOU CAN'T DEFEAT A MOTHER'S LOVE.

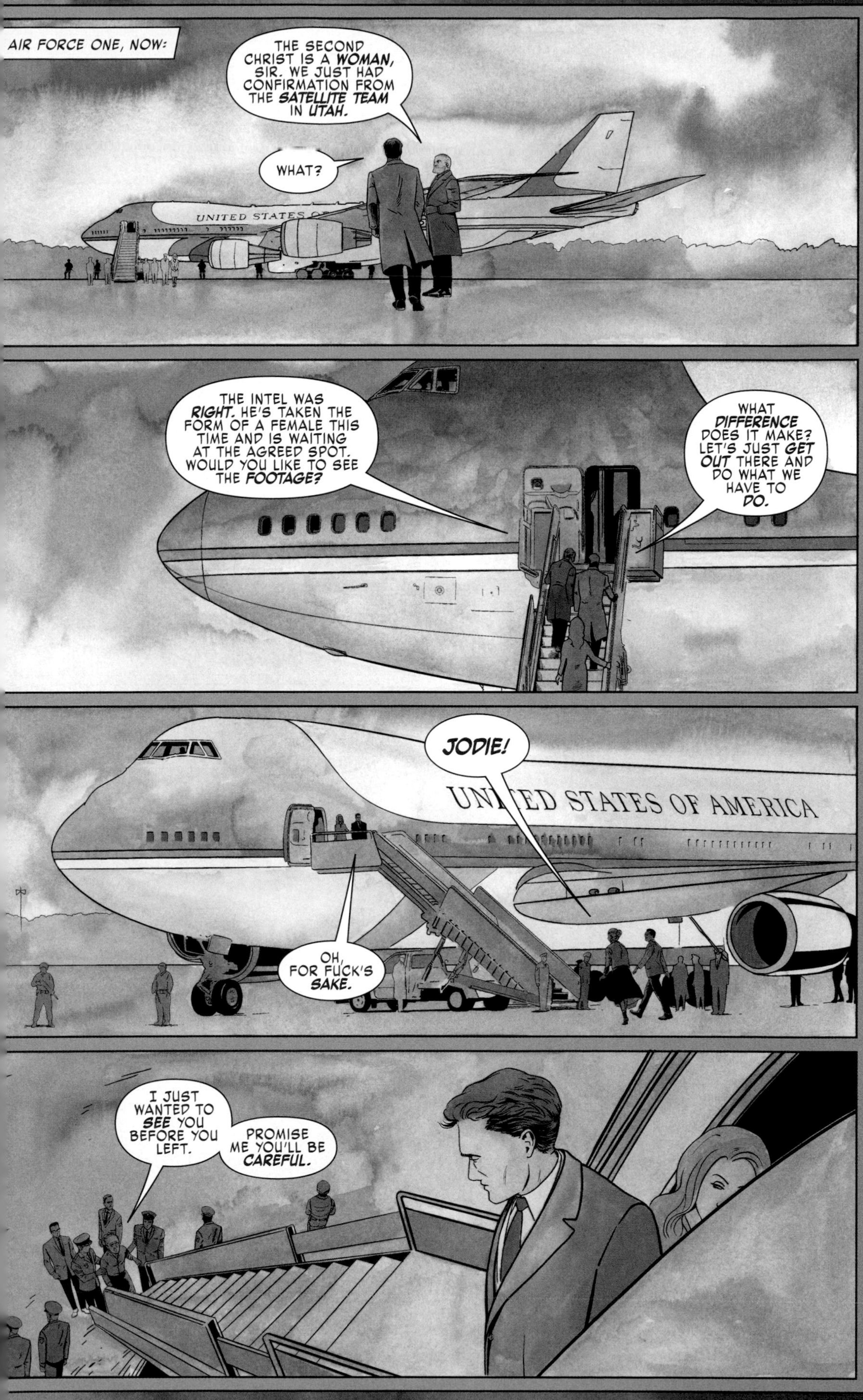
AIR FORCE ONE, NOW:
THE SECOND CHRIST IS A WOMAN, SIR. WE JUST HAD CONFIRMATION FROM THE SATELLITE TEAM IN UTAH.
WHAT?
UNITED STATES
THE INTEL WAS RIGHT. HE'S TAKEN THE FORM OF A FEMALE THIS TIME AND IS WAITING AT THE AGREED SPOT. WOULD YOU LIKE TO SEE THE FOOTAGE?
WHAT DIFFERENCE DOES IT MAKE? LET'S JUST GET OUT THERE AND DO WHAT WE HAVE TO DO.
JODIE!
UNITED STATES OF AMERICA
OH, FOR FUCK'S SAKE.
I JUST WANTED TO SEE YOU BEFORE YOU LEFT.
PROMISE ME YOU'LL BE CAREFUL.

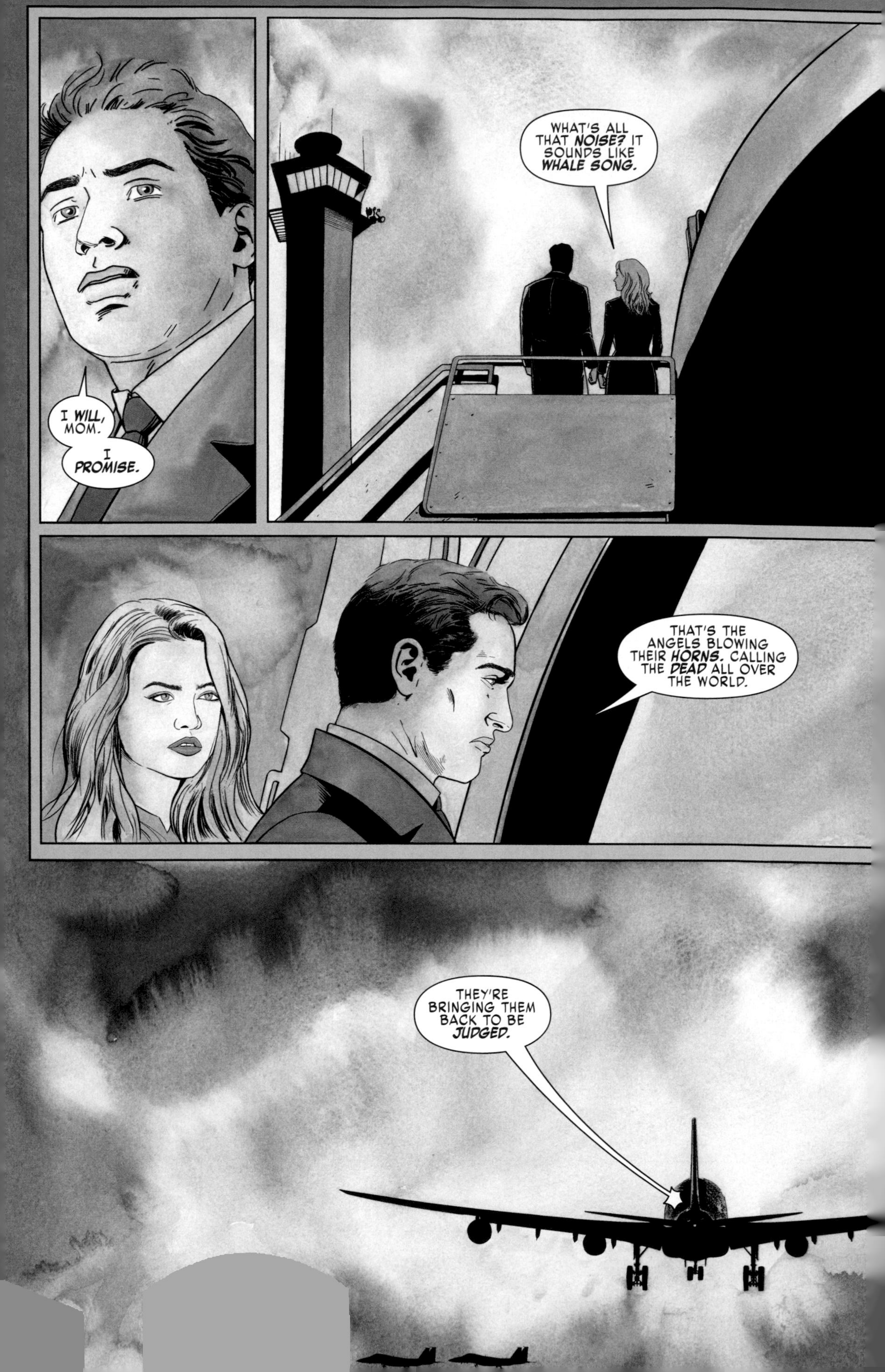
I WILL, MOM.
I PROMISE.
WHAT'S ALL THAT NOISE? IT SOUNDS LIKE WHALE SONG.
THAT'S THE ANGELS BLOWING THEIR HORNS. CALLING THE DEAD ALL OVER THE WORLD.
THEY'RE BRINGING THEM BACK TO BE JUDGED.

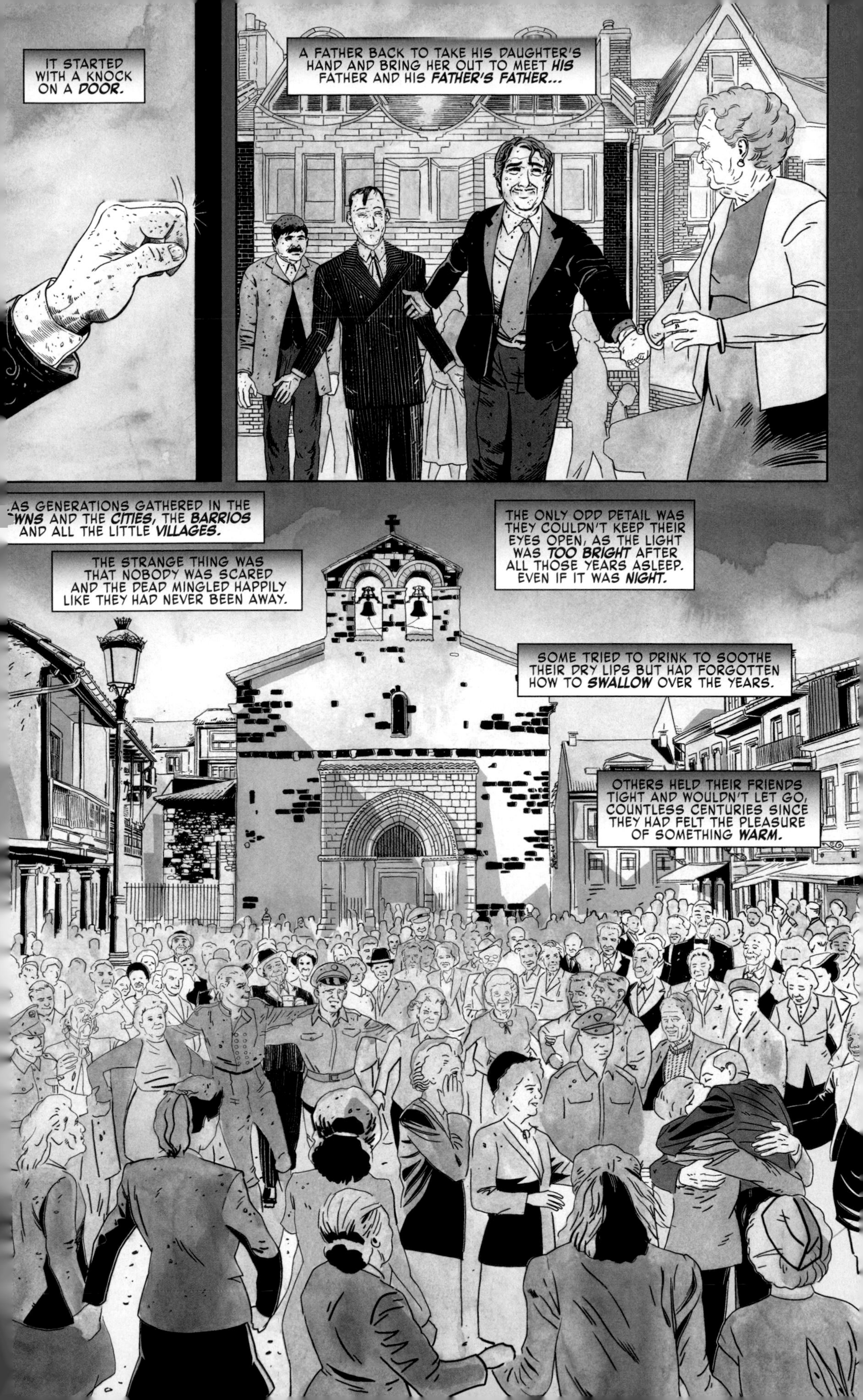
IT STARTED WITH A KNOCK ON A *DOOR*.
A FATHER BACK TO TAKE HIS DAUGHTER'S HAND AND BRING HER OUT TO MEET *HIS* FATHER AND HIS *FATHER'S FATHER...*
.AS GENERATIONS GATHERED IN THE WNS AND THE *CITIES*, THE *BARRIOS* AND ALL THE LITTLE *VILLAGES*.
THE STRANGE THING WAS THAT NOBODY WAS SCARED AND THE DEAD MINGLED HAPPILY LIKE THEY HAD NEVER BEEN AWAY.
THE ONLY ODD DETAIL WAS THEY COULDN'T KEEP THEIR EYES OPEN, AS THE LIGHT WAS *TOO BRIGHT* AFTER ALL THOSE YEARS ASLEEP. EVEN IF IT WAS *NIGHT*.
SOME TRIED TO DRINK TO SOOTHE THEIR DRY LIPS BUT HAD FORGOTTEN HOW TO *SWALLOW* OVER THE YEARS.
OTHERS HELD THEIR FRIENDS TIGHT AND WOULDN'T LET GO, COUNTLESS CENTURIES SINCE THEY HAD FELT THE PLEASURE OF SOMETHING *WARM*.

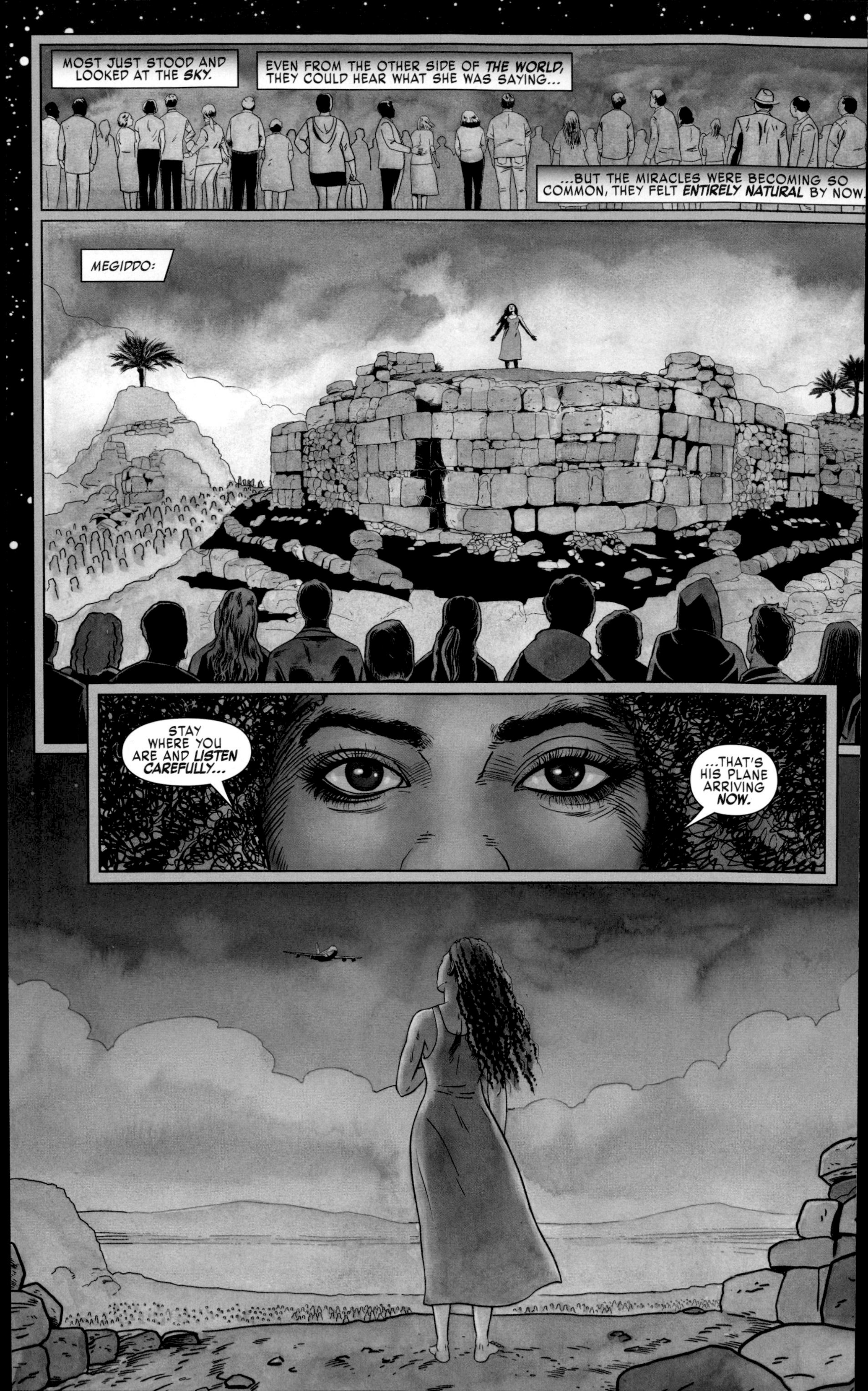
MOST JUST STOOD AND LOOKED AT THE SKY.
EVEN FROM THE OTHER SIDE OF THE WORLD, THEY COULD HEAR WHAT SHE WAS SAYING...
...BUT THE MIRACLES WERE BECOMING SO COMMON, THEY FELT ENTIRELY NATURAL BY NOW.
MEGIDDO:
STAY WHERE YOU ARE AND LISTEN CAREFULLY...
...THAT'S HIS PLANE ARRIVING NOW.

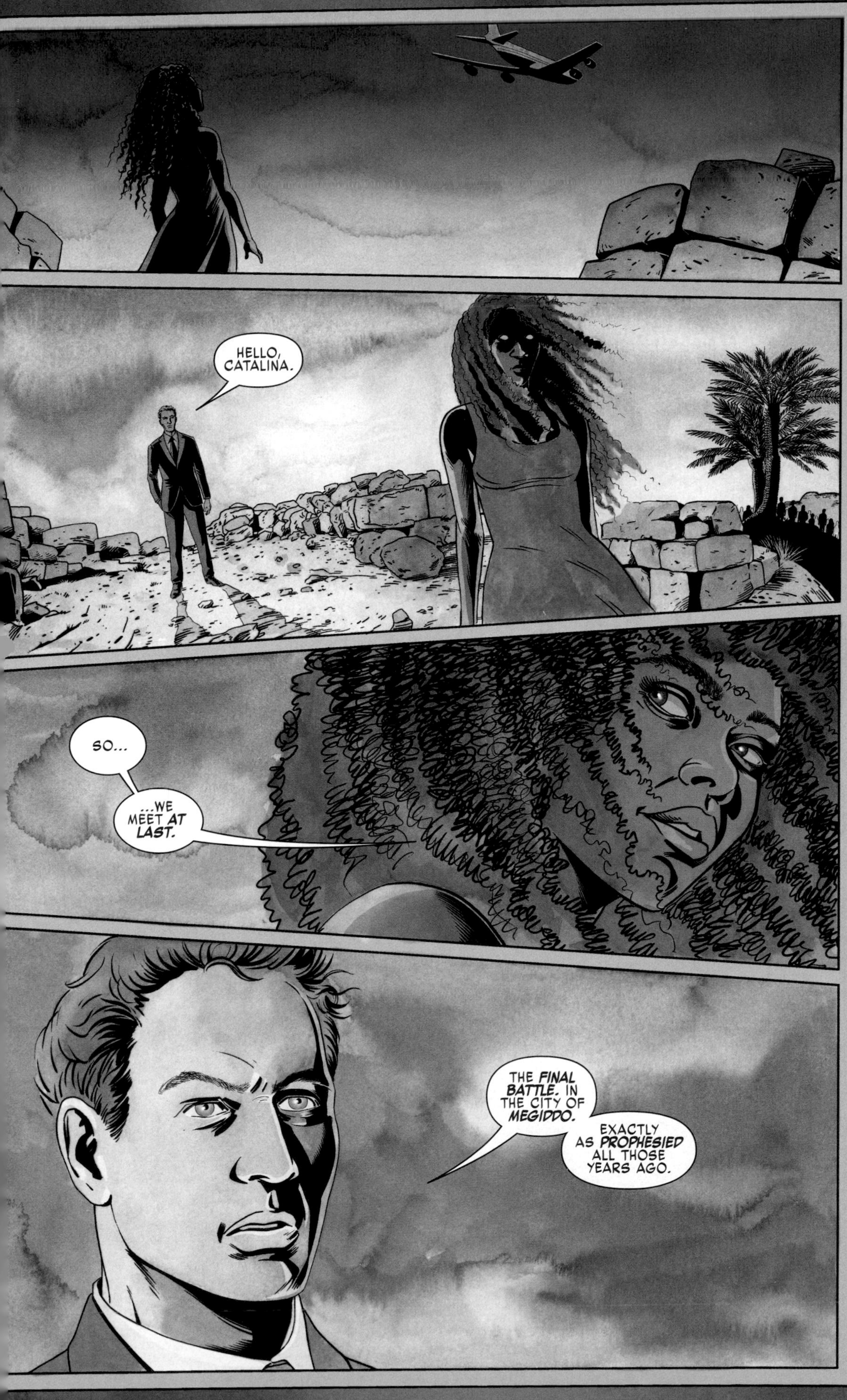
HELLO, CATALINA.
SO...
...WE MEET AT LAST.
THE FINAL BATTLE. IN THE CITY OF MEGIDDO.
EXACTLY AS PROPHESIED ALL THOSE YEARS AGO.

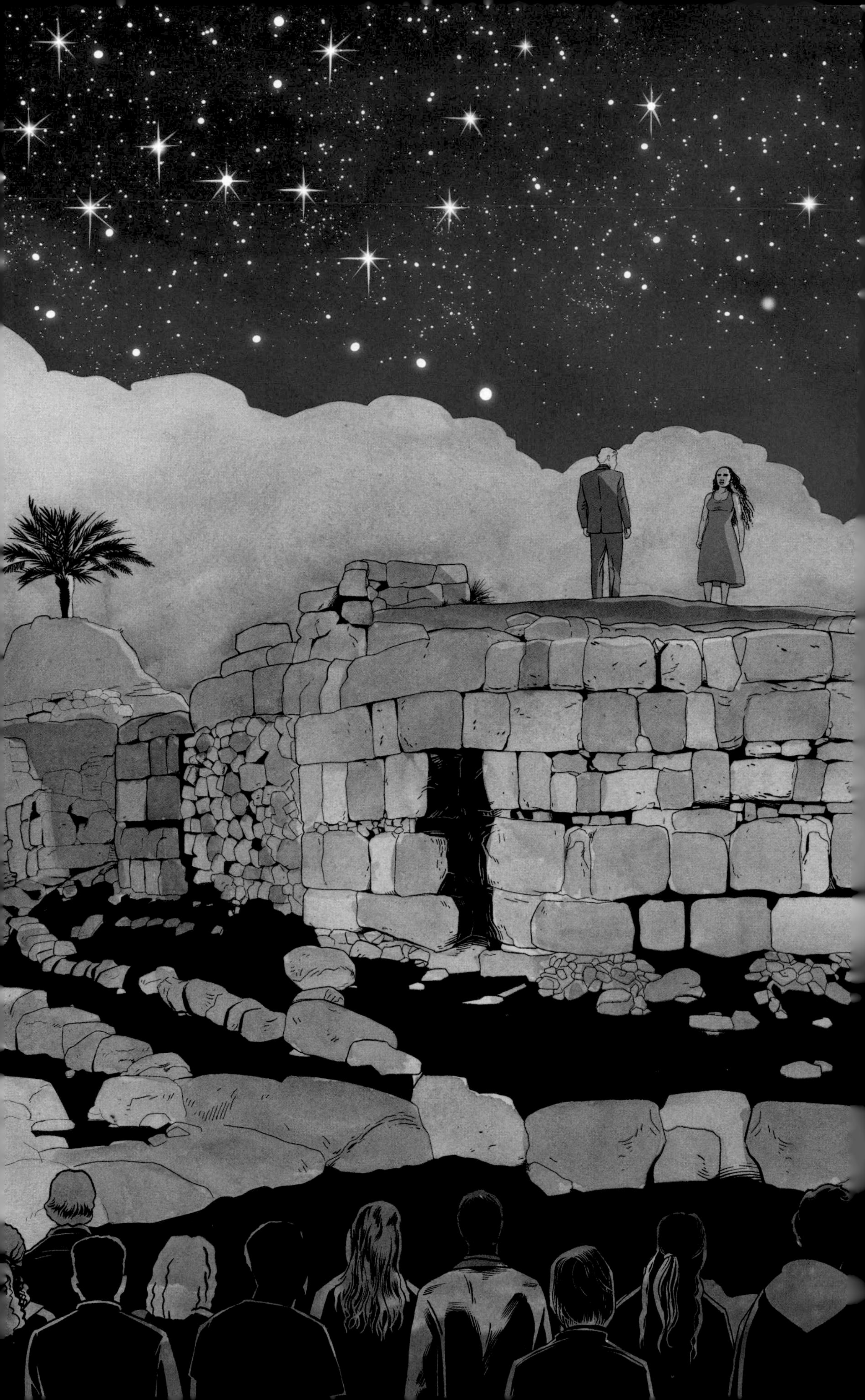

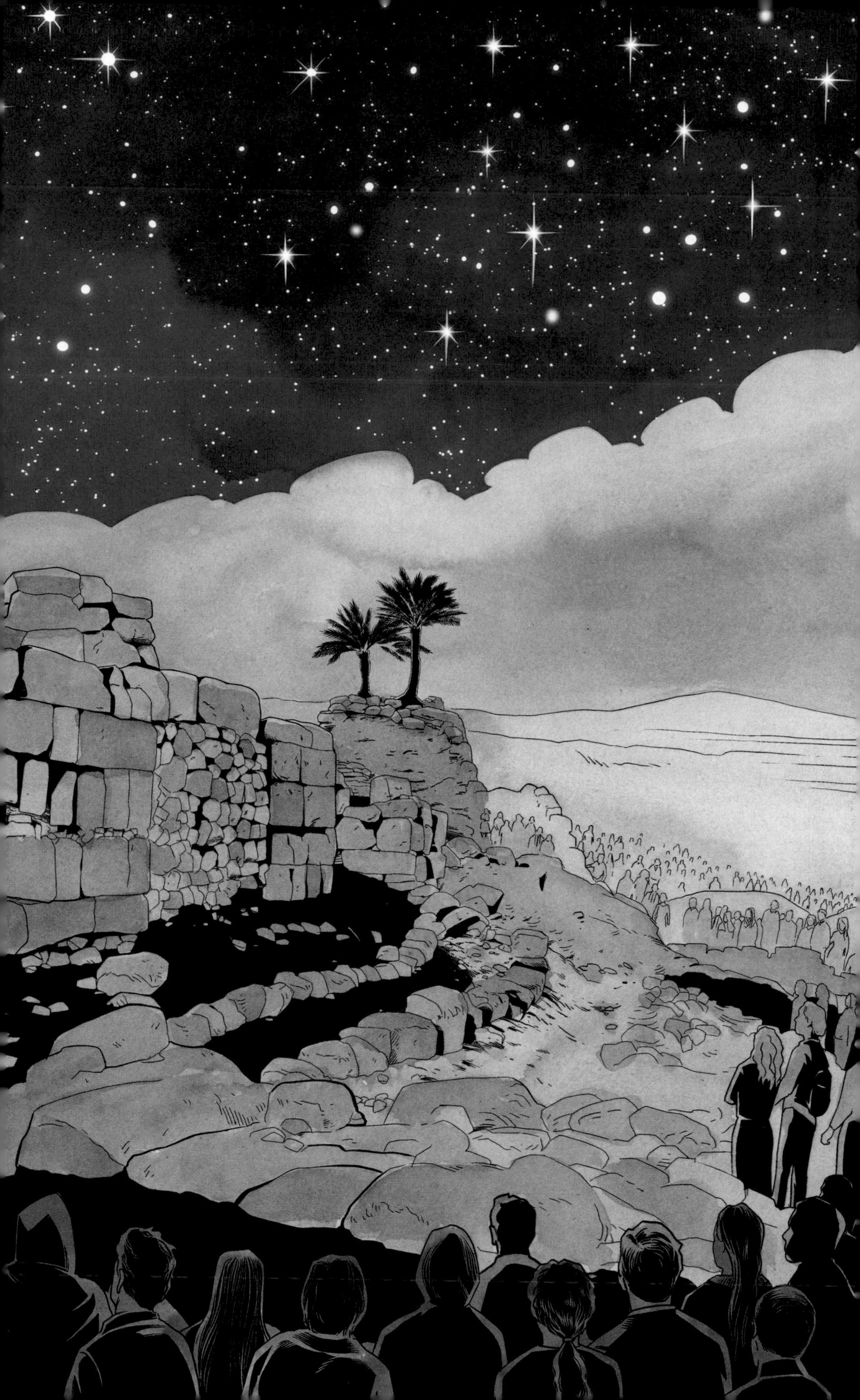

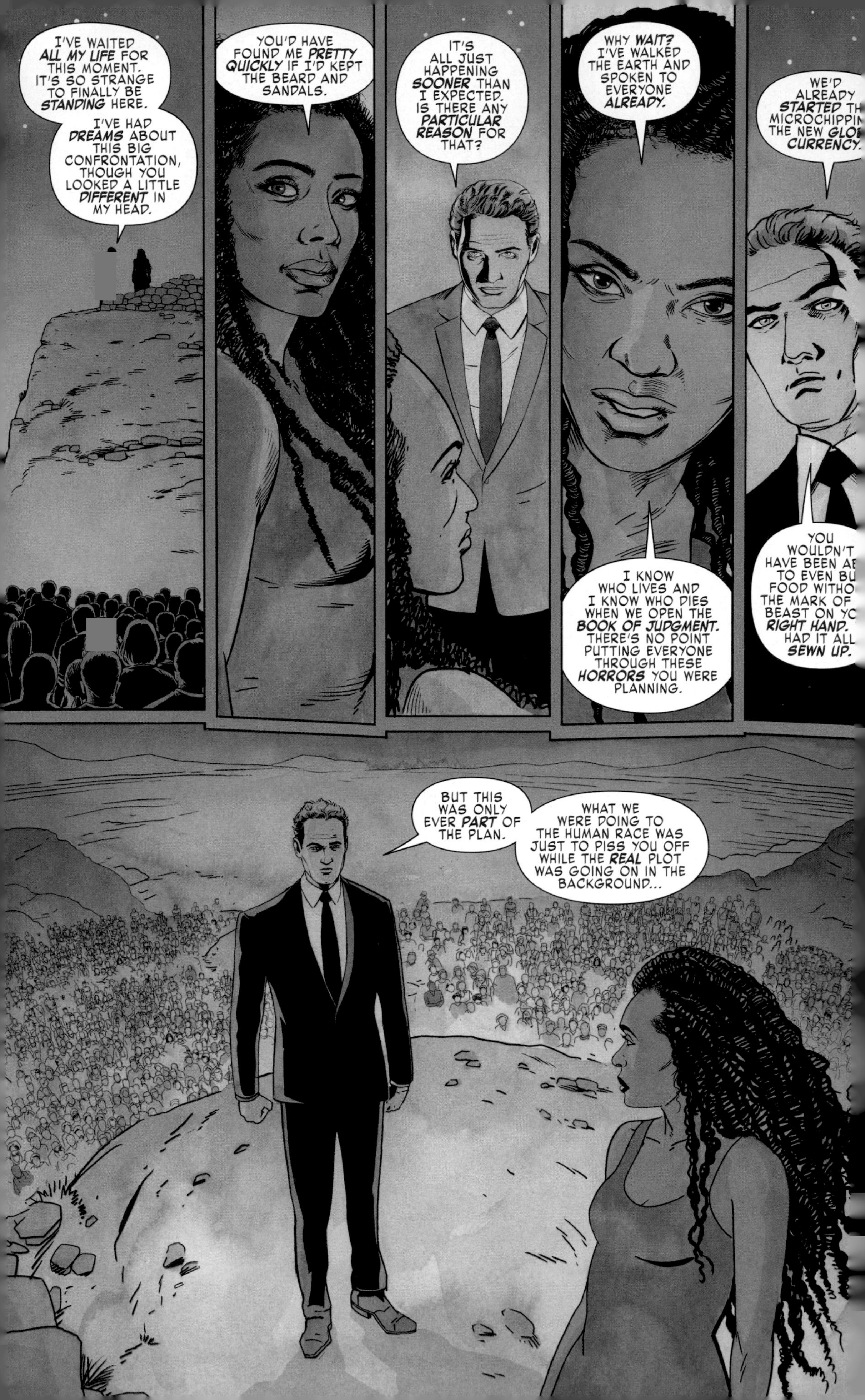
I'VE WAITED ALL MY LIFE FOR THIS MOMENT. IT'S SO STRANGE TO FINALLY BE STANDING HERE.
I'VE HAD DREAMS ABOUT THIS BIG CONFRONTATION, THOUGH YOU LOOKED A LITTLE DIFFERENT IN MY HEAD.
YOU'D HAVE FOUND ME PRETTY QUICKLY IF I'D KEPT THE BEARD AND SANDALS.
IT'S ALL JUST HAPPENING SOONER THAN I EXPECTED. IS THERE ANY PARTICULAR REASON FOR THAT?
WHY WAIT? I'VE WALKED THE EARTH AND SPOKEN TO EVERYONE ALREADY.
I KNOW WHO LIVES AND I KNOW WHO DIES WHEN WE OPEN THE BOOK OF JUDGMENT. THERE'S NO POINT PUTTING EVERYONE THROUGH THESE HORRORS YOU WERE PLANNING.
WE'D ALREADY STARTED TH MICROCHIPPIN THE NEW GLOB CURRENCY.
YOU WOULDN'T HAVE BEEN AB TO EVEN BU FOOD WITHO THE MARK OF BEAST ON YO RIGHT HAND. HAD IT ALL SEWN UP.
BUT THIS WAS ONLY EVER PART OF THE PLAN.
WHAT WE WERE DOING TO THE HUMAN RACE WAS JUST TO PISS YOU OFF WHILE THE REAL PLOT WAS GOING ON IN THE BACKGROUND...

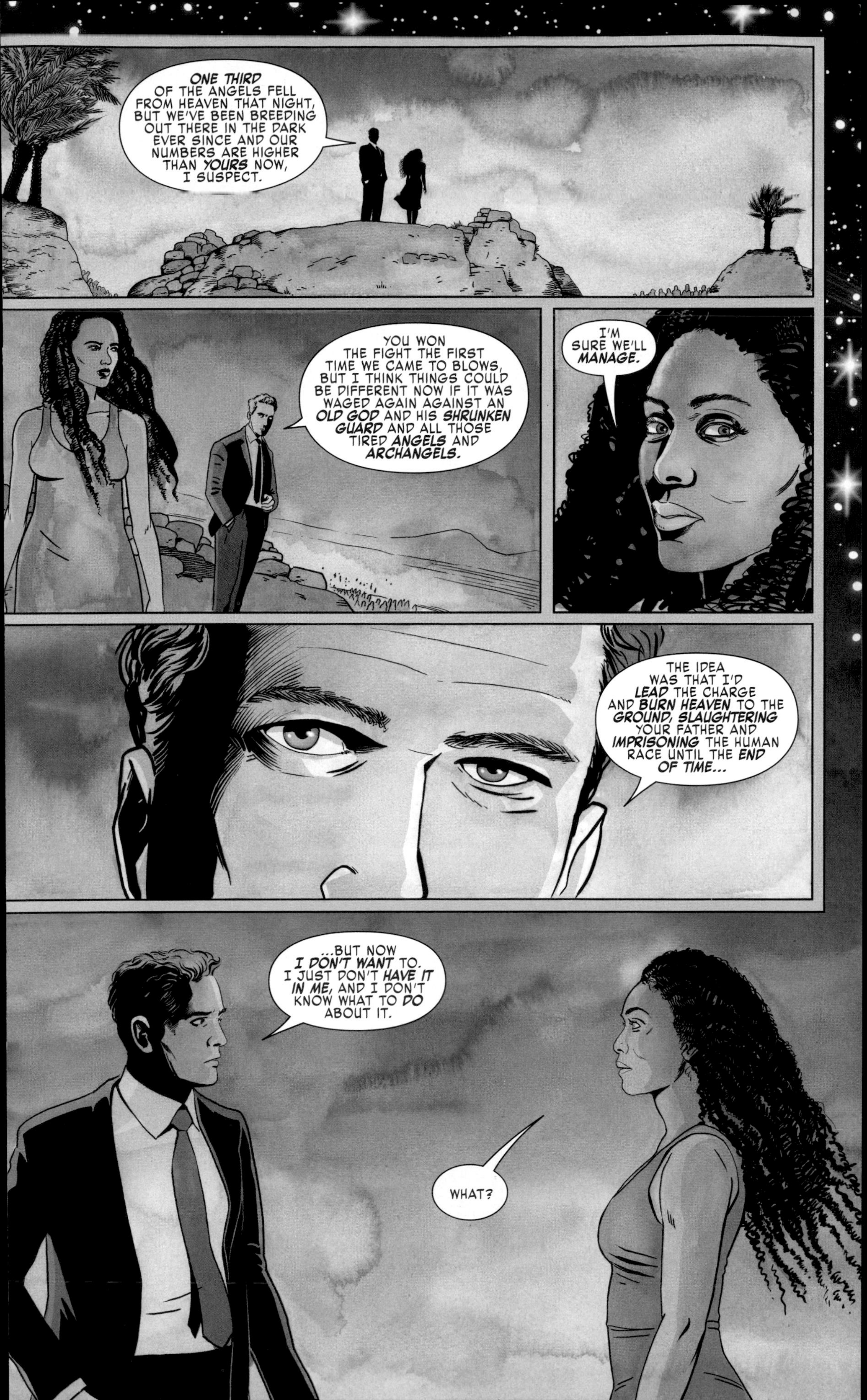
ONE THIRD OF THE ANGELS FELL FROM HEAVEN THAT NIGHT, BUT WE'VE BEEN BREEDING OUT THERE IN THE DARK EVER SINCE AND OUR NUMBERS ARE HIGHER THAN YOURS NOW, I SUSPECT.
YOU WON THE FIGHT THE FIRST TIME WE CAME TO BLOWS, BUT I THINK THINGS COULD BE DIFFERENT NOW IF IT WAS WAGED AGAIN AGAINST AN OLD GOD AND HIS SHRUNKEN GUARD AND ALL THOSE TIRED ANGELS AND ARCHANGELS.
I'M SURE WE'LL MANAGE.
THE IDEA WAS THAT I'D LEAD THE CHARGE AND BURN HEAVEN TO THE GROUND, SLAUGHTERING YOUR FATHER AND IMPRISONING THE HUMAN RACE UNTIL THE END OF TIME...
...BUT NOW I DON'T WANT TO. I JUST DON'T HAVE IT IN ME, AND I DON'T KNOW WHAT TO DO ABOUT IT.
WHAT?

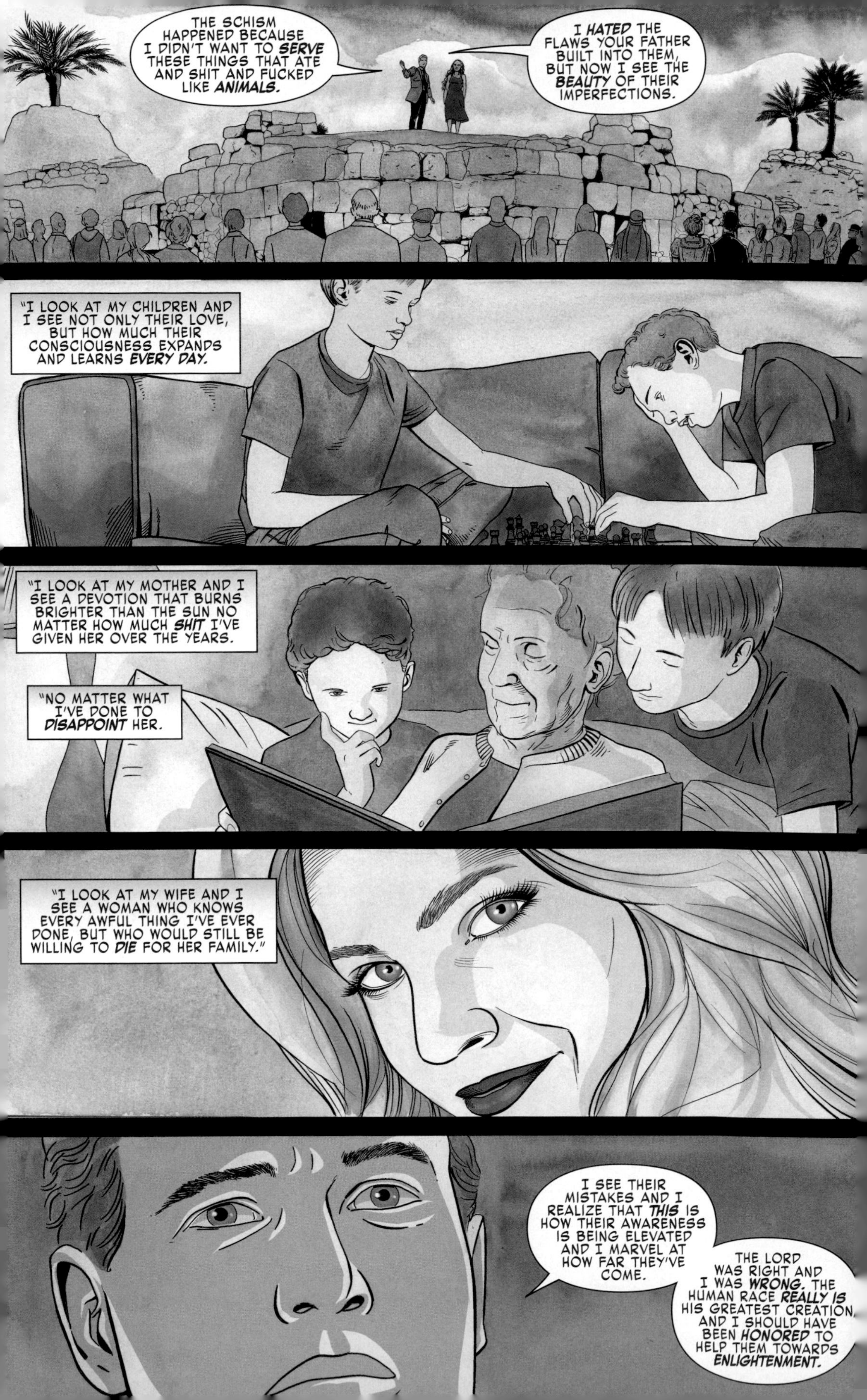
THE SCHISM HAPPENED BECAUSE I DIDN'T WANT TO SERVE THESE THINGS THAT ATE AND SHIT AND FUCKED LIKE ANIMALS.
I HATED THE FLAWS YOUR FATHER BUILT INTO THEM, BUT NOW I SEE THE BEAUTY OF THEIR IMPERFECTIONS.
"I LOOK AT MY CHILDREN AND I SEE NOT ONLY THEIR LOVE, BUT HOW MUCH THEIR CONSCIOUSNESS EXPANDS AND LEARNS EVERY DAY.
"I LOOK AT MY MOTHER AND I SEE A DEVOTION THAT BURNS BRIGHTER THAN THE SUN NO MATTER HOW MUCH SHIT I'VE GIVEN HER OVER THE YEARS.
"NO MATTER WHAT I'VE DONE TO DISAPPOINT HER.
"I LOOK AT MY WIFE AND I SEE A WOMAN WHO KNOWS EVERY AWFUL THING I'VE EVER DONE, BUT WHO WOULD STILL BE WILLING TO DIE FOR HER FAMILY."
I SEE THEIR MISTAKES AND I REALIZE THAT THIS IS HOW THEIR AWARENESS IS BEING ELEVATED AND I MARVEL AT HOW FAR THEY'VE COME.
THE LORD WAS RIGHT AND I WAS WRONG. THE HUMAN RACE REALLY IS HIS GREATEST CREATION, AND I SHOULD HAVE BEEN HONORED TO HELP THEM TOWARDS ENLIGHTENMENT.

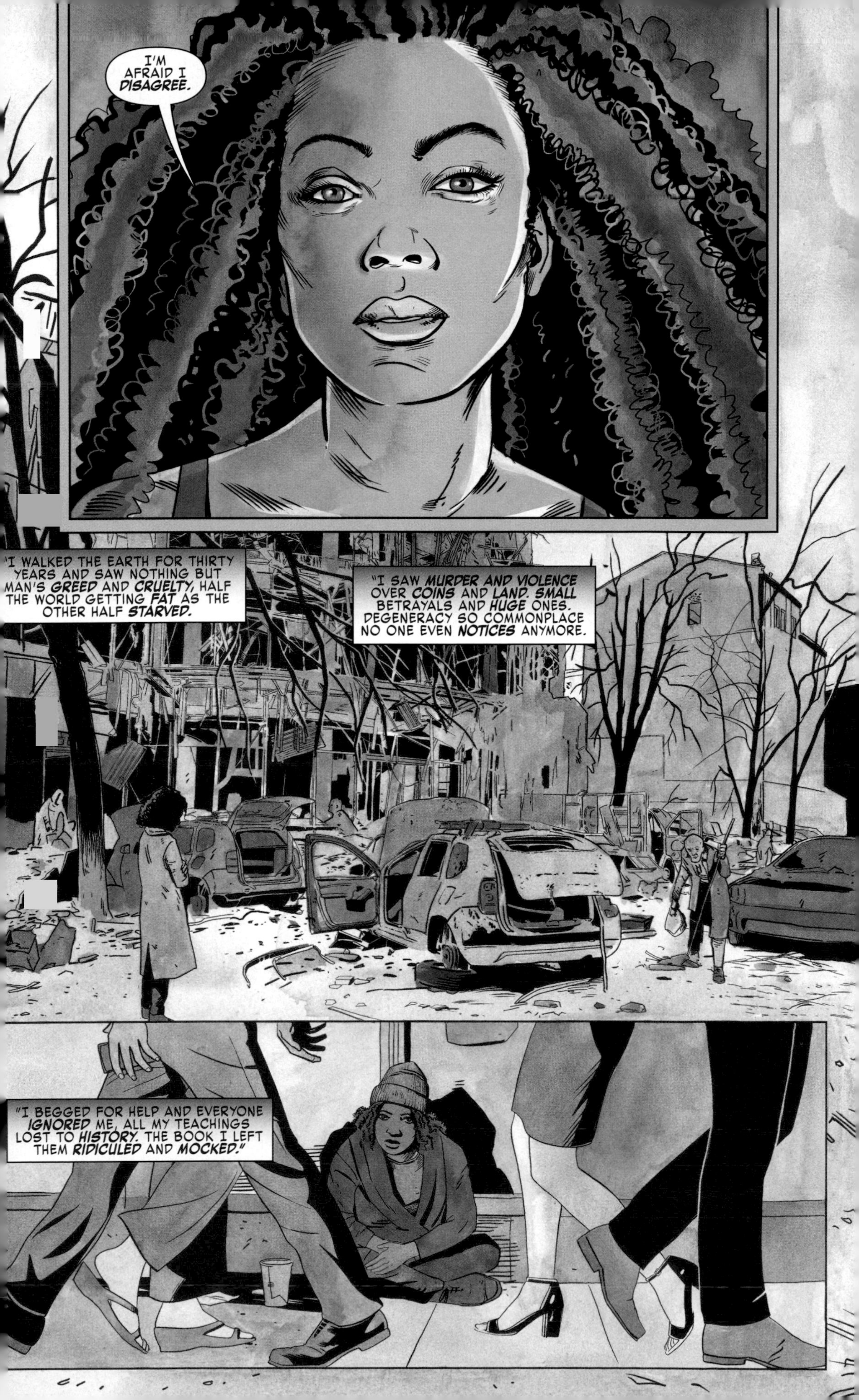
I'M AFRAID I DISAGREE.
"I WALKED THE EARTH FOR THIRTY YEARS AND SAW NOTHING BUT MAN'S GREED AND CRUELTY, HALF THE WORLD GETTING FAT AS THE OTHER HALF STARVED.
"I SAW MURDER AND VIOLENCE OVER COINS AND LAND. SMALL BETRAYALS AND HUGE ONES. DEGENERACY SO COMMONPLACE NO ONE EVEN NOTICES ANYMORE.
"I BEGGED FOR HELP AND EVERYONE IGNORED ME, ALL MY TEACHINGS LOST TO HISTORY. THE BOOK I LEFT THEM RIDICULED AND MOCKED."

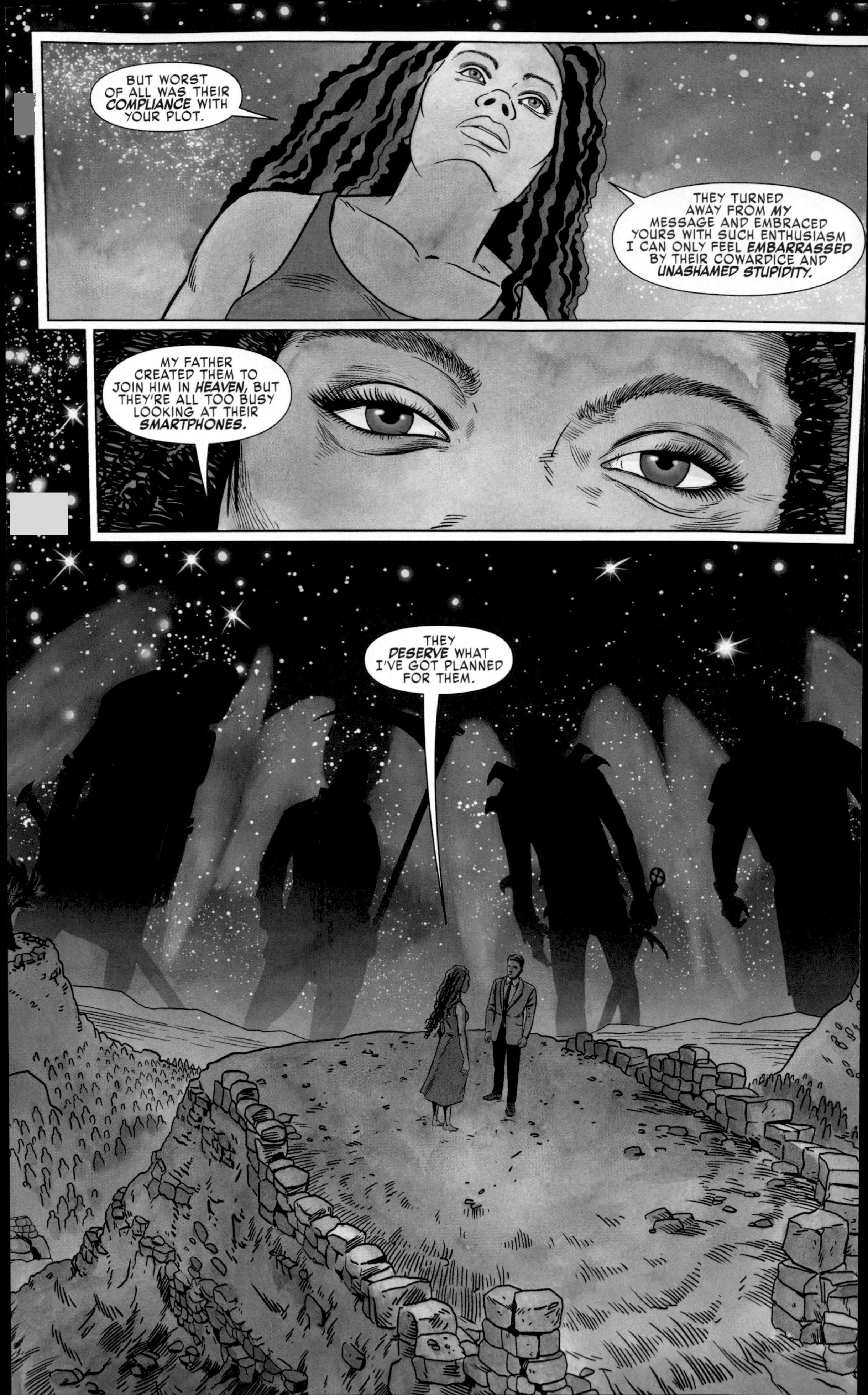
BUT WORST OF ALL WAS THEIR COMPLIANCE WITH YOUR PLOT.
THEY TURNED AWAY FROM MY MESSAGE AND EMBRACED YOURS WITH SUCH ENTHUSIASM I CAN ONLY FEEL EMBARRASSED BY THEIR COWARDICE AND UNASHAMED STUPIDITY.
MY FATHER CREATED THEM TO JOIN HIM IN HEAVEN, BUT THEY'RE ALL TOO BUSY LOOKING AT THEIR SMARTPHONES.
THEY DESERVE WHAT I'VE GOT PLANNED FOR THEM.

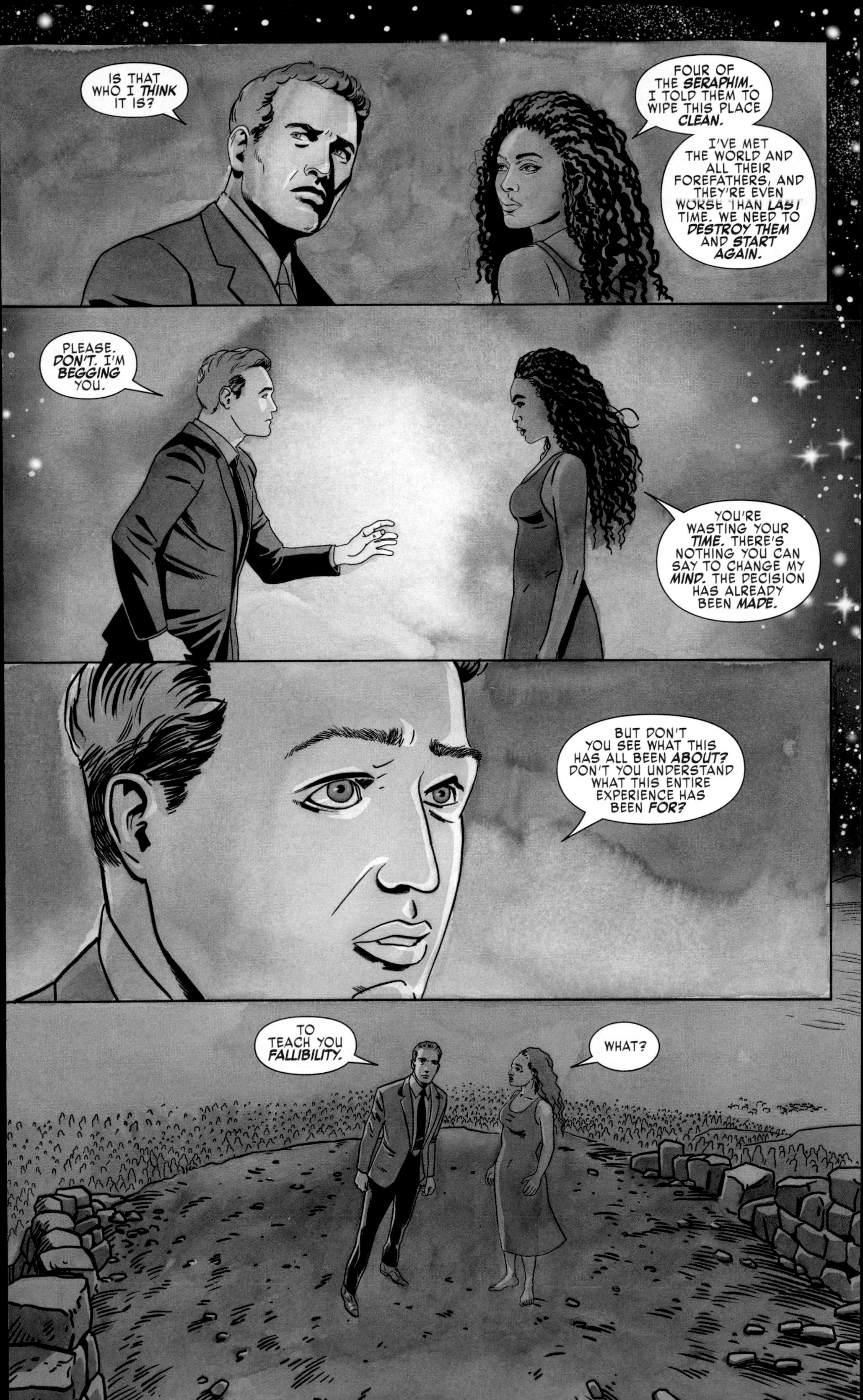
IS THAT WHO I THINK IT IS?
FOUR OF THE SERAPHIM. I TOLD THEM TO WIPE THIS PLACE CLEAN.
I'VE MET THE WORLD AND ALL THEIR FOREFATHERS, AND THEY'RE EVEN WORSE THAN LAST TIME. WE NEED TO DESTROY THEM AND START AGAIN.
PLEASE. DON'T. I'M BEGGING YOU.
YOU'RE WASTING YOUR TIME. THERE'S NOTHING YOU CAN SAY TO CHANGE MY MIND. THE DECISION HAS ALREADY BEEN MADE.
BUT DON'T YOU SEE WHAT THIS HAS ALL BEEN ABOUT? DON'T YOU UNDERSTAND WHAT THIS ENTIRE EXPERIENCE HAS BEEN FOR?
TO TEACH YOU FALLIBILITY.
WHAT?

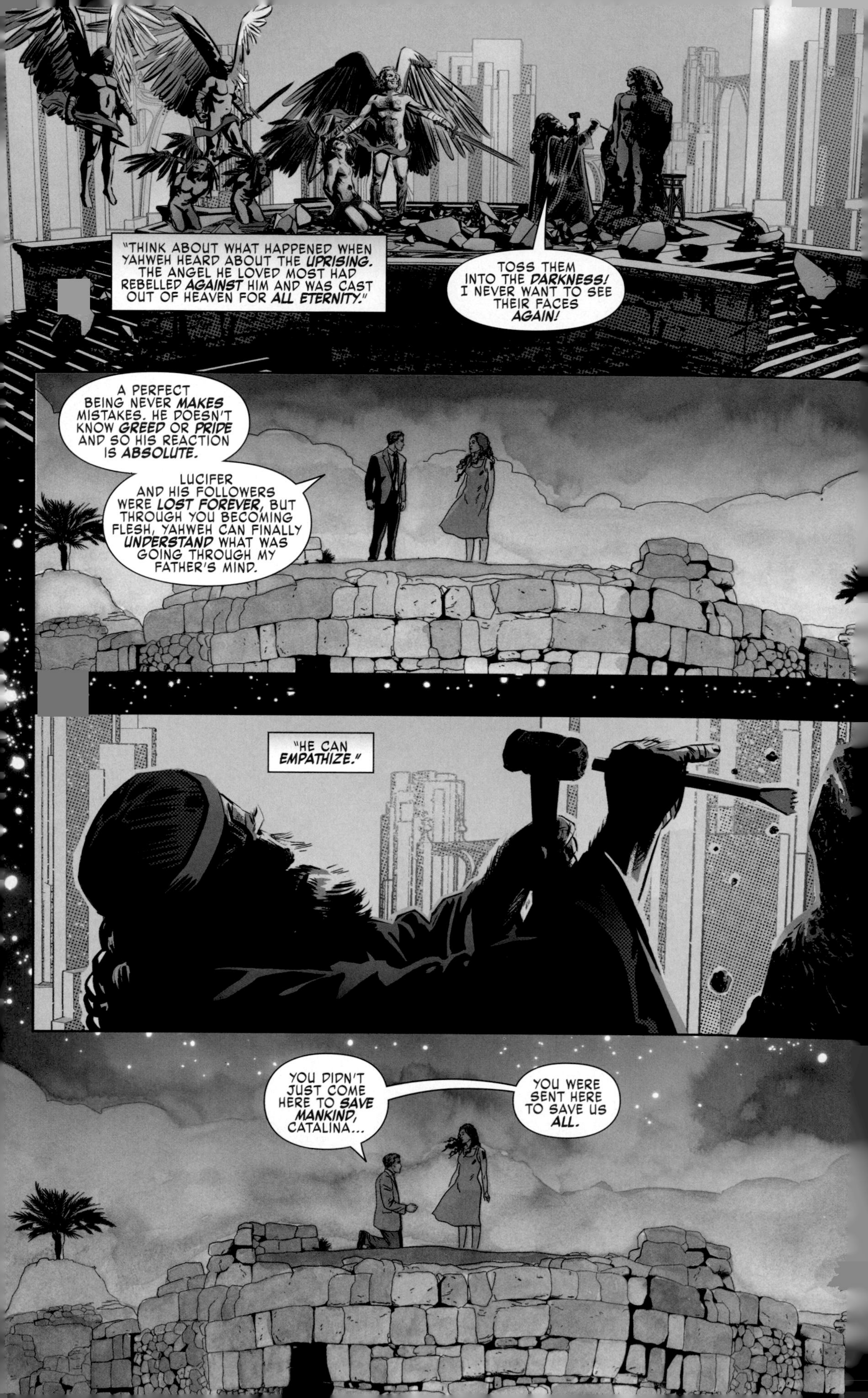
"THINK ABOUT WHAT HAPPENED WHEN YAHWEH HEARD ABOUT THE UPRISING. THE ANGEL HE LOVED MOST HAD REBELLED AGAINST HIM AND WAS CAST OUT OF HEAVEN FOR ALL ETERNITY."
TOSS THEM INTO THE DARKNESS! I NEVER WANT TO SEE THEIR FACES AGAIN!
A PERFECT BEING NEVER MAKES MISTAKES. HE DOESN'T KNOW GREED OR PRIDE AND SO HIS REACTION IS ABSOLUTE.
LUCIFER AND HIS FOLLOWERS WERE LOST FOREVER, BUT THROUGH YOU BECOMING FLESH, YAHWEH CAN FINALLY UNDERSTAND WHAT WAS GOING THROUGH MY FATHER'S MIND.
"HE CAN EMPATHIZE."
YOU DIDN'T JUST COME HERE TO SAVE MANKIND, CATALINA...
YOU WERE SENT HERE TO SAVE US ALL.

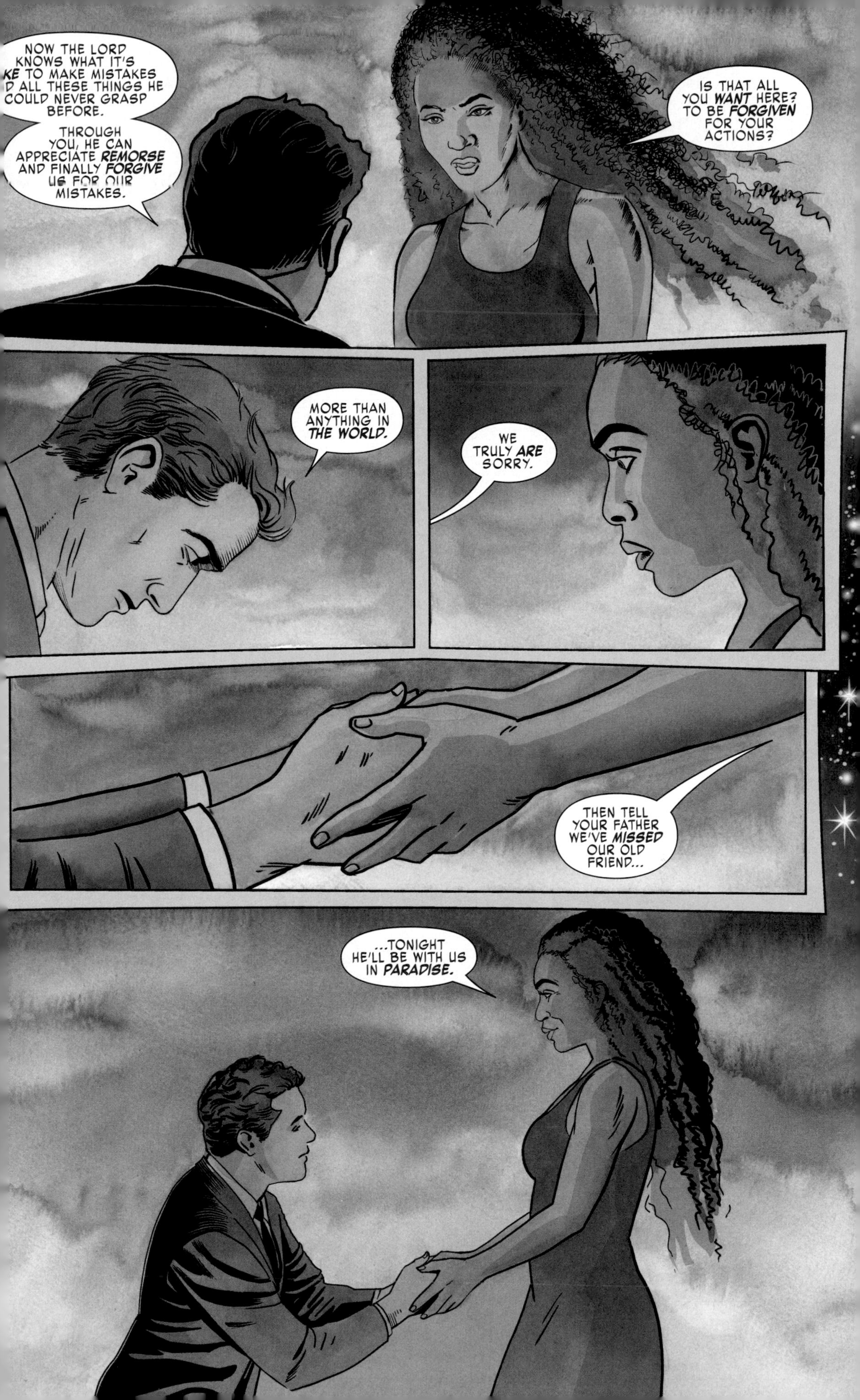
NOW THE LORD KNOWS WHAT IT'S KE TO MAKE MISTAKES D ALL THESE THINGS HE COULD NEVER GRASP BEFORE.
THROUGH YOU, HE CAN APPRECIATE REMORSE AND FINALLY FORGIVE US FOR OUR MISTAKES.
IS THAT ALL YOU WANT HERE? TO BE FORGIVEN FOR YOUR ACTIONS?
MORE THAN ANYTHING IN THE WORLD.
WE TRULY ARE SORRY.
THEN TELL YOUR FATHER WE'VE MISSED OUR OLD FRIEND...
...TONIGHT HE'LL BE WITH US IN PARADISE.

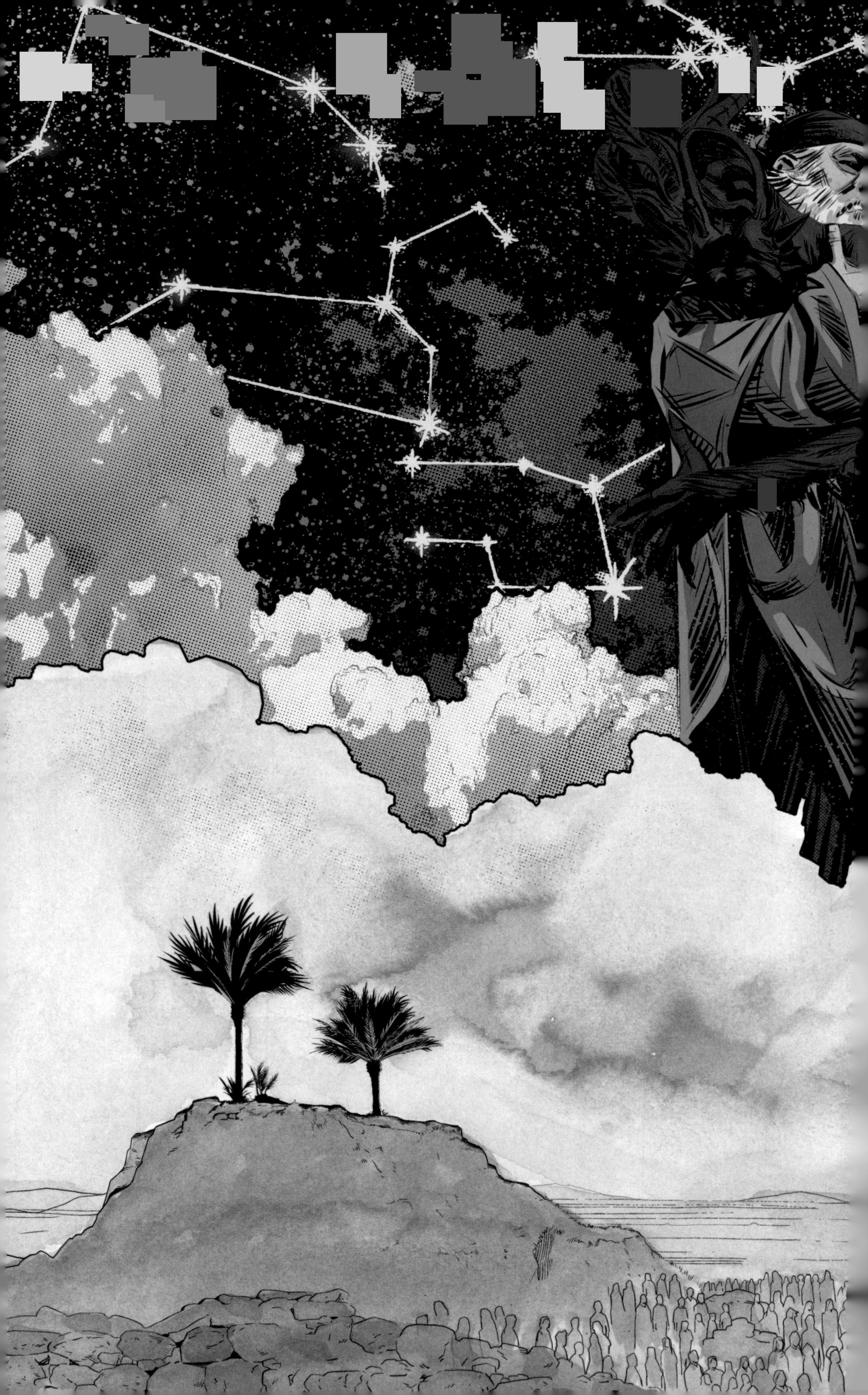

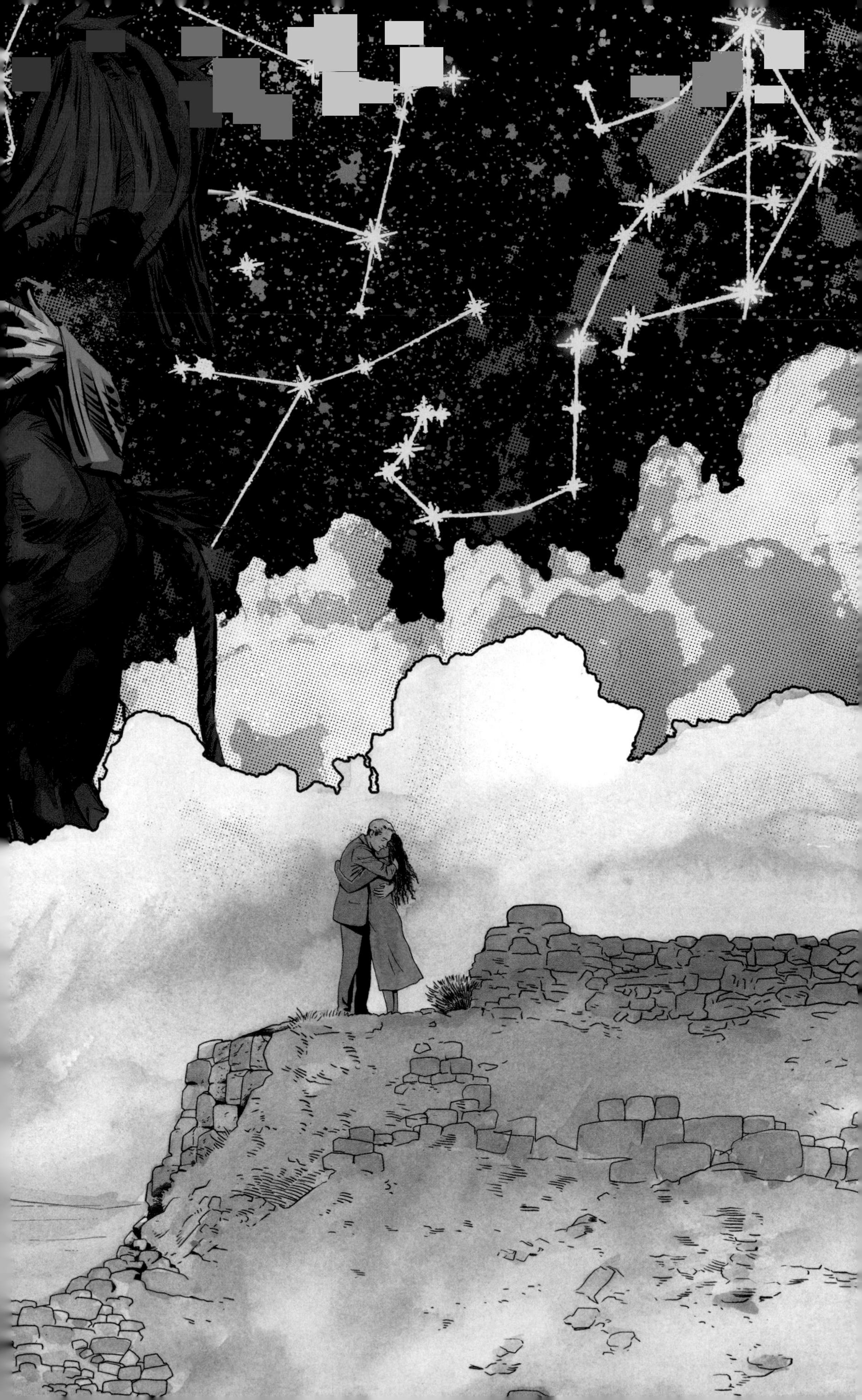

1969:
THEY THINK THEY'RE GOING TO WIN BECAUSE THEY'RE SMARTER THAN I AM, JODIE.
BECAUSE THEY WENT TO ALL THOSE FANCY UNIVERSITIES AND HAVE BEEN PLANNING THIS FOR YEARS.
BUT THERE'S ONE THING THEY'LL NEVER HAVE, AND THAT'S YOU, BABY. I'M GOING TO LOVE YOU LIKE NO CHILD HAS BEEN LOVED BEFORE, AND I'M GOING TO MAKE YOU INTO THE BEST KID I KNOW.
THEY'RE GOING TO TEMPT YOU WITH SO MANY TERRIBLE THINGS, BUT I'M GOING TO TEACH YOU RIGHT FROM WRONG.
1983:
ARE YOU EVER SCARED WHEN YOU READ THE BIBLE, JODIE? WHEN YOU SEE WHAT YOU'LL BE UP AGAINST AT THE APOCALYPSE AND STUFF?
NOPE. BECAUSE GOOD ALWAYS WINS IN THE END, MAGGIE.

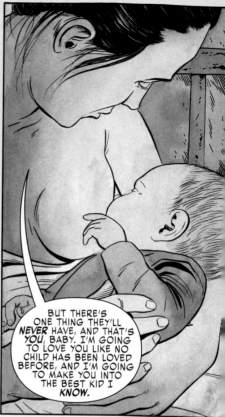

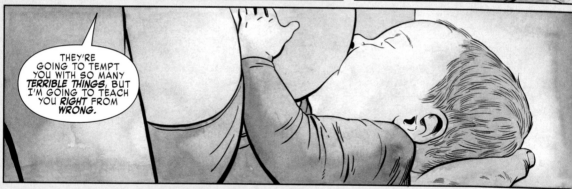

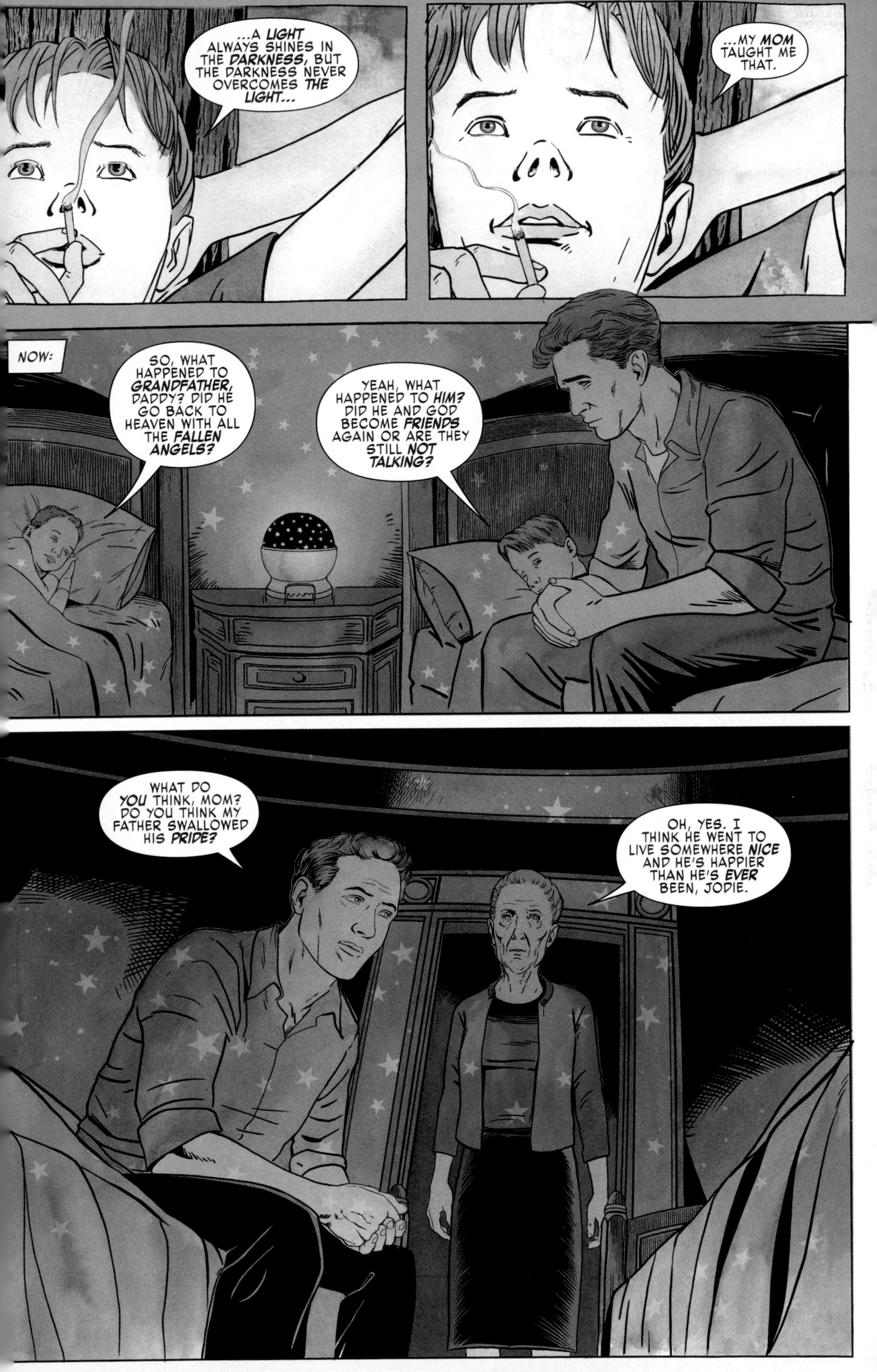
...A LIGHT ALWAYS SHINES IN THE DARKNESS, BUT THE DARKNESS NEVER OVERCOMES THE LIGHT...
...MY MOM TAUGHT ME THAT.
NOW:
SO, WHAT HAPPENED TO GRANDFATHER, DADDY? DID HE GO BACK TO HEAVEN WITH ALL THE FALLEN ANGELS?
YEAH, WHAT HAPPENED TO HIM? DID HE AND GOD BECOME FRIENDS AGAIN OR ARE THEY STILL NOT TALKING?
WHAT DO YOU THINK, MOM? DO YOU THINK MY FATHER SWALLOWED HIS PRIDE?
OH, YES. I THINK HE WENT TO LIVE SOMEWHERE NICE AND HE'S HAPPIER THAN HE'S EVER BEEN, JODIE.

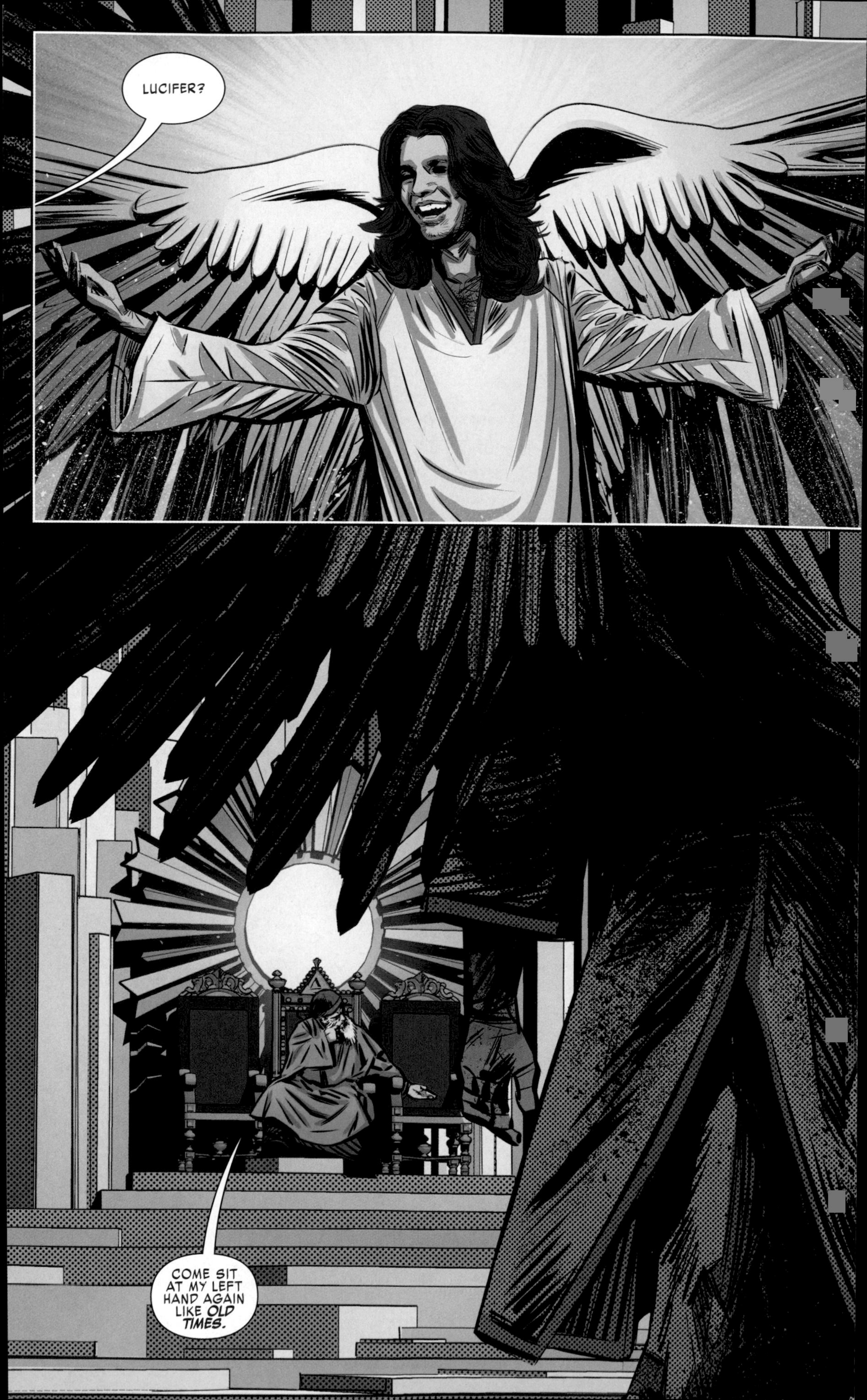
LUCIFER?
COME SIT AT MY LEFT HAND AGAIN LIKE OLD TIMES.

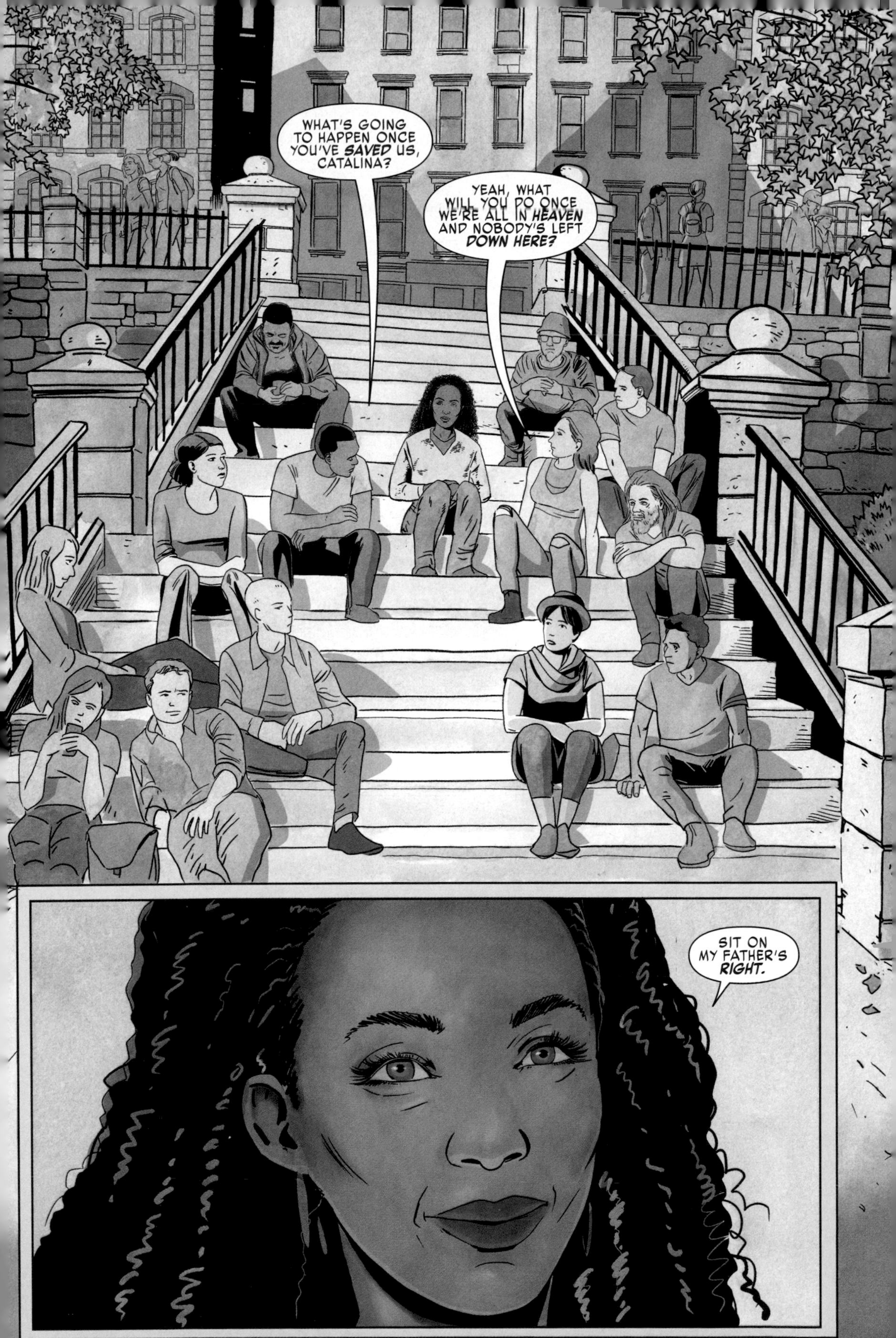
WHAT'S GOING TO HAPPEN ONCE YOU'VE SAVED US, CATALINA?
YEAH, WHAT WILL YOU DO ONCE WE'RE ALL IN HEAVEN AND NOBODY'S LEFT DOWN HERE?
SIT ON MY FATHER'S RIGHT.

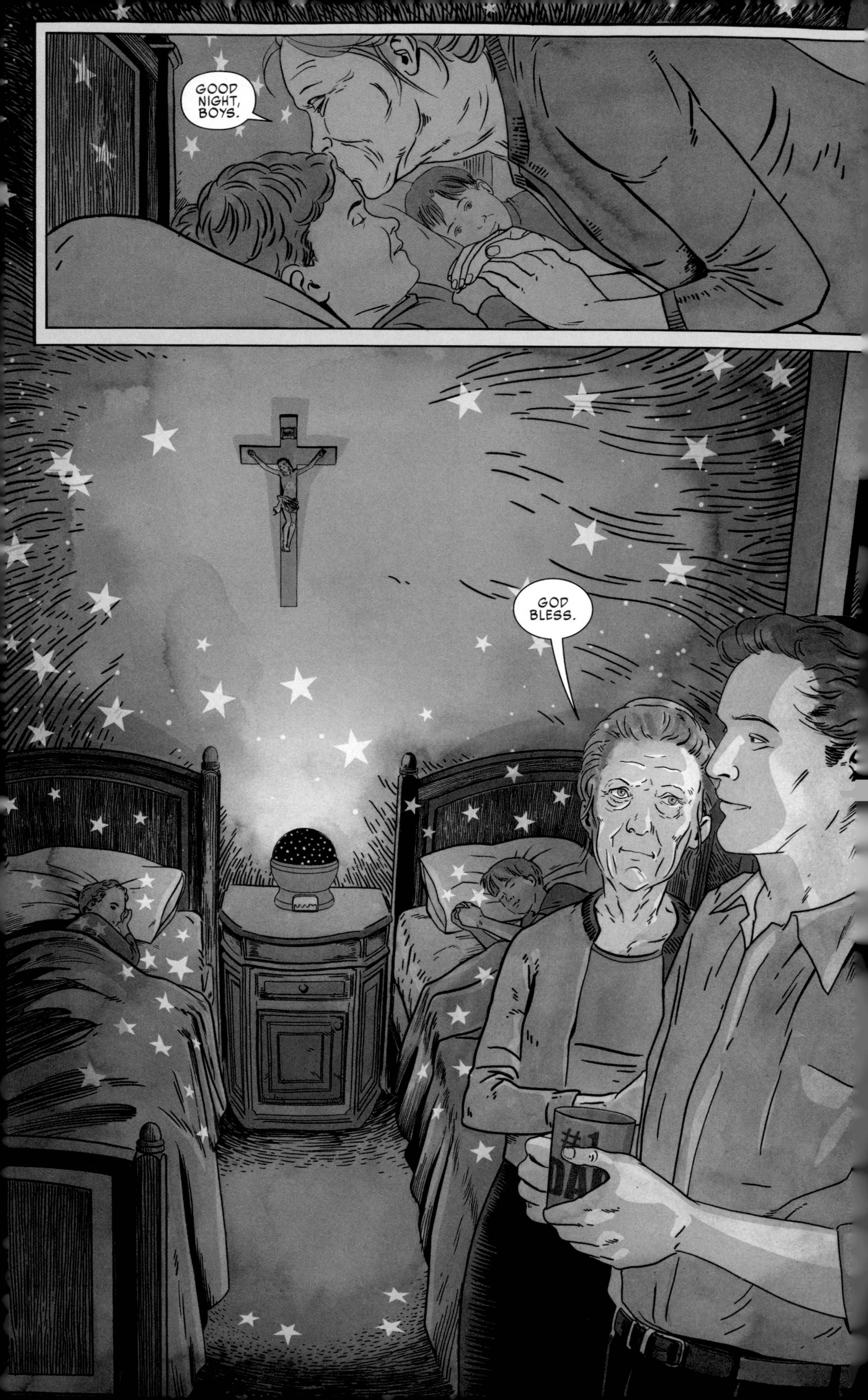
GOOD NIGHT, BOYS.
GOD BLESS.

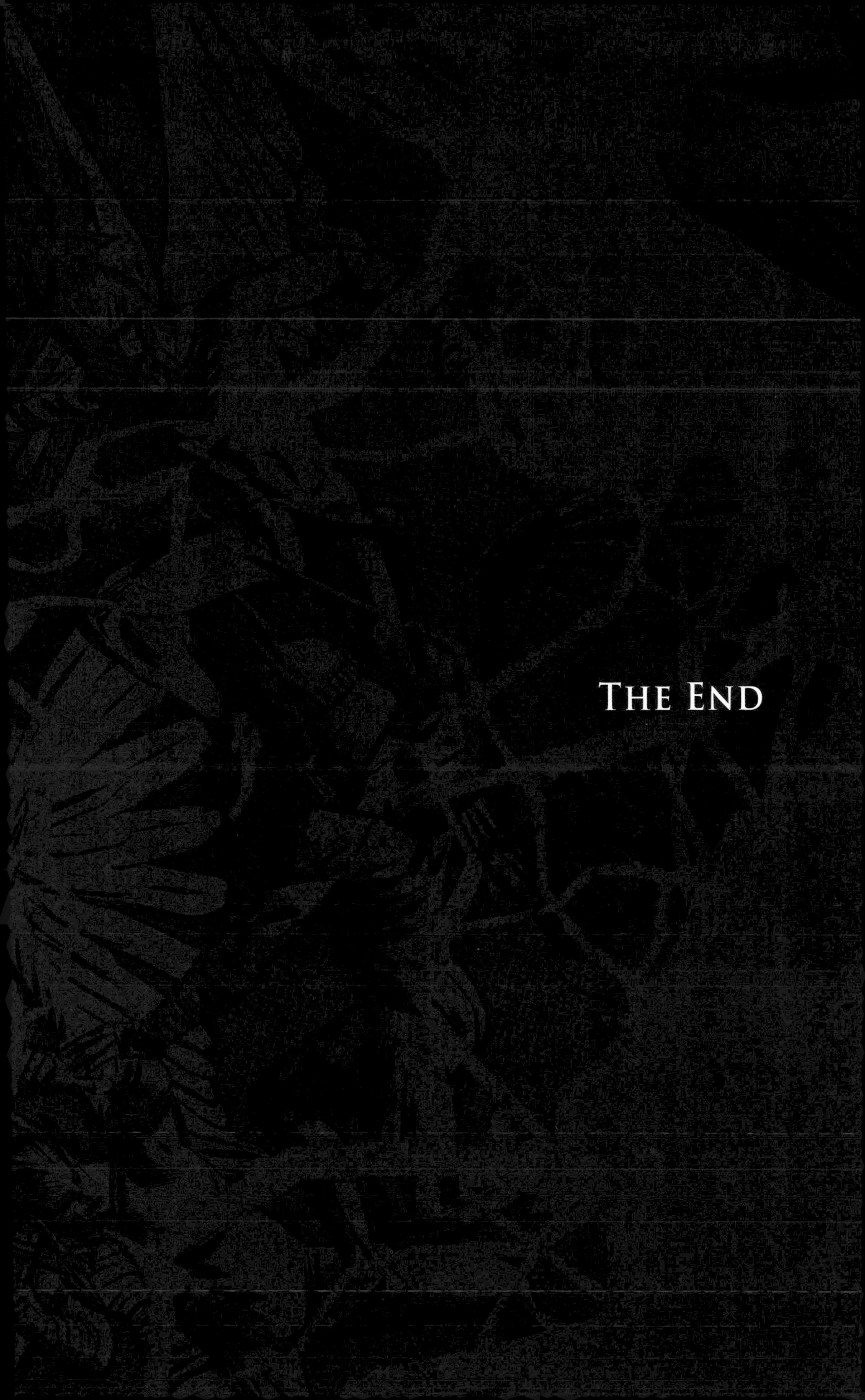
THE END

MILLAR AND GROSS:
THE FINAL TESTAMENT

MARK MILLAR: Well, Peter. Here we are for the final back and forth. Nineteen years in the making. I was literally the same age as Joe Jonas when we started this.

PETER GROSS: I was more like Father O'Higgins when we started!

MM: I just googled famous 33-year-olds and picked Joe Jonas over Daniel Radcliffe and Taylor Swift, but it's only just dawned on me I could have said Jesus himself, of course. How did I miss that?

PG: Even I knew Jesus was 33. I had to look up Joe Jonas to figure it out! I thought you'd be more of a Jesus expert at this point.

MM: I know we're getting old when Harry Potter is the same age as Jesus! But this has been quite a journey. I was looking for the perfect partner for this and it's my old DC editor Stuart Moore who suggested you when I emailed him after San Diego Con 2003. I needed someone whose art didn't look too American. This couldn't be a splashy guy who did double-page spreads and Kirby dots. This needed a very specific look, or it wouldn't have worked at all. As always, Stuart made the right call. You were perfect for this, and I remember feeling it as the first pages came in. I knew I was in good hands.

PG: I'm definitely not the high-energy superhero artist that people might associate with your work! Less true back then than now, when you're associated with most of the top-tier artists in the biz. It's sometimes a bit intimidating to be the most understated artist in the Millarworld pantheon.

MM: Understated is elegant. You don't always want too much flesh on show! This book needed a maturity and a quietness, which made the expanding story over the three volumes, this build-up to the end of the world, such a challenge. We talked

about so many versions of this over the years as it couldn't just descend into the Michael Bay version with the skies ripped open and a billion fiery swords descending from the Heavens, great beasts with seven heads rising from the ocean. A comedian pal of mine said years back that a comedy or a horror that costs a lot of money is neither funny nor scary and he was right. The *American Jesus* story, deep down, is a horror and it had to stay human. There had to be that ordinary way in for people or all the big stuff just becomes the third act of a Marvel movie, and you zone out with all the CGI. The first *Omen* film of course did this perfectly, taking these huge ideas and showing them through the prism of a low-budget slasher movie structure.

PG: That pretty well sums up my approach. I always look for the little human moments in stories and try to stress those even in the midst of cosmic goings-on. I may have mentioned this before somewhere, but I had a painting professor in college who, when looking at some portraits and still lifes I had done, said that I painted beautiful women like they were potatoes, and potatoes like they were beautiful women! I'm not sure if he meant it as a compliment, but I took it as one, and it's become a sort of credo for me over the years.

MM: We should use that quote for the back of the trade (laughs). But the amount of time this took obviously meant several different iterations in our conversations over the years as your thoughts change and styles change too. I think the whole thing actually feels remarkably consistent. It doesn't feel like the *Stand By Me* of the first volume suddenly becoming an unrecognizable *Avengers Endgame* by the third. Even the human race being raised from the dead on the Day of Judgement starts small where it's just a man who died fifty years ago knocking on an old lady's door and embracing her. St. John's vision of the Apocalypse is literally the biggest story ever told and it's never quite been dramatized (for obvious budgetary reasons) so keeping it small and personal was a challenge. Bringing it down to two people and a reprise of what Lucifer's fall from grace really was - an argument between two friends - was key. The final issue was the first time they'd spoken to each other again for the entirety of human history. If we take that measure as the existence of Homo Genus, that's 2 million years, human beings the start of their argument.

PG: I love that the end of this story took a 180-degree turn from what the readers probably expected, and what you had set up as the confrontation to end all confrontations. It plays against type in a way. It makes me curious as to, at this point in your career, what would you say is characteristic of a "Mark Millar story"? And does *American Jesus*

play against that or fall into it? I always felt like you'd been carrying the *American Jesus* story in you for a long time, and it was a bit special and apart from other things you had written.

MM: It's hard to really get the measure of my own tones and themes as it's always in a state of flux from project to project. My favourite movies will range from Billy Wilder and Michael Curtiz to *Sinbad and The Eye of the Tiger*. I think it just depends how you're feeling at the time. Something like *Huck* is the complete antithesis of *Wanted*, but I loved doing them both and they're both very much me. Everything I think any creative person does deep down is an ode to something we loved growing up. The original Superman was a tribute to Doc Savage and Batman was created by guys who loved The Shadow and Sherlock Holmes. Even the Roman myths are just inspired by people who loved the Greek heroes (laughs). *Chosen*

was always a massive tribute to *The Omen* for me, a Richard Donner buff who loved his *Lethal Weapon* and his antichrist movies almost as much as I loved his Superman. But I think the DNA of all my projects, if I had to boil it down, is a big, even abstract idea told in a style that anyone can understand. Donner did this brilliantly and Stan Lee was the absolute master. It's not reductive in any way. Simplicity can be the hardest thing to do. But this ending was a real process, the ideas just constantly refined over literally a decade and a half. I remember having breakfast and talking it through with my friend Nacho Vigalondo, the Spanish film director, a decade ago when he was staying with me in Glasgow. He was amazing with advice and suggestions, and we talked about how the most important part of this story was the reconciliation between God and Lucifer. That's never been done before, as far as I'm aware, in comics, movies, TV or prose. I think it's a new idea and that had us

really animated over breakfast. But there's several versions of this leading up to that point. The new Jesus could have been a man again just as he was 2000 years ago and I was really weighing this up for a few years. On the one hand, there's a power to seeing someone who looks like the Biblical Jesus walking into the Vatican and pulling it down or melting the statue of the bull on Wall Street. I had all these scenes sketched out when I did the first volume. But at the same time, I kind of liked the idea of the returned Jesus being a woman this time as she'd be in hiding and would need to look different in her early days or she'd be caught immediately. One of the writer / producers on the show, Leopoldo Gout, urged me to go the female route and his reason was that Netflix already had a returned Jesus show coming up with a guy who looked like the traditional bearded Christ. The show was American and very different from ours, but even so. It was still too close, and this nudged me in the direction of Catalina. But we had so many versions of this, didn't we? What ended up the first issue of volume two was going to be three issues for a while, but I realised it could be tighter and so I stripped the script back to just one issue. There were so many different ways this could have gone. Do you remember the idea I had where Jodie ACTUALLY WAS the returned Jesus and the Satanists had taken him away and tricked him into believing he was the Antichrist? It's kind of cool, especially as there's a little confusion in Revelation itself, where the Antichrist appears and pretends to be the returned Christ for four years. I liked the idea at first, but it all just felt a little convoluted and this was so much cleaner. I felt it also devalued the twist at the end of volume one, so I scrapped it pretty quickly.

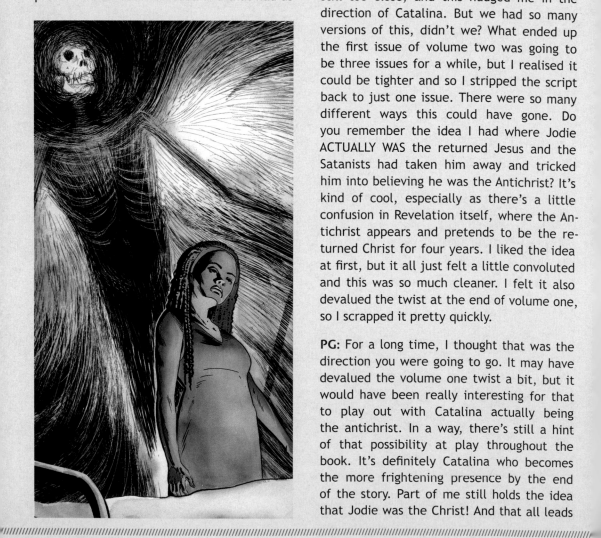

PG: For a long time, I thought that was the direction you were going to go. It may have devalued the volume one twist a bit, but it would have been really interesting for that to play out with Catalina actually being the antichrist. In a way, there's still a hint of that possibility at play throughout the book. It's definitely Catalina who becomes the more frightening presence by the end of the story. Part of me still holds the idea that Jodie was the Christ! And that all leads

to my favorite character in the book: Father O'Higgins. All his scenes were my favorites to work on, and I just felt him to be a very compelling character — especially seeing him as he aged so much from Volume 1 to his return in 3.

MM: It's a good twist, but it didn't work with that ending of reconciliation between Lucifer and God, which was the ultimate destination for the story. It just pulls it too much in another direction and so I had to give it up, sadly. It's weird that when we first started talking to a studio about this, I think the first conversation was Sony Screen Gems, Philip Seymour Hoffman was who we all wanted for the priest, which would have been amazing. I won't name names, but there was also a *Twilight* version of this around 2010/11. They wanted to do it as a romance all set in one town with returned Jesus and Jodie the Antichrist all playing out in a *Smallville* kind of setting. I was sort of into it as their track record was really good, but it's probably for the best that one fizzled out. When Netflix bought Millarworld this quite neatly had no script drafts or producers attached and so they were able to start with a blank piece of paper. As we talk now, it's January 2023 and *The Chosen One* hasn't been seen yet. It should be pretty close by the time this trade paperback collection is out, but I think it was a really smart idea to go Spanish language with this. It's a huge market for the company with things like *Money Heist* and *Narcos* and, a

great point made in our early meetings, is that the Catholicism seems more authentic, the mythology more real, in a Spanish language setting. English-speaking countries like America and the UK are too secular now. It's probably forty or fifty years since something with a major religious basis has really resonated in the traditional Hollywood market as God and church is now too far away for them, sadly. But I love the power this has in a climate where saints and demons are as real as they are to me. As a practicing Catholic, I know I'm a rarity now, but it's exciting to see how this could play in territories closer to mine in terms of ideology. It's being treated very seriously. This isn't a parody or anything cheesy. If Christopher Nolan can do Batman with an entrenched realism and respect for the material, we can do the Apocalypse with the same grown-up head.

PG: Does that mean we're losing all the "American" in the show? Funny how it's gone closer back to the original title of "Chosen" that you had with volume one. I can't remember what expectations I had of the story when you first emailed me about it. I think I was game with whatever your one-line pitch might have been. I'm sure I didn't know that you were a practicing Catholic at the time too, especially given the irreverent sort of tone to much of your work. But as I learned you were a practicing believer, it brought an element to the whole story that I enjoyed reading. I think the expectation was that this would be an irreverent take on the story,

like *The Magic Order* as they wanted to expand their potential franchise base. Either way I knew it was something I wanted to do, but my producer head from *Wanted*, *Kick-Ass*, *Kingsman* and so on still had genuine ambitions, and so after *Jupiter's Legacy* came out I made sure I was an active producer on everything going forward. *The Chosen One* Season 1 is probably the last project where I wasn't in there picking the team with the other execs from the start. *Super Crooks* was a Japanese team and I worked with them a little. *Jupiter's* I had pretty much nothing to do with at all until a few months before it came out and the second showrunner was gone. Everything since I've sat in on every pitch meeting from writers and talked casting and directors every day with our team, really heavily involved, but *The Chosen One* was done almost entirely by our Mexican team and neither me nor the rest of the American side of the company had even read the final, translated scripts until it was just about ready to shoot. So, I'm going into this as a relatively fresh pair of eyes. I've seen the first cuts of the first two episodes, but as of right now that's all I've seen and it's exciting. I'll be much more involved in season 2 as I've built a relationship with the Mexican side of the company now and they're really terrific. Some of these guys worked on *Narcos* so it's a really high-end bunch of creatives and I really love the Gout Brothers. The actual look of this thing is just beautiful. It's almost like an art house picture. I think you're going to be really pleased when you see it. The cast are all fantastic too, especially the wee boy who plays Jodie. He looks like one of your drawings come to life.

but it really wasn't, until the end anyway. Where do you feel your story falls within the canon of Catholicism? Are you trying to one-up the Bible by suggesting a different outcome?

MM: As mad as it sounds, I always saw this as the sequel. We had a great trailer 2000 years ago with the Book of Revelation and here we are (laughs). Yes, the show starts for a scene or two in the United States and then Jodie's mum heads south with the baby so everything that happens to the kid in the book happens south of the border instead of the US small town we had. It actually makes a lot of sense. If you're hiding from these huge forces who want to kill your baby, you'll go somewhere as remote as possible. So she heads for this faraway place in Mexico and these beautiful beaches and amazing colour where she can just get lost and raise the boy safely. Until that truck lands on his head and everybody realizes he's not what they thought he was. It's the same story, but with a different backdrop. When you, me and all the other artists sold Millarworld to Netflix a few years back I wasn't really sure what my new executive job would entail, and I was suddenly a member of staff. All I knew was I was a movie exec within this huge organisation, but I assumed it would really just be writing all the sequels they wanted me to write so they had complete stories and creating the new stuff in-house

PG: I'm looking forward to seeing it, but always with a bit of trepidation to see someone else's take on a story I worked on! I'm glad that you mentioned the adaptation has amazing color, because that was one of the highlights of working on the book for me. Having my partner (now wife) Jeanne McGee color the series in watercolor with an approach that had little to do with traditional comics was really fun and challenging to do. And I think it really caught people's attention, especially when the first volume came out.

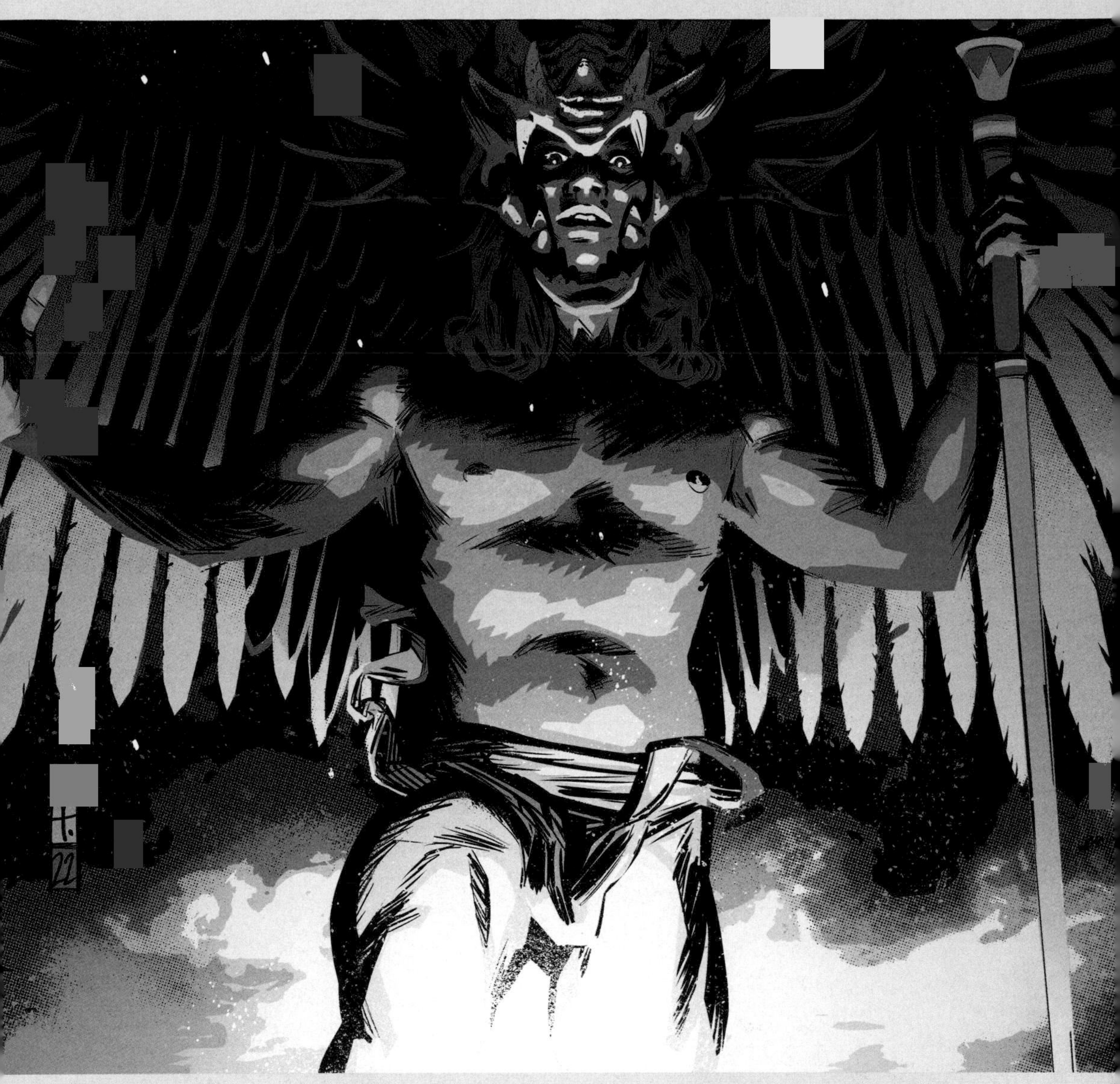

MM: Jeanne's colors have been great. The whole thing has really felt like a little family business, this tiny handful of us working away relatively quietly for years and now it's going to be seen by the wider mainstream and it hopefully brings a ton of these people to the books too. It's been a huge part of our lives, so fingers crossed for the show itself as that's how most people are going to think about it once it becomes flesh and blood actors instead of drawings. It's been an absolute blast, Peter, and I could not have had a better partner and co-creator. The only sad bit is that this is the end of the story, but it lives on in the trade and the inevitable big bumper hardcover with all these little extras we can charge extra money for at the back. I'm really proud of this book and couldn't be happier with what we've done here. It really has been a pleasure and I can only hope there's another world religion out there somewhere who want us to give them a sequel.

PG: I just hope this isn't the last time we get to chat about *American Jesus*, because it's always a pleasure to ramble on with you. And I hope that high priced hardcover has the leather embossed, Bible-like cover we always dreamt of!

END

MARK MILLAR is a NEW YORK TIMES bestselling author, Hollywood producer, and now president of his own division at Netflix after selling his publishing company to the world's biggest streamer in 2017. He also signed on to exclusively create new comics, TV series, and movies in-house as a senior executive. Adaptations of JUPITER'S LEGACY and a Japanese anime of SUPER CROOKS have already been released. THE MAGIC ORDER, REBORN, SHARKEY THE BOUNTY HUNTER, PRODIGY, KING OF SPIES, EMPRESS, MPH, HUCK and a live-action SUPER CROOKS are currently being put together now. AMERICAN JESUS (adapted as THE CHOSEN ONE) will be released in 2023.

Previously, Mark worked at Marvel comics where he created THE ULTIMATES, which was selected by TIME MAGAZINE as the comic book of the decade, and described by screenwriter Zak Penn as his major inspiration for THE AVENGERS movie. Millar also created WOLVERINE: OLD MAN LOGAN and MARVEL CIVIL WAR. CIVIL WAR was the basis of the third Captain America movie, and OLD MAN LOGAN was the inspiration for Fox's LOGAN.

CIVIL WAR remains Marvel's biggest-selling graphic novel of all time and his seminal SUPERMAN: RED SON the highest-selling Superman graphic novel in history. In 2021, RED SON was also released as an animated feature.

Mark has been an executive producer on all adaptations of his books, and worked as a creative consultant to Fox Studios on their Marvel slate of movies.

His much-anticipated autobiography, THE GREATEST STORY EVER TOLD, will be published next year.

PETER GROSS is an Eisner-nominated and NY TIMES bestselling comic artist. He started his career with the creator-owned series EMPIRE LANES, and went on to illustrate three of DC/Vertigo's longest running series: BOOKS OF MAGIC, LUCIFER, and THE UNWRITTEN (co-created with Mike Carey),

Peter was one of the initial artists to join up with Mark Millar on the original launch of Millarworld, illustrating AMERICAN JESUS/CHOSEN. Other recent work includes THE HIGHEST HOUSE and THE DOLLHOUSE FAMILY.

Peter lives in Minneapolis, Minnesota with his wife Jeanne McGee, who is also the colorist on AMERICAN JESUS. They have one daughter, Alice, who Peter hopes will one day write a comic for him to draw.

Born and raised in San Francisco, **JEANNE MCGEE** is a printmaker who works in a variety of mediums, and occasionally colors comics. You can find more of her work at jeannemcgee.com and follow her on Instagram: @jeannemcgeeart

TOMM COKER began his career as a comic book artist while still in high school. Since then, he has provided artwork for a variety of characters ranging from **THE AVENGERS** to **XMEN**. Tomm is currently working on **THE BLACK MONDAY MURDERS** (Image Comics) with writer, Jonathan Hickman.

DANIEL FREEDMAN is a comic book creator, colorist, screenwriter, film editor and director. Daniel splits his time writing for both print and screen, best known for the hit series **UNDYING LOVE** and the original graphic novels **RAIDERS**, **BIRDKING** and **KALI**. He is a Los Angeles native.

CORY PETIT is an artist residing in Brooklyn, New York with his still half-feral cat Fluff. A twenty-plus year vet of the comic book industry, who just can't seem to figure out how not to let random animals walk into his apartment. Like, who just lets racoons, opossums, skunks etc in for a bite of dinner?

You've skimmed past his name on the credits on other titles such as **AVENGERS**, **JESSICA JONES**, **GUARDIANS OF THE GALAXY**, **MILES MORALES**, **WOLVERINE**...and a couple of others.

Over the last 10 years, **SARAH UNWIN** has worked in film production on titles including **AVENGERS: AGE OF ULTRON**, **FANTASTIC BEASTS AND WHERE TO FIND THEM**, **TOMB RAIDER**, **POKÉMON: DETECTIVE PIKACHU** and **THE MIDNIGHT SKY**.

In 2022, she moved in-house at Netflix into the Millarworld Division as Editorial Production Manager to focus on the publishing of their wide variety of books.

MELINA MIKULIC is a well-known graphic designer in Croatia's comic scene; she has designed many editions for all leading Croatian comic publishers. She came on board the Millar team in 2015 and has stayed since then, working on design and production on many of Millar's projects.

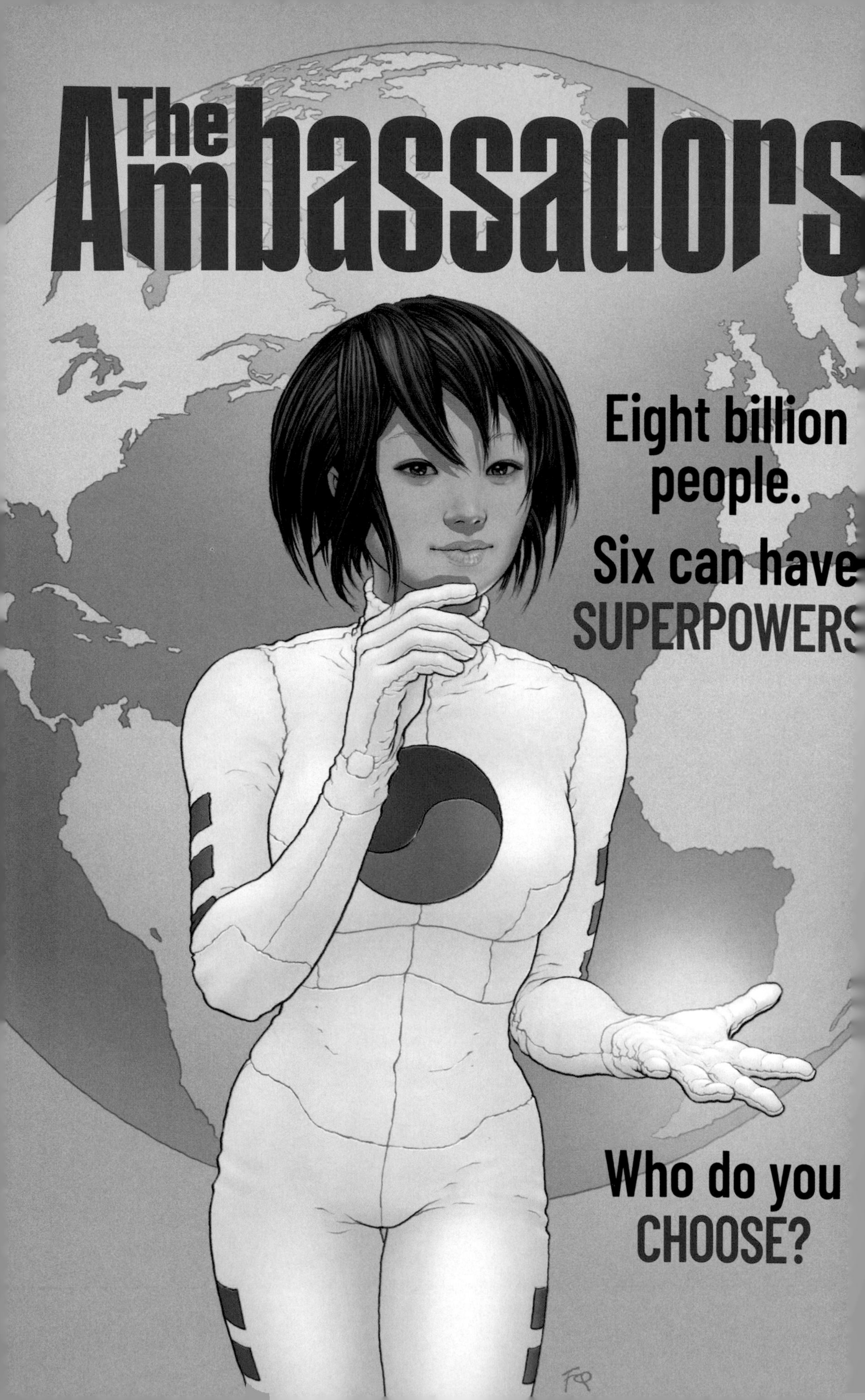
The Ambassadors
Eight billion people.
Six can have SUPERPOWERS
Who do you CHOOSE?
FQ

MARK MILLAR
FRANK QUITELY
TRAVIS CHAREST
OLIVIER COIPEL
MATTEO BUFFAGNI
MATTEO SCALERA
KARL KERSCHL

The Ambassadors

MARCH 2023

THE MARK MILLAR COLLECTION

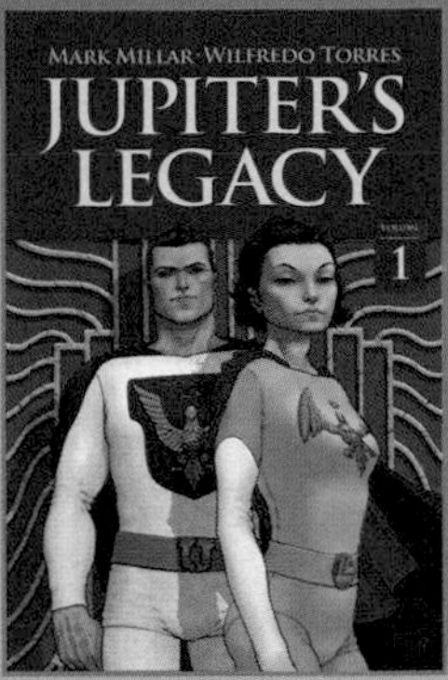
MARK MILLAR · WILFREDO TORRES
JUPITER'S LEGACY
1
Jupiter's Legacy 1-5

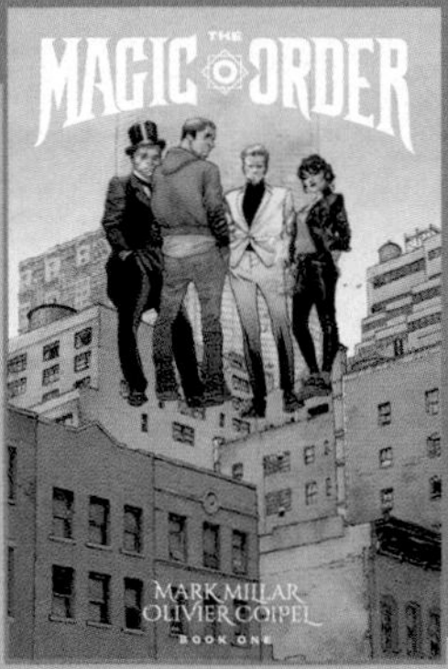
THE MAGIC ORDER
MARK MILLAR
OLIVIER COIPEL
BOOK ONE
The Magic Order 1-3

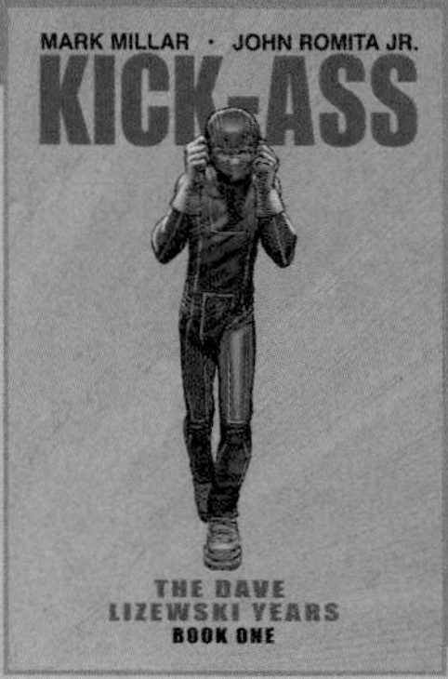
MARK MILLAR · JOHN ROMITA JR.
KICK-ASS
THE DAVE LIZEWSKI YEARS
BOOK ONE
Kick-Ass 1-4

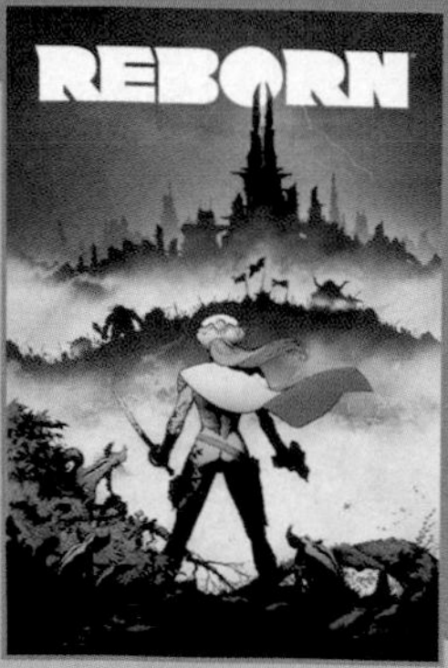
REBORN
Reborn

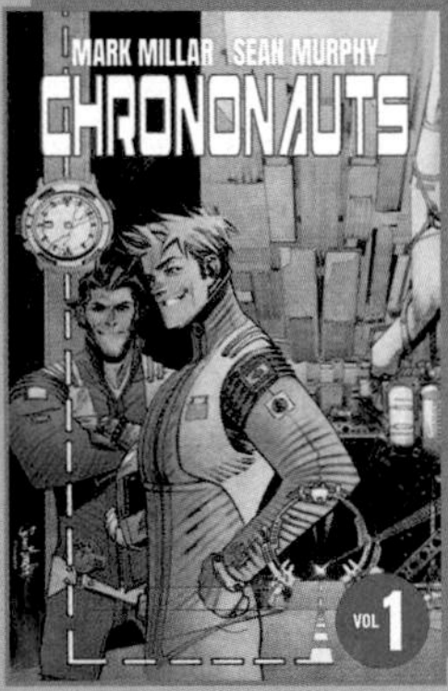
MARK MILLAR SEAN MURPHY
CHRONONAUTS
VOL 1
Chrononauts 1-2

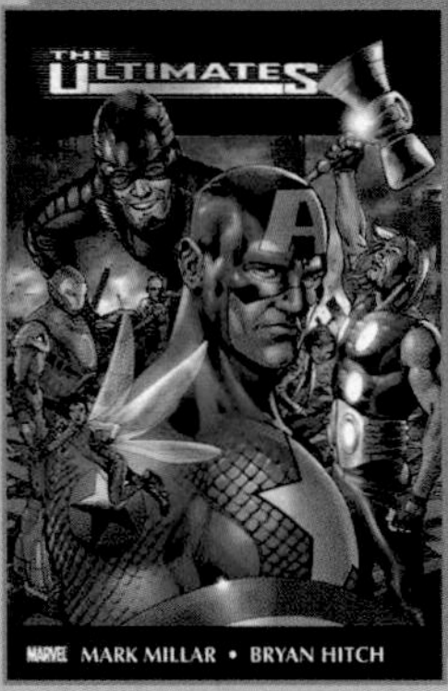
THE ULTIMATES
MARK MILLAR • BRYAN HITCH
The Ultimates 1-2

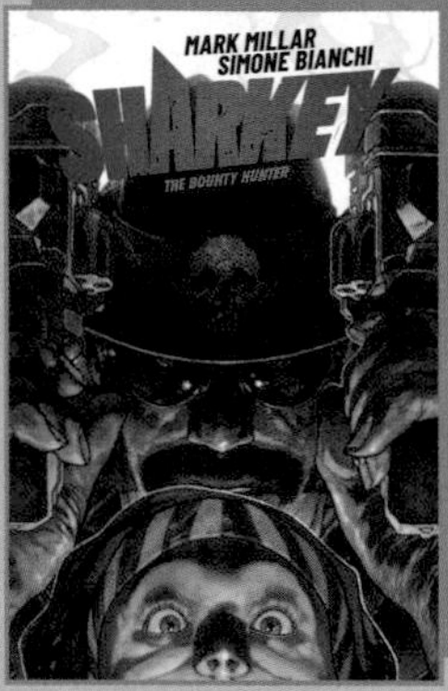
MARK MILLAR
SIMONE BIANCHI
THE BOUNTY HUNTER
Sharkey The Bounty Hunter

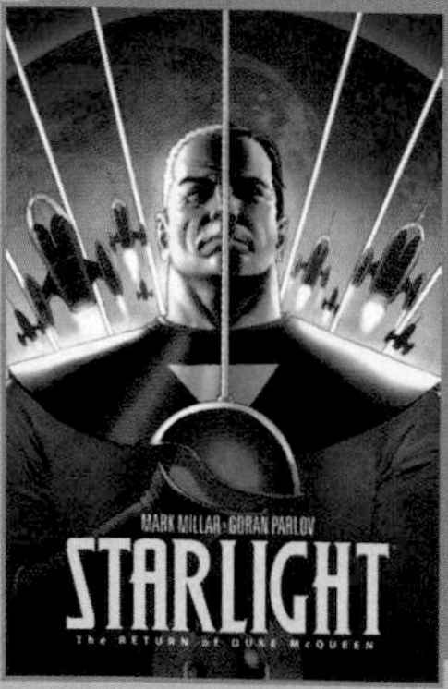
MARK MILLAR · GORAN PARLOV
STARLIGHT
Starlight

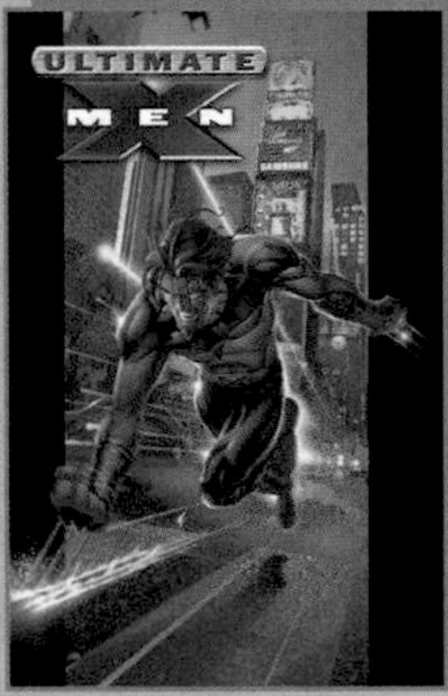
ULTIMATE
X
MEN
Ultimate X-Men 1-6

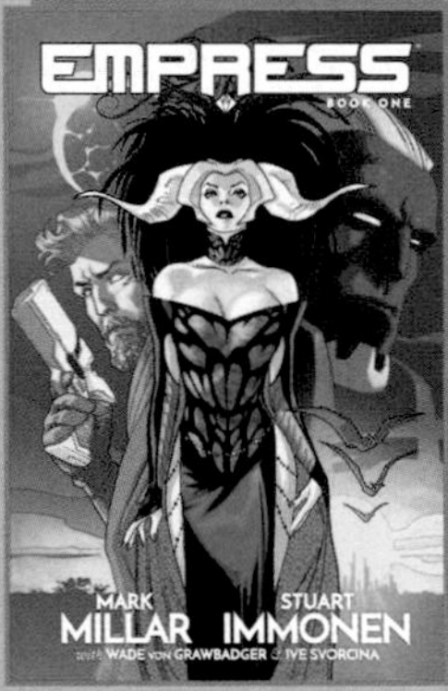
EMPRESS
BOOK ONE
MARK MILLAR
STUART IMMONEN
WADE VON GRAWBADGER
IVE SVORCINA
Empress

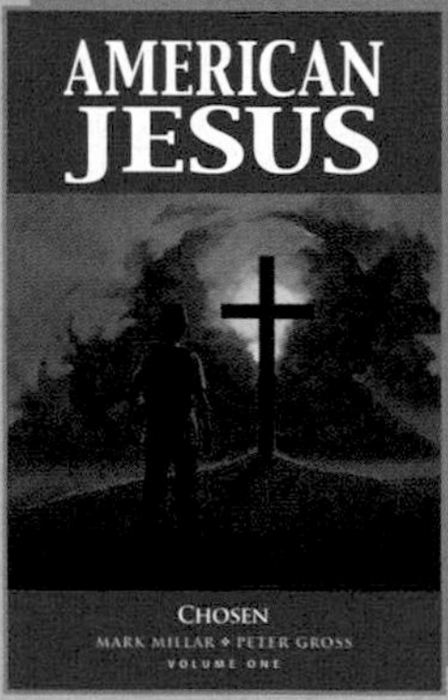
AMERICAN JESUS
CHOSEN
MARK MILLAR ✦ PETER GROSS
VOLUME ONE
American Jesus 1-3

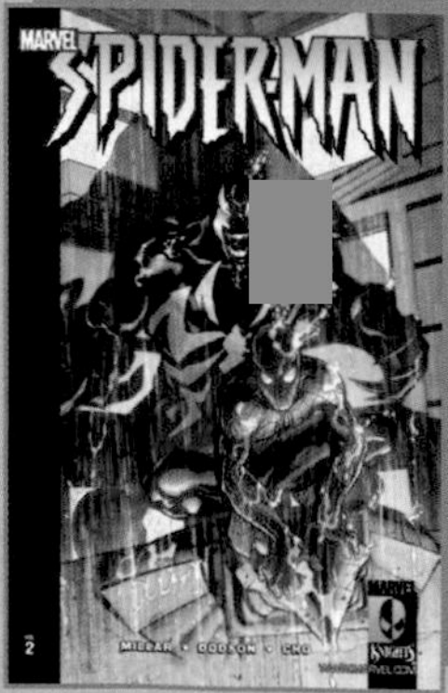
MARVEL
SPIDER-MAN
2
Marvel Knights Spider-Man

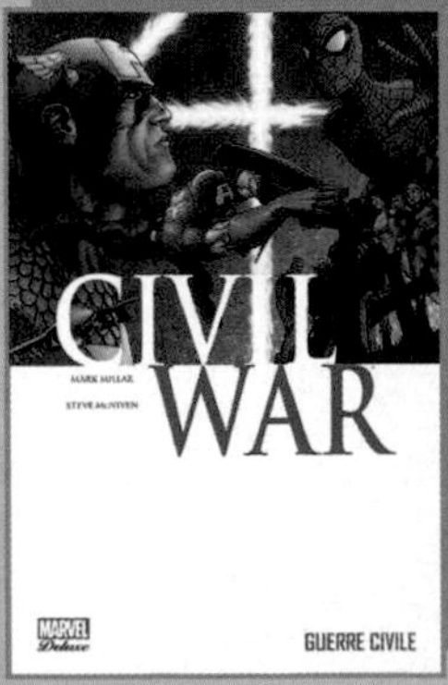
CIVIL WAR
MARVEL Deluxe
GUERRE CIVILE
Civil War

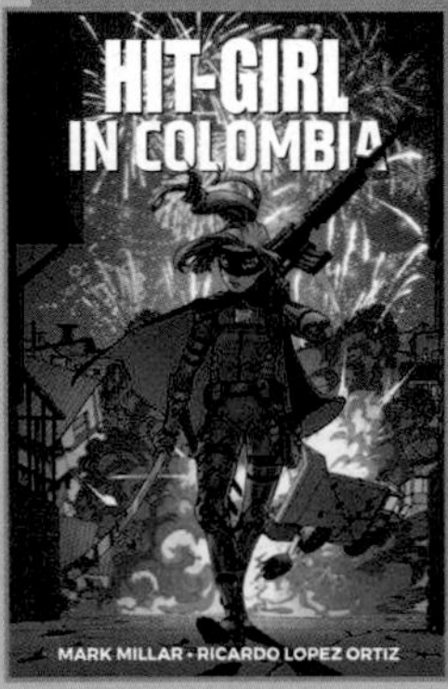
HIT-GIRL
IN COLOMBIA
MARK MILLAR · RICARDO LOPEZ ORTIZ
Hit-Girl 1-6

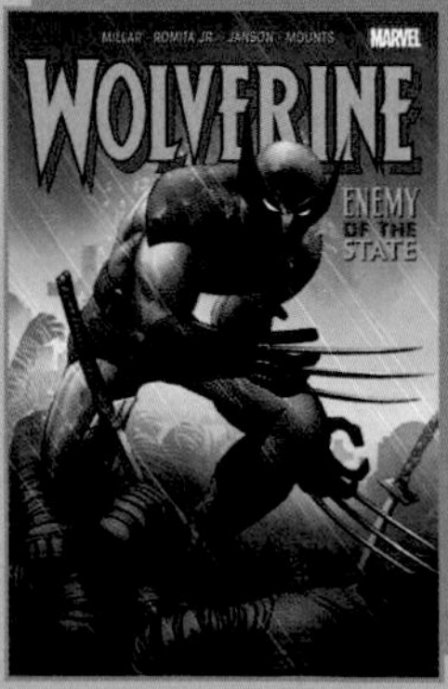
MARVEL
WOLVERINE
ENEMY OF THE STATE
Wolverine: Enemy of the State 1-2

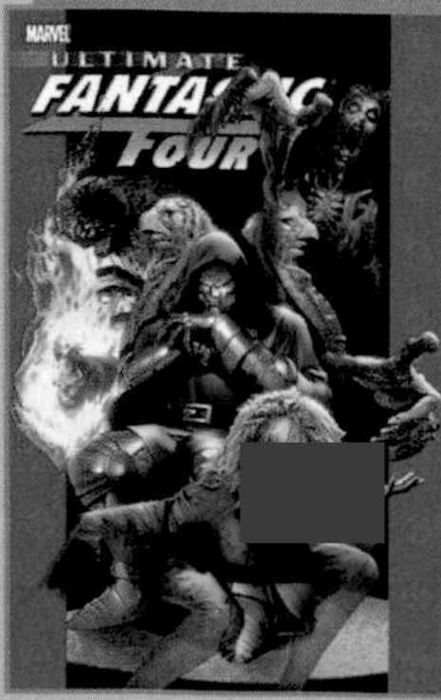
MARVEL
ULTIMATE
FOUR
Ultimate Fantastic Four

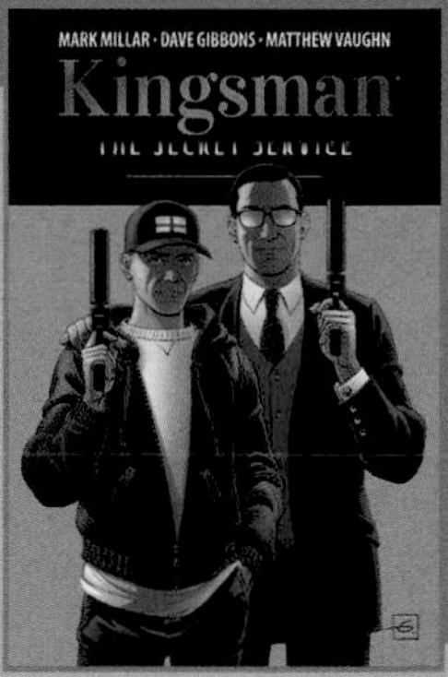
MARK MILLAR · DAVE GIBBONS · MATTHEW VAUGHN
Kingsman
THE SECRET SERVICE
Kingsman 1-2

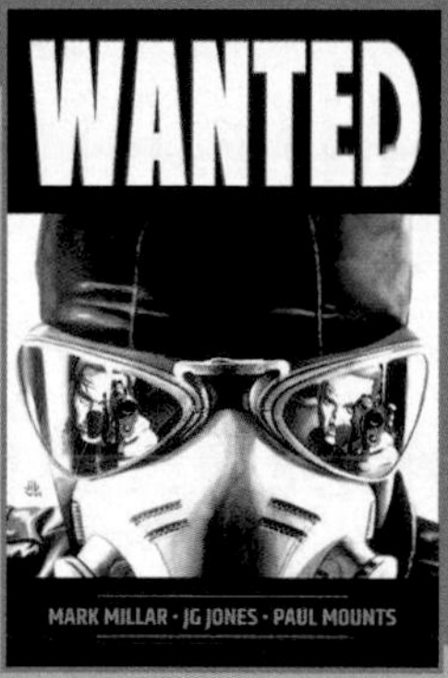
WANTED
MARK MILLAR · JG JONES · PAUL MOUNTS
Wanted

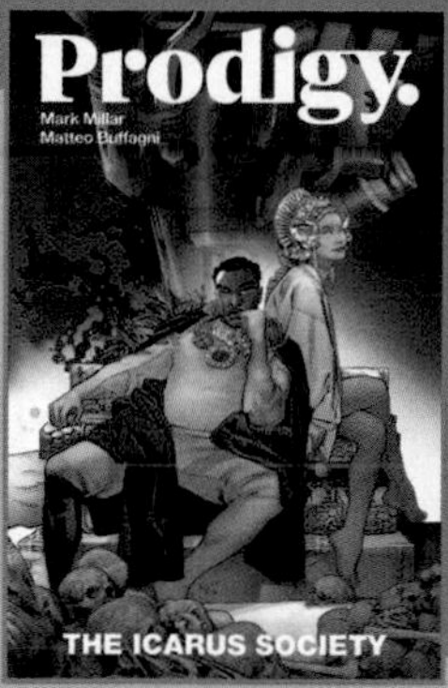
Prodigy.
Mark Millar
Matteo Buffagni
THE ICARUS SOCIETY
Prodigy 1-2

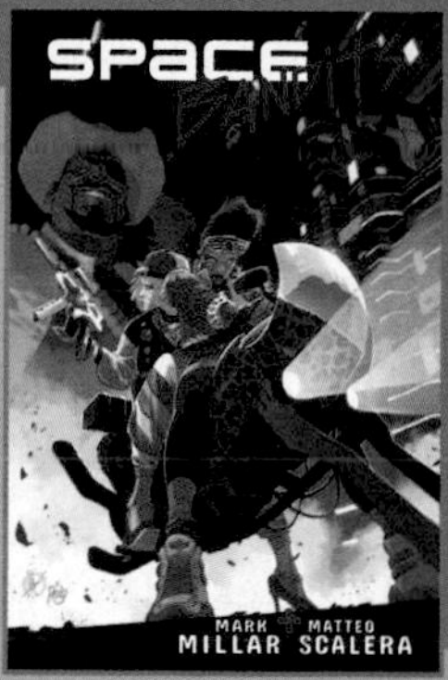
SPACE
MARK MILLAR
MATTEO SCALERA
Space Bandits

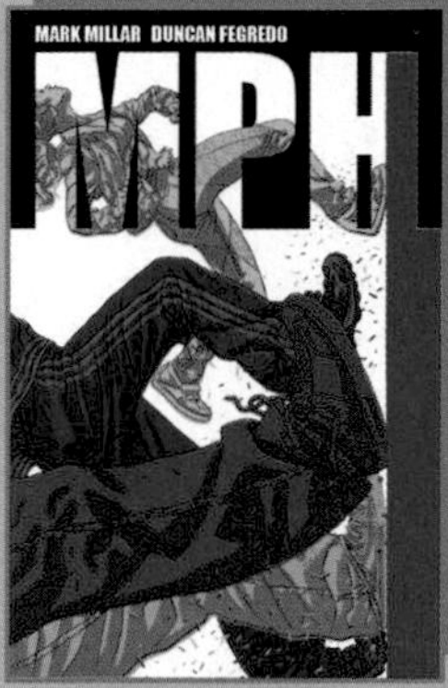
MARK MILLAR DUNCAN FEGREDO
MPH
MPH

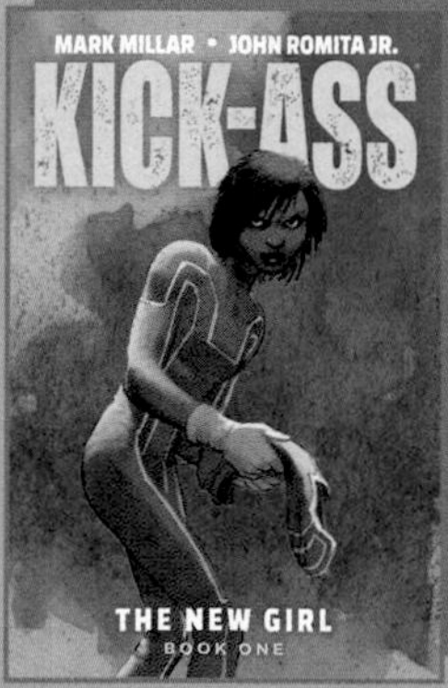
MARK MILLAR · JOHN ROMITA JR.
KICK-ASS
THE NEW GIRL
BOOK ONE
Kick-Ass: The New Girl 1-4

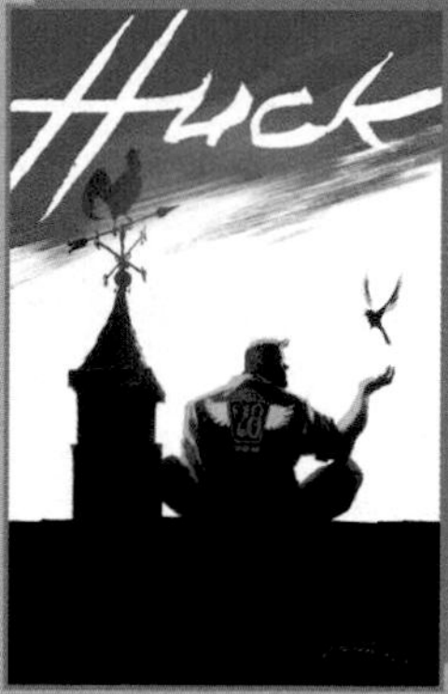
Huck
Huck

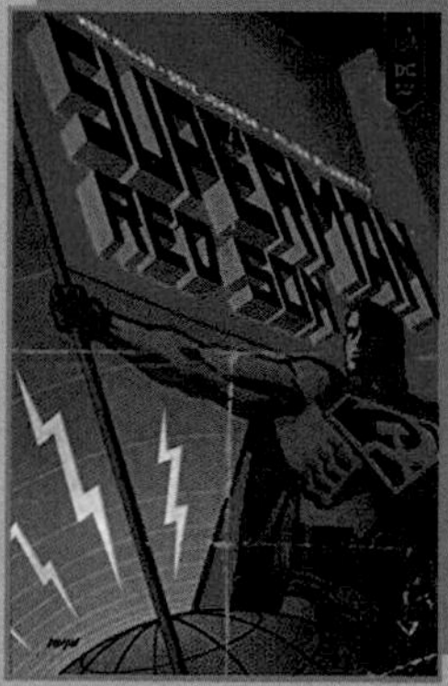
SUPERMAN
RED SON
Superman Red Son

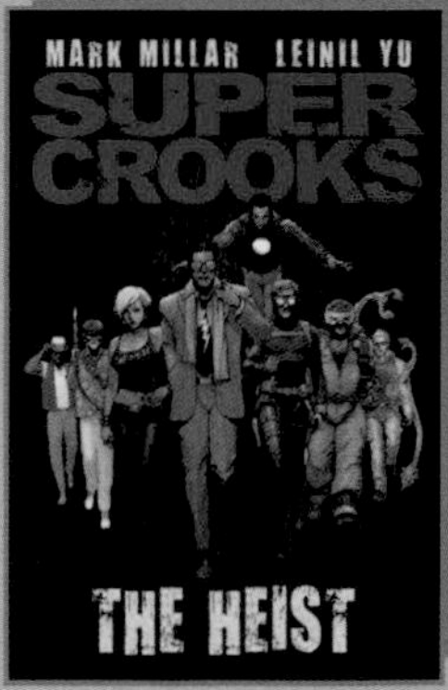
MARK MILLAR LEINIL YU
SUPER
CROOKS
THE HEIST
Super Crooks

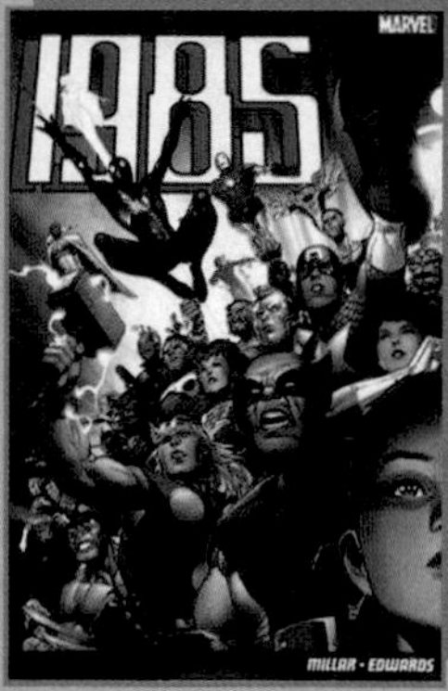
MARVEL
1985
MILLAR · EDWARDS
1985

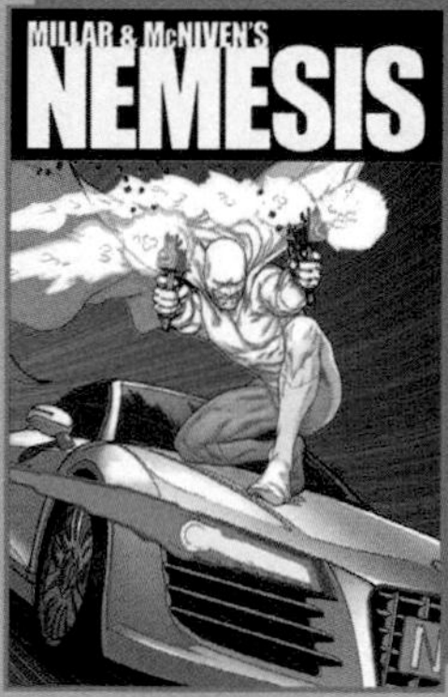
MILLAR & McNIVEN'S
NEMESIS
Nemesis

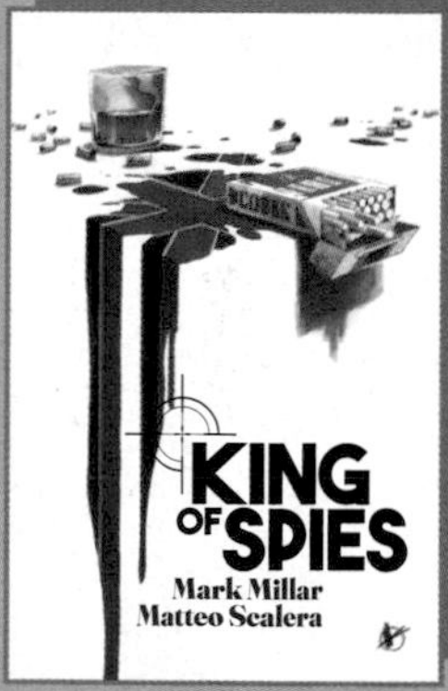
KING
OF SPIES
Mark Millar
Matteo Scalera
King of Spies

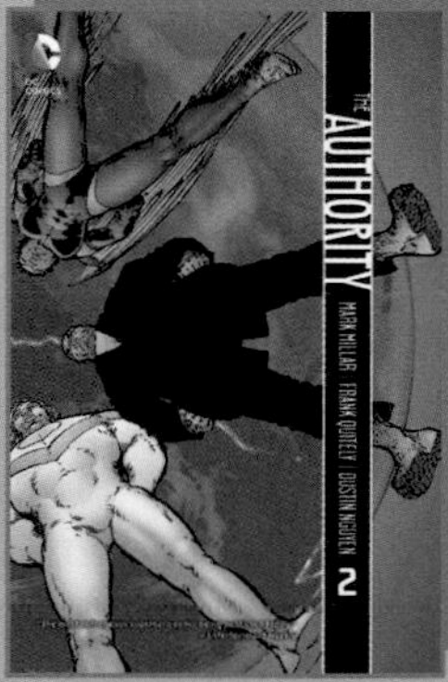
THE AUTHORITY
MARK MILLAR
FRANK QUITELY
DUSTIN NGUYEN
2
The Authority

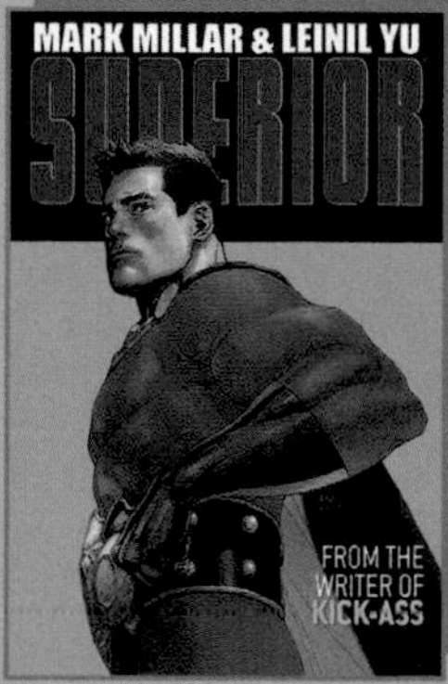
MARK MILLAR & LEINIL YU
SUPERIOR
FROM THE
WRITER OF
KICK-ASS
Superior

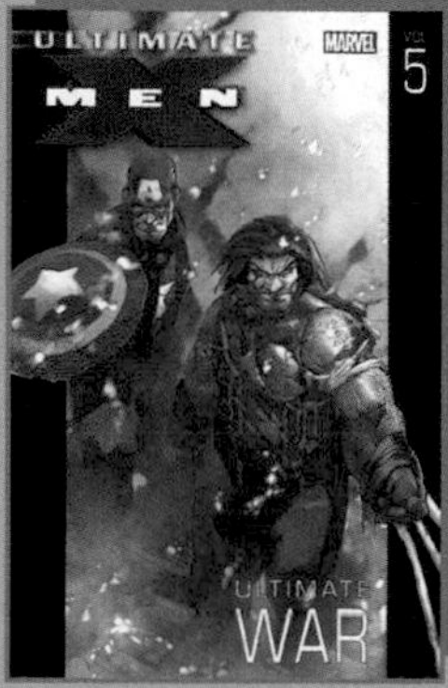
ULTIMATE
X
MEN
MARVEL
5
ULTIMATE
WAR
Ultimate War

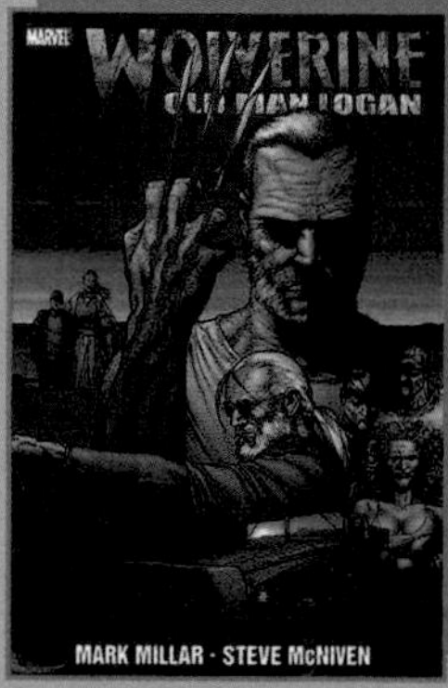
MARVEL
WOLVERINE
OLD MAN LOGAN
MARK MILLAR · STEVE McNIVEN
Wolverine: Old Man Logan

BE THE FIRST
FOR TRAILERS AND PREVIEWS

SIGN UP TO THE MILLARWORLD NEWSLETTER AT

WWW.MRMARKMILLAR.COM

YOU CAN
ALSO FIND
US ON

MILLAR TIME

VISIT **MILLAR TIME** on
YouTube EVERY WEEK

NETFLI